3rd Edition

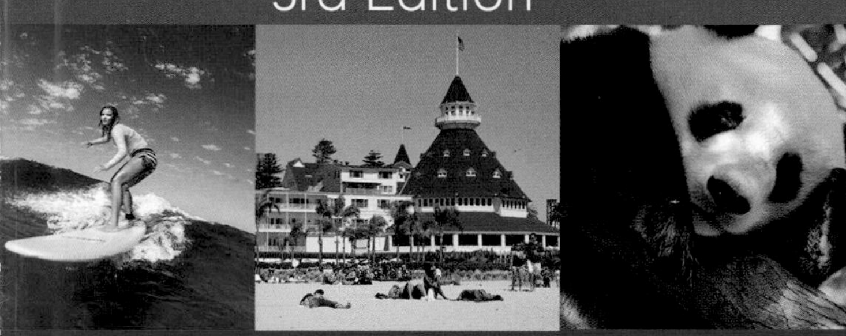

by Maribeth Mellin

FrommerMedia LLC

Contents

18 Favorite Moments 1

1 The Best Full-Day Tours 7
The Best in One Day 8
The Best in Two Days 12
The Best in Three Days 16

2 The Best Special-Interest Tours 19
Balboa Park 20
San Diego with Kids 28
Historic San Diego 34
The Best Golf Courses 40

3 The Best Neighborhood Walks 43
Gaslamp Quarter 44
Old Town 50
Embarcadero 54
La Jolla 58
Hillcrest 62
Coronado 66

4 The Best Shopping 69
Shopping Best Bets 70
Shopping A to Z 74

5 The Best of San Diago Outdoors 81
The Best Beaches 82
Cabrillo National Monument 88
The Best Hiking 92
Mission Bay Park 96

6 **The Best Dining 99**
Dining Best Bets 100
Dining A to Z 104

7 **The Best Nightlife 113**
Nightlife Best Bets 114
Nightlife A to Z 117

8 **The Best Arts & Entertainment 123**
Arts & Entertainment Best Bets 124
Arts & Entertainment A to Z 126

9 **The Best Lodging 131**
Lodging Best Bets 132
Lodging A to Z 136

10 **The Best Day Trips 145**
North County 146
Julian 150
Tijuana 154

The Savvy Traveler 159
Before You Go 160
Getting There 164
Getting Around 166
Fast Facts 168
A Brief History 173

Index 176

Published by:
Frommer Media LLC

ISBN 978-1-62887-302-3 (paper), 978-1-62887-303-0 (e-book)

Editorial Director: Pauline Frommer
Editor: Michael Kelly
Production Editor: Heather Wilcox
Photo Editor: Meghan Lamb
Cartographer: Roberta Stockwell
Compositor: Heather Pope
Indexer: Maro RioFrancos

Front cover photos, left to right: Surfing in Del Mar, Courtesy of L'Auberge Del Mar; Coronado Hotel, © meunierd/Shutterstock.com; sleeping panda at San Diego Zoo, © Nadia Borisevich

Back cover photo: Jet-skiing in Mission Bay, Courtesy of Paradise Point Resort

For information on our other products and services, please go to Frommers.com.

Frommer's also publishes its books in a variety of electronic formats. Some content that appears in print may not be available in electronic formats.

Manufactured in China

5 4 3 2 1

About This Guide

Organizing your time. That's what this guide is all about.

Other guides give you long lists of things to see and do and then expect you to fit the pieces together. The Day by Day guides are different. These guides tell you the best of everything, and then they show you how to see it in the smartest, most time-efficient way. Our authors have designed detailed itineraries organized by time, neighborhood, or special interest. And each tour comes with a bulleted map that takes you from stop to stop.

Hoping to wiggle your toes in the oceanside sand in San Diego's year-round perfect weather? Sample some killer street tacos or observe the giant pandas at one of the nation's finest zoos? How about strolling along the Embarcadero, off San Diego Bay, or through the historic Gaslamp Quarter, where San Diego's urban revival began? Whatever your interest or schedule, the Day by Days give you the smartest routes to follow. Not only do we take you to the top attractions, hotels, and restaurants, but we also help you access those special moments that locals get to experience—those "finds" that turn tourists into travelers.

The Day by Days are also your top choice if you're looking for one complete guide for all your travel needs. The best hotels and restaurants for every budget, the greatest shopping values, the wildest nightlife—it's all here.

Why should you trust our judgment? Because our authors personally visit each place they write about. They're an independent lot who say what they think and would never include places they wouldn't recommend to their best friends. They're also open to suggestions from readers. If you'd like to contact them, please send your comments our way at feedback@frommers.com, and we'll pass them on.

Enjoy your Day by Day guide—the most helpful travel companion you can buy. And have the trip of a lifetime.

About the Author

Maribeth Mellin is an award-winning journalist and photographer based in San Diego. She has received Mexico's prestigious Pluma de Plata award as well as commendations from Cancún, Cozumel, Acapulco, and other destinations. In addition, her articles on medical, social, and legal issues have garnered numerous awards from journalism organizations. Mellin has authored several travel books, and her articles and photos have appeared in the *San Diego Union-Tribune, Los Angeles Times, Dallas Morning News, Endless Vacation magazine, San Francisco Chronicle,* and other publications. She also has contributed to multiple websites, including Concierge.com and TravelCNN.com. When not traveling the globe, she enjoys time at home with her husband near the beach and border in San Diego.

An Additional Note

Please be advised that travel information is subject to change at any time—and this is especially true of prices. We therefore suggest that you write or call ahead for confirmation when making your travel plans. The authors, editors, and publisher cannot be held responsible for the experiences of readers while traveling. Your safety is important to us, however, so we encourage you to stay alert and be aware of your surroundings.

Star Ratings, Icons & Abbreviations

Every hotel, restaurant, and attraction listing in this guide has been ranked for quality, value, service, amenities, and special features using a **star-rating system.** Hotels, restaurants, attractions, shopping, and nightlife are rated on a scale of zero stars (recommended) to three stars (exceptional). In addition to the star-rating system, we also use a **kids icon** to point out the best bets for families. Within each tour, we recommend cafes, bars, or restaurants where you can take a break. Each of these stops appears in a shaded box marked with a coffee-cup-shaped bullet.

The following **abbreviations** are used for credit cards:

AE	American Express	DISC	Discover	V	Visa
DC	Diners Club	MC	MasterCard		

Frommers.com

Now that you have this guidebook to help you plan a great trip, visit our website at **www.frommers.com** for additional travel information on more than 4,000 destinations. We update features regularly to give you instant access to the most current trip-planning information available. At Frommers.com, you'll find scoops on the best airfares, lodging rates, and car rental bargains. You can even book your travel online through our reliable travel booking partners. Other popular features include:

- Online updates of our most popular guidebooks
- Vacation sweepstakes and contest giveaways
- Newsletters highlighting the hottest travel trends
- Online travel message boards with featured travel discussions

A Note on Prices

In the "Take a Break" (☕) and "Best Bets" sections of this book, we have used a system of dollar signs to show a range of costs for 1 night in a hotel (the price of a double-occupancy room) or the cost of an entree at a restaurant. Use the following table to decipher the dollar signs:

Cost	Hotels	Restaurants
$	under $130	under $15
$$	$130–$200	$15–$30
$$$	$200–$300	$30–$40
$$$$	$300–$395	$40–$50
$$$$$	over $395	over $50

How to Contact Us

In researching this book, we discovered many wonderful places—hotels, restaurants, shops, and more. We're sure you'll find others. Please tell us about them, so we can share the information with your fellow travelers in upcoming editions. If you were disappointed with a recommendation, we'd love to know that, too. Please write to: Contact@FrommerMedia.com

18 Favorite **Moments**

18 Favorite **Moments**

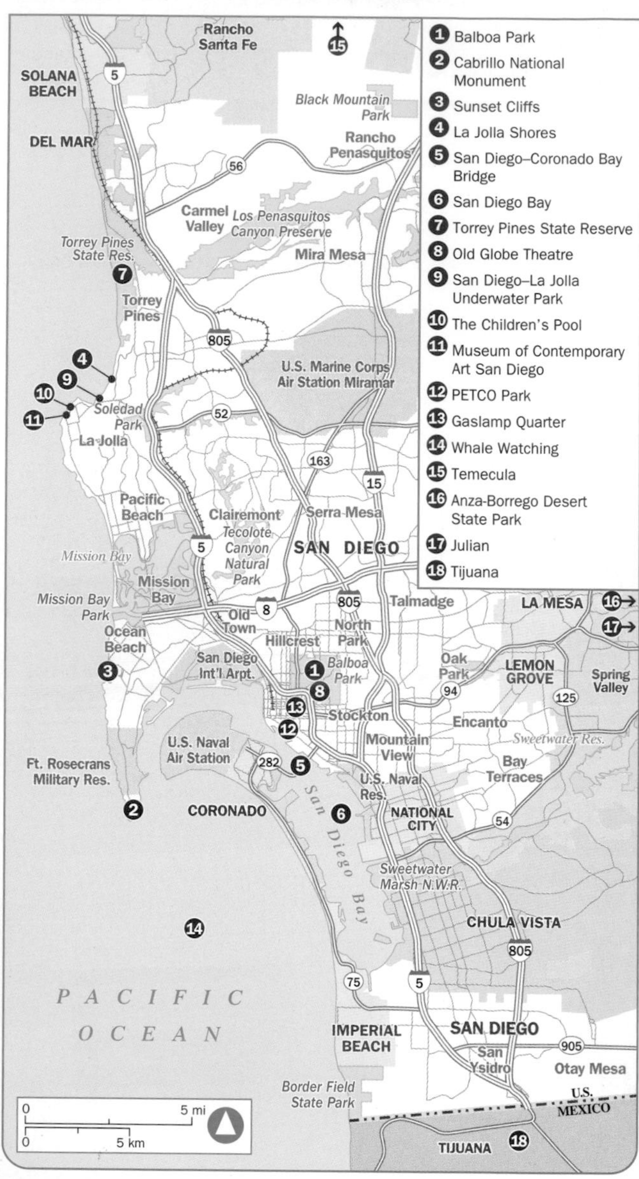
1 Balboa Park
2 Cabrillo National Monument
3 Sunset Cliffs
4 La Jolla Shores
5 San Diego–Coronado Bay Bridge
6 San Diego Bay
7 Torrey Pines State Reserve
8 Old Globe Theatre
9 San Diego–La Jolla Underwater Park
10 The Children's Pool
11 Museum of Contemporary Art San Diego
12 PETCO Park
13 Gaslamp Quarter
14 Whale Watching
15 Temecula
16 Anza-Borrego Desert State Park
17 Julian
18 Tijuana
Rancho Santa Fe
SOLANA BEACH
DEL MAR
Black Mountain Park
Rancho Penasquitos
Carmel Valley
Los Penasquitos Canyon Preserve
Mira Mesa
Torrey Pines State Res.
Torrey Pines
U.S. Marine Corps Air Station Miramar
Soledad Park
La Jolla
Pacific Beach
Clairemont
Serra Mesa
Tecolote Canyon Natural Park
SAN DIEGO
Mission Bay
Mission Bay Park
Old Town
Talmadge
LA MESA
Ocean Beach
Hillcrest
North Park
San Diego Int'l Arpt.
Balboa Park
Oak Park
LEMON GROVE
Spring Valley
Stockton
Encanto
Sweetwater Res.
U.S. Naval Air Station
Mountain View
Bay Terraces
Ft. Rosecrans Military Res.
U.S. Naval Res.
CORONADO
NATIONAL CITY
San Diego Bay
Sweetwater Marsh N.W.R.
CHULA VISTA
PACIFIC OCEAN
IMPERIAL BEACH
SAN DIEGO
San Ysidro
Otay Mesa
Border Field State Park
U.S.
MEXICO
TIJUANA
0 5 mi
0 5 km

Previous page: Downtown San Diego from Coronado Island.

If you think San Diego is just about wiggling your toes in the sand or cooing over cuddly panda bears, think again. Combining big-city style with small-town heart, this seaside destination offers an embarrassment of riches: stunning natural beauty, high-octane nightlife, world-class cultural organizations, family-friendly attractions, and sophisticated dining. Oh, did I mention it has the country's best weather as well? San Diego is also perched on the border with Mexico, creating a powerful bi-national culture in everything from street food to art and commerce.

❶ **Spending an idyllic day in Balboa Park.** This is one of the world's great urban cultural parks, home to more than a dozen of the city's top museums. It offers dazzling gardens, glorious Spanish Colonial Revival architecture, and the world-famous San Diego Zoo as well. Balboa Park is San Diego's crown jewel. *See p 9.*

❷ **Taking in the city's best panorama.** Cabrillo National Monument not only offers a whirlwind history tour—beginning with San Diego's European discovery in 1542—it also provides unsurpassed 360-degree views of downtown and beyond. From its location at the tip of Point Loma—422 feet (129m) above sea level—it's also a great vantage point from which to watch migrating Pacific gray whales in the winter. *See p 13.*

❸ **Watching for the green flash.** There's no better place to watch for the storied "green flash"—when the sun sinks beneath the horizon—than Sunset Cliffs, the rugged, crumbling sandstone lookout points above secret surf spots in Ocean Beach.

❹ **Wiggling your toes in the sand.** Seriously, how could you not spend time at the beach? Choose La Jolla Shores for the total family, surfer, beachcomber, sunbathing, and kayaking experience. After all, some of the world's finest oceanographers are based here. *See p 85.*

❺ **Zipping across the San Diego–Coronado Bay Bridge.** Roll down the windows, put the top down, and let the wind blow through your hair as you cruise along this graceful engineering marvel. It's always a

Balboa Park.

bit of a rush, and the views are spectacular, so try to keep your eyes on the road. *See p 66.*

❻ **Cruising the bay.** Whether it's a weekend-brunch sightseeing tour, a chartered sailboat excursion, or just a water-taxi ride to Coronado, don't miss an opportunity to spend some time on San Diego Bay. Spanish conquistador Sebastián Vizcaíno described it in 1602 as "a port which must be the best to be found in all the South Sea." Discover it for yourself. *See p 168.*

❼ **Escaping to Torrey Pines State Natural Reserve.** Dramatically set atop 300-foot (91m) cliffs overlooking the Pacific, this reserve is home to the rarest pine tree in North America. Short trails crisscross the delicate landscape, which also incorporates one of San Diego's best beaches. *See p 93.*

❽ **Being a groundling.** You won't have to stand like they did in William Shakespeare's day, but you can see the Bard's works al fresco at the Old Globe Theatre's summer Shakespeare Festival. The Tony Award–winning Old Globe performs Shakespeare's work in true repertory style, alternating three different productions at its open-air theater. *See p 21.*

Enjoy views of downtown from Cabrillo National Monument.

Ocean Beach Pier at sunset.

❾ **Paddling with the fishes.** The calm surfaces and clear waters of the San Diego–La Jolla Underwater Park are the ultimate local spot for a little kayaking. This ecological reserve features sea caves and vibrant marine life, including California's state marine fish, the electric-orange Garibaldi. *See p 84.*

❿ **Communing with seals and sea lions.** The Children's Pool, a picturesque cove in La Jolla, was named for the toddlers who could safely frolic behind its protective, manmade seawall. A colony of pinnipeds came to like it equally, and now the beach is shared—sometimes a little uneasily—between humans and seals. *See p 60.*

⓫ **Challenging your perception.** The city's most intriguing museum is the Museum of Contemporary Art San Diego (MCASD). With a flagship space in La Jolla and two downtown annexes, this internationally prominent museum offers ongoing exhibitions of cutting-edge art as well as a roster of special events. A visit to any of

MCASD's facilities is guaranteed to be a thought-provoking experience. *See p 56.*

⓬ **Buying some peanuts and Cracker Jack.** San Diego's Major League Baseball team, the Padres, play at PETCO Park, a state-of-the-art ballpark that opened in 2004. Incorporating seven buildings that date as far back as 1909, PETCO's clever design and downtown location have made it a fan favorite. *See p 129.*

⓭ **Strolling the Gaslamp Quarter.** For dining, shopping, dancing, drinking, or just soaking up some local flavor, this is the place to be. People-watching opportunities abound—if you can manage to take your eyes off the exquisitely restored Victorian commercial buildings in this 16½-block district. *See p 44.*

⓮ **Scouting for whales.** Every year, from December through March, Pacific gray whales pass through San Diego waters, making their way to and from breeding lagoons in Mexico. There are ample opportunities to observe these gentle giants from both land and sea as they undertake one of the longest migrations of any mammal. *See p 32.*

The Padres in action at PETCO Park.

⓯ **Toasting the good life.** Just across the county line in Temecula, about 60 miles (97km) north of downtown San Diego, are some two dozen wineries. They range from mom-and-pop operations with minimal amenities to slick commercial ventures with fancy tasting rooms, retail boutiques, and restaurants. Cheers. *See p 148.*

⓰ **Witnessing the desert's spring fling.** For a period of several weeks—usually late February through March—Anza-Borrego Desert State Park magically comes

Watching sea lions in La Jolla.

alive with a carpet of blooming wildflowers. A brilliant palette of pink, lavender, red, orange, and yellow transforms the rugged landscape into a colorful oasis. *See p 95.*

⑰ **Getting in touch with your pioneer spirit.** The mountain hamlet of Julian was founded as a gold-mining town in the 1860s, but it gained fame for another mother lode: apples. Today, this rustic community has a distinctly Victorian, Old West charm, redolent of hot apple pies. *See p 150.*

⑱ **Making a run for the border.** What a difference a line makes. Once you cross it, you're instantly immersed in the chaotic vibrancy of Mexico's fourth-largest city. Just a 20-minute drive from downtown, Tijuana has a raucous tourist zone with plentiful shopping as well as an array of cultural and culinary delights. *See p 154.* ●

Gaslamp Quarter.

1 The Best **Full-Day Tours**

The Best in **One Day**

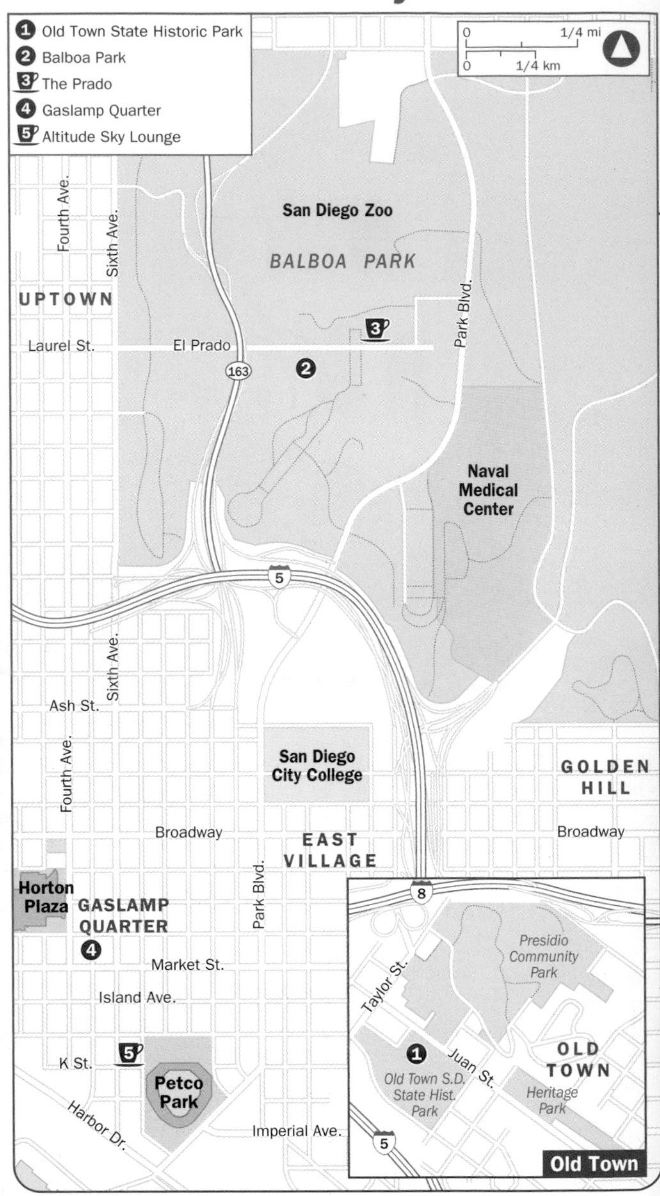

Previous page: The Immaculate Conception Church in Old Town San Diego.

If you have only 24 hours in San Diego, you may be tempted to blow the whole day on the beach or at the zoo. While it's hard to argue with that approach, it would deprive you of experiencing San Diego's robust and unusual heritage as the birthplace of California, with deep ties to Spain, Mexico, Wild West history, and the U.S. military. Besides, you'll still get plenty of sun as you tour through Old Town, and you just might hear the animals squawk and roar from the zoo as you explore Balboa Park next door. **START: Blue or Green Line trolley to Old Town Transit Center.**

1 ★ Old Town State Historic Park. Dedicated to re-creating the early life of the city from 1821 to 1872, this is where San Diego's Mexican heritage is best celebrated. It features more than a dozen structures (some original, some reconstructed), including the home of a wealthy family circa 1872 and the fledgling town's one-room schoolhouse. Memorabilia and exhibits are on view in some buildings; visitor-oriented shops and restaurants are incorporated into the rest. On Wednesdays and Saturdays from 10am to 4pm, costumed park volunteers reenact life in the 1800s with cooking and crafts demonstrations, a working blacksmith, and parlor singing. Free 1-hour walking tours leave daily at 11am and 2pm from the Robinson-Rose House. ⏲ *At least 1 hr. The park is bordered by Juan, Congress, Twiggs & Wallace sts.* ☎ *619/220-5422. www.parks.ca.gov. Free admission. Museums daily 10am–5pm; most restaurants until 9pm. Trolley: Blue or Green Line to Old Town.*

The Skyfari aerial cable car over San Diego Zoo, one of the many features in Balboa Park.

2 ★★★ kids Balboa Park. Like New York's Central Park and San Francisco's Golden Gate Park, the emerald in San Diego's crown is Balboa Park, a 1,174-acre (475-hectare) city-owned playground and the largest urban cultural park in the nation. The park's most distinctive features are its mature landscaping, the architectural beauty of the Spanish colonial revival–style buildings lining the pedestrian thoroughfare (byproducts of expositions in 1915 and 1935), and more than a dozen engaging and diverse museums. You'll also find rose, cactus, and flower gardens; walkways; 4½ miles (7km) of hiking trails in Florida Canyon; an ornate pavilion with the world's largest outdoor organ; an old-fashioned carousel; an IMAX domed theater; the acclaimed Old Globe Theatre; and the San Diego Zoo. ⏲ *At least*

2 hr. (or more, depending on which museums pique your interest). Primary entrances are at Sixth Ave. & Laurel St. on the west side & Park Blvd. & Presidents Way on the east side. ☎ 619/239-0512. www.balboapark.org. Museum prices vary; free organ concerts are presented every Sun at 2pm & Mon at 7:30pm in summer; free as well as paid self-guided tours are available from the Visitor Center, daily 9:30am–4:30pm. Attraction hours vary, but many are 10am–5pm. Bus: 7, 120 & 215; a free tram operates within the park daily 9am–6pm (extended hours in summer).

3 **The Prado,** Balboa Park's sophisticated-but-casual restaurant, is a great place to catch your breath and set a spell, whether you're stopping in for lunch, dinner, or just some drinks and appetizers. This sprawling restaurant complex in the baroque House of Hospitality has lovely patio dining (it overlooks a garden popular for weddings), a lounge where you often find live entertainment, and special event spaces. *1549 El Prado. ☎ 619/557-9441. www.cohnrestaurants.com. $15–$36.*

4 ★★ Gaslamp Quarter. Where others had seen only dismal mudflats melting into a shallow bay, businessman Alonzo Horton saw untapped potential. In 1867, he undertook an audacious plan to lure citizens away from Old Town with the founding of "New Town," several miles to the south. New Town is now known as the Gaslamp Quarter, and it's become more successful than anything Alonzo could have hoped for. It comprises 16½ blocks of restored historic buildings housing dozens of restaurants, bars, clubs, and boutiques—this is where you'll find San Diego's most vigorous nightlife, fabulous Victorian architecture, and excellent people-watching. Begin your tour of the area at Horton Plaza shopping center, where you can not only shop and dine but also catch a play or a movie. 🕓 *At least 1 hr. (not including dining or entertainment options). The district is bounded by Broadway on the north, L St. & the waterfront to the south, Fourth Ave. to the west, & Sixth Ave. to the east. Gaslamp Quarter Association ☎ 619/233-5227. www.gaslamp.org. Mall stores tend to stay open until 9pm weekdays, 7 or 8pm weekends; independent stores are generally open*

The Gaslamp Quarter, extending from Broadway to Harbor Drive.

San Diego at sunset from the Altitude Sky Lounge.

until 7pm Sun–Thurs, 8 or 9pm Fri–Sat. Restaurants usually serve until 10pm Sun–Thurs, with longer hours Fri–Sat. Bars are usually open until 2am daily; most clubs are open until 2am Thurs–Sat. Crowds are thick Thurs–Sat & whenever there's a large convention in town or a baseball game at PETCO Park. Parking structures are available at Horton Plaza; Market St. & Sixth Ave.; Sixth Ave. & K St. Trolley: Green, Blue & Orange Lines. Bus: Any downtown route.

Finish off your day by rising above it all for a nightcap at the open-air 5 **Altitude Sky Lounge,** 22 floors up from the Gaslamp commotion. This long, narrow space is in the Gaslamp Quarter Marriott overlooking PETCO Park and the Convention Center. It offers fire pits, lounges, and DJ-spun grooves as well as appetizers from the first-floor restaurant. As with many Gaslamp Quarter venues, lines begin forming around 10pm on weekends (2 hr. before game time when the Padres are playing). *660 K St. (btw. Sixth & Seventh aves.). ☎ 619/696-0234. www.altitudeskybar.com. Daily 5pm–1:30am; open 2 hr. before Padres games. $10–$19.*

The Best in **Two Days**

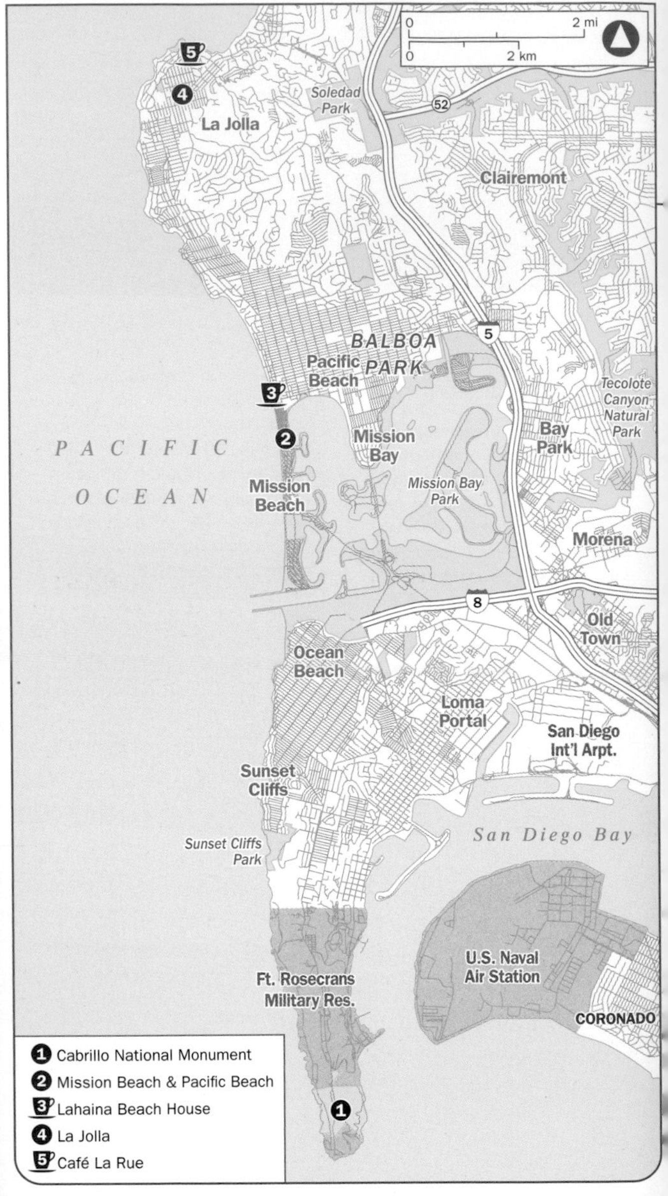
0
2 mi
0
2 km
La Jolla
Soledad Park
52
Clairemont
5
BALBOA PARK
Pacific Beach
Tecolote Canyon Natural Park
Bay Park
Mission Bay
PACIFIC OCEAN
Mission Beach
Mission Bay Park
Morena
8
Old Town
Ocean Beach
Loma Portal
San Diego Int'l Arpt.
Sunset Cliffs
San Diego Bay
Sunset Cliffs Park
U.S. Naval Air Station
Ft. Rosecrans Military Res.
CORONADO
1 Cabrillo National Monument
2 Mission Beach & Pacific Beach
3 Lahaina Beach House
4 La Jolla
5 Café La Rue

You don't have to venture far for stunning natural settings in San Diego, which means it's easy to season your nature romps with a little history, great food, and even some shopping. This itinerary showcases the extremes of SoCal coastal living, from rollicking Pacific Beach to refined La Jolla. You'll really need your sunscreen today, though. A car is in order too. Although it is possible to tackle this itinerary via public transportation, it's much more practical to have your own set of wheels. START: **Bus route 84 to Cabrillo National Monument.**

❶ ★★★ kids Cabrillo National Monument. Breathtaking views mingle with the early history of San Diego—specifically, the arrival of Juan Rodríguez Cabrillo in 1542. His statue is prominently featured here, along with a historic lighthouse built in 1855, a small museum, the remnants of World War II artillery batteries, a visitor center with lots of books and souvenirs for sale, and a theater screening short videos about local natural history and the age of exploration. The park's setting 422 feet (129m) above sea level at the tip of Point Loma makes it a great vantage point for watching migrating Pacific gray whales December through March. National Park Service rangers also lead walks at the monument, and there are tide pools to explore at the base of the peninsula. The Bayside Trail is an easy hike (3.2 miles/5km round-trip) along an interpreted walkway that leads to a lookout over the bay. *At least 1 hr. There are great picnicking spots here, but no food facilities, so pack a lunch. 1800 Cabrillo Memorial Dr. ☎ 619/557-5450. www.nps.gov/cabr. Admission $10 per vehicle, $5 for walk-ins. Daily 9am–5pm. Bus: Route 84.*

Cabrillo National Monument's historic lighthouse.

❷ ★★ Mission Beach and Pacific Beach. This is it: ground zero for the party-hearty, freewheeling, Southern California beach lifestyle. These two beaches form a 3-mile (5km) stretch of sand paralleled by a cement boardwalk that hosts a nonstop parade of surfers, skaters, bikers, joggers, and plain old beach lovers. South Mission Beach is where you'll find serious beach volleyball and a seaside basketball court. Farther north is Belmont Park, an amusement park whose star attraction is a 1925 wooden roller coaster. Another 1925 holdover is Crystal Pier at the foot of Garnet Avenue in Pacific Beach (or PB, as it's known). This 400 foot-long (122m) wooden pier now supports rental cottages but is open daily to the public, offering great views of the local surfers. The streetside action in these beach zones takes place primarily on Mission Boulevard (heading north from

The boardwalk at Mission Beach.

Belmont Park) and Garnet Avenue (running east from Mission Blvd.), both overflowing with restaurants, clubs, and retailers. Rent a bike and join the parade. ⌚ *At least 1 hr. (or more, depending on how much frolicking in the surf you want to do). Discover Pacific Beach: ☎ 858/273-3303. www.pacificbeach.org. Bus: Route 8/9 from Old Town Transit Center.*

An old beach bungalow transformed into a simple, unpretentious, utterly rockin' eatery and bar, **3 Lahaina Beach House** has been a Pacific Beach institution for generations. Its weathered wooden deck, just inches from the boardwalk, is standing-room-only on sunny weekends and provides a sensory overload of sights and sounds. The food is basic—omelets, burgers, fish tacos—but the atmosphere is pure beach party. Cash only. *710 Oliver Ave. (along the boardwalk btw. Reed Ave. & Pacific Beach Dr.). ☎ 858/270-3888. 9am–9pm. $7–$11.*

4 ★★★ La Jolla. About the only thing La Jolla shares in common with the beach communities to the south is the Pacific Ocean. Locals refer to La Jolla's principal shopping and dining district as "the village," and it's one of the classiest villages you could imagine. High-end boutiques, antiques stores, art galleries, and fine restaurants line the streets; just steps away, a dramatic coastline of sandstone cliffs and picturesque coves with tropical-blue waters awaits. And this beauty has brains, too—La Jolla is a center for local arts and culture, providing a home for the University of California, San Diego (where you'll find the Tony Award–winning La Jolla Playhouse and the Stuart Collection of site-specific art); the flagship space for the Museum of Contemporary Art San Diego; and the Athenaeum Music and Arts Library, which presents concerts and art exhibits. La Jolla is a Southern California Riviera. ⌚ *3 hr. (or more if you want to enjoy an exhibit or show). ☎ 858/454-5718. www.lajollabythesea.com. Bus: Route 30 from Mission Blvd. & Grand Ave. in PB.*

Surfers heading to sea at Mission Beach.

Sunset from La Jolla Pier.

La Valencia Hotel is the grande dame of La Jolla. The Pink Lady originally opened in 1926, and its Mediterranean style and killer location made it a favorite of celebs like Greta Garbo, Charlie Chaplin, and a second generation of movie stars brought in by La Jolla native Gregory Peck, who co-founded the La Jolla Playhouse. A major redo completed in 2014 transformed the hotel's clubby, legendary watering hole into the chic 5 ★ **Café La Rue,** whose paintings of Paris circa 1947 and menu of fromages, charcuterie, and mussels play off the hotel's European panache. Linger at a sidewalk table for the full effect. *1132 Prospect St. (at Herschel Ave.). ☎ 858/551-3761 or 858/454-0771. www.lavalencia.com. 8am–midnight. $14–$29.*

La Valencia Hotel.

The Best in **Three Days**

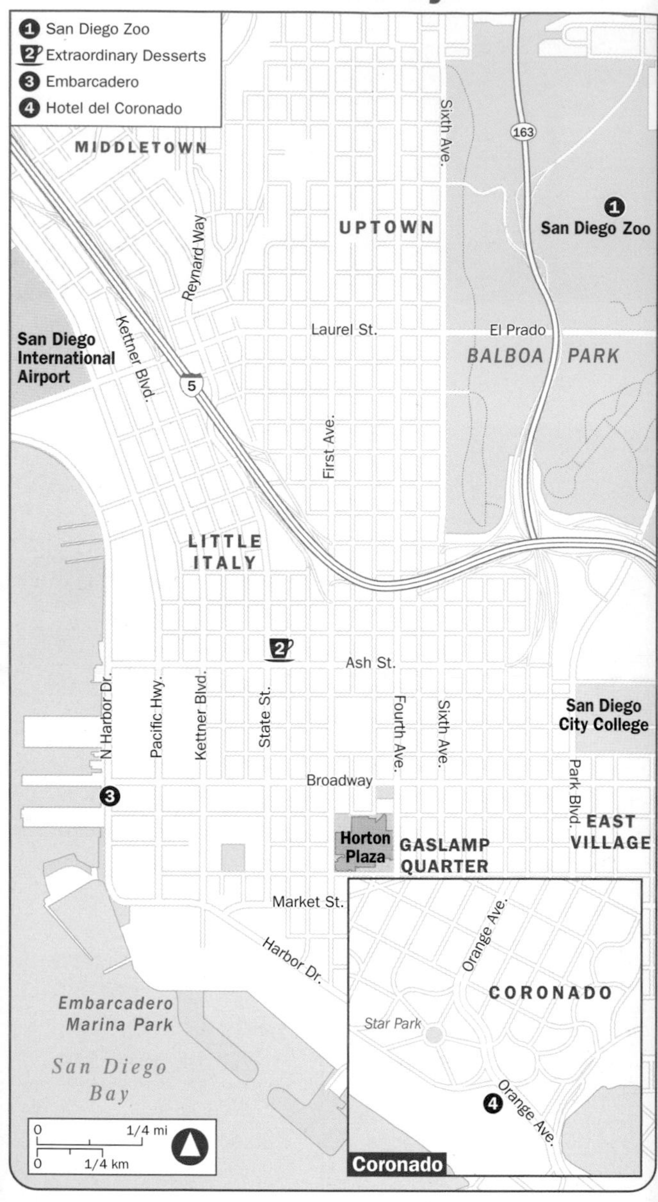
1 San Diego Zoo
2 Extraordinary Desserts
3 Embarcadero
4 Hotel del Coronado
MIDDLETOWN
UPTOWN
San Diego Zoo
Sixth Ave.
163
Reynard Way
Kettner Blvd.
San Diego International Airport
5
Laurel St.
El Prado
BALBOA PARK
First Ave.
LITTLE ITALY
Ash St.
N Harbor Dr.
Pacific Hwy.
Kettner Blvd.
State St.
Fourth Ave.
Sixth Ave.
San Diego City College
Park Blvd.
Broadway
EAST VILLAGE
Horton Plaza
GASLAMP QUARTER
Market St.
Harbor Dr.
Orange Ave.
CORONADO
Star Park
Embarcadero Marina Park
San Diego Bay
Orange Ave.
0
1/4 mi
0
1/4 km
Coronado

Now that you have an overview of the city—from its Spanish colonial and Mexican-American frontier roots to its high-octane nightlife and lively, lovely beach communities—it's time to go where the wild things are. Put on a pair of comfortable shoes and head to San Diego's best-known attraction, the San Diego Zoo. Then cap your day with a visit to the area's most iconic structure: the Hotel del Coronado. START: **Bus 7 to the San Diego Zoo.**

❶ ★★★ kids **San Diego Zoo.** "World famous" often precedes any mention of the San Diego Zoo, and for good reason. Established in 1916, the zoo was a pioneer in developing naturalistic, humane enclosures. It's also a global leader in endangered-species preservation with its breeding programs. Among the most popular wildlife sightings are the giant pandas. The zoo's most recent addition is **Elephant Odyssey,** featuring a herd of Asian elephants as well as life-size replicas of prehistoric animals that roamed the San Diego region. Other highlights include the **Panda Trek** exhibit, where grownups and kids munch bamboo and roll down hillsides; the **Monkey Trails** and **Forest Tales,** the zoo's largest, most elaborate habitat, re-creating a wooded forest filled with a variety of rare creatures; **Gorilla Tropics,** housing two troops of lowland gorillas; and the Tasmanian devils and kangaroos in the **Australian Outback.** ◷ *At least 3 hr. 2920 Zoo Dr.* ☎ *619/234-3153 (recorded info), or 619/231-1515. www.sandiegozoo.org. Admission $50 adults, $40 children 3–11, free for active-duty military (U.S. & foreign); discounted 2-day passes can be used for both the zoo & Safari Park (see p 30). Sept to mid-June daily 9am–4pm (grounds close at 5 or 6pm); mid-June to Aug daily 9am–8pm (grounds close at 9pm). Bus: 7.*

The Australian Outback exhibit at the San Diego Zoo.

You've earned this one, after all the walking you've done. Head toward downtown and the Embarcadero, but stop on the way for a sinful creation from ❷ ★★★ **Extraordinary Desserts.** Set in an architecturally striking space, this local standout also serves panini, salads, and artisan cheeses as well as wine and beer. Chef/proprietor Karen Krasne sells her own line of jams, confections, and syrups, too, if you want to take a taste of San Diego home. Take Bus 7 to Broadway and Union Street, and then walk 4 blocks north. *1430 Union St.* ☎ *619/294-7001. www.extraordinarydesserts.com. Mon–Thurs 8:30am–11pm; Fri 8:30am–midnight; Sat 10am–midnight; Sun 10am–11pm. $6–$15.*

❸ **Embarcadero.** Take a leisurely stroll down San Diego's waterfront, where the sights include the flotilla of historic vessels that make up the San Diego Maritime Museum. Most impressive is the *Star of India*, which was originally put to sea in 1863, making it the world's oldest active ship. Continue to the Broadway Pier, where you can catch the ferry to Coronado. ⏲ *30 min. Broadway Pier, 1050 N. Harbor Dr., at the intersection of Broadway.* ☎ *800/442-7847 or 619/234-4111. www.flagshipsd.com. Ferries run on the hour Sun–Thurs 9am–9pm & Fri–Sat 9am–10pm. They return from the Ferry Landing in Coronado to the Broadway Pier every hour on the half-hour Sun–Thurs 9:30am–9:30pm & Fri–Sat 9:30am–10:30pm. The ride takes 15 min. The fare is $4.75 each way. Buy tickets at the Harbor Excursion kiosk on Broadway Pier or at the Ferry Landing in Coronado. The ferries do not accommodate cars.*

Hotel del Coronado.

The Passion Fruit Pavlova from Extraordinary Desserts.

❹ ★★★ **Hotel del Coronado.** This is the last of California's stately old seaside hotels. In continuous operation since 1888, the Del is a monument to Victorian grandeur, boasting cupolas, turrets, and gingerbread trim, making it San Diego's most recognizable property. There is plenty here to engage a nonguest, including a gallery devoted to the hotel's history, a shopping arcade, and several wonderful options for drinks or dining—not to mention the fact the hotel sits on Coronado Beach, one of San Diego's finest stretches of sand. ⏲ *1 hr. 1500 Orange Ave.* ☎ *800/468-3533 or 619/435-6611. www.hoteldel.com. Bus: 904 from the Ferry Landing.* ●

2 The Best Special-Interest Tours

Balboa Park

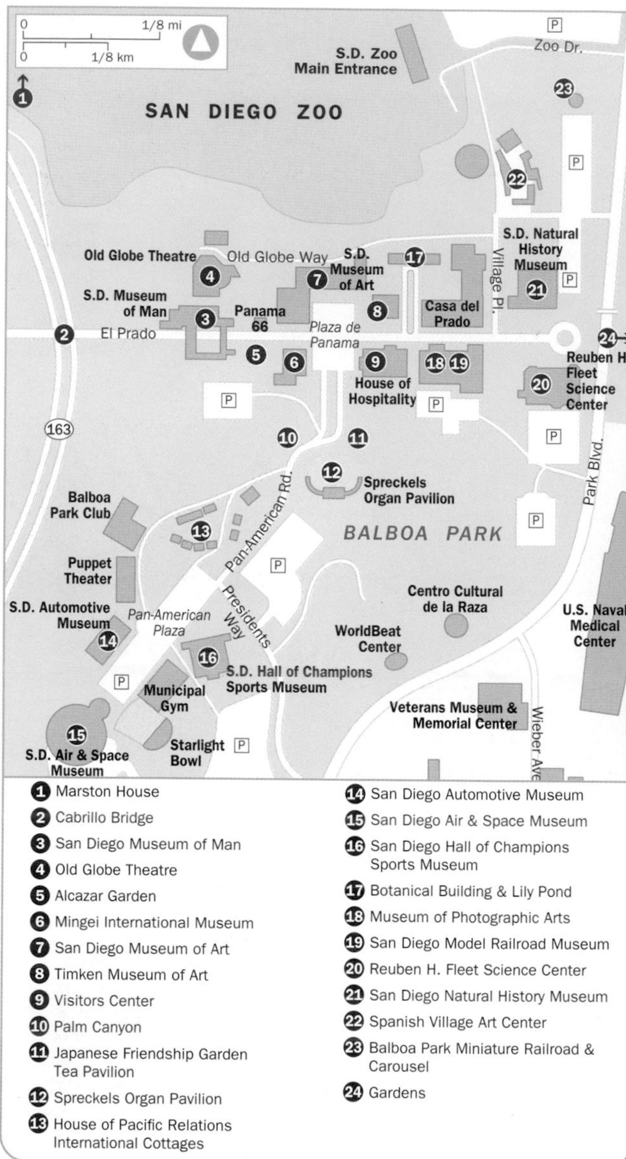
0 1/8 mi
0 1/8 km
S.D. Zoo Main Entrance
Zoo Dr.
SAN DIEGO ZOO
S.D. Natural History Museum
Village Pl.
Old Globe Theatre
Old Globe Way
S.D. Museum of Art
S.D. Museum of Man
Panama 66
Casa del Prado
El Prado
Plaza de Panama
Reuben H. Fleet Science Center
House of Hospitality
163
Spreckels Organ Pavilion
Park Blvd.
Balboa Park Club
BALBOA PARK
Pan-American Rd.
Puppet Theater
Centro Cultural de la Raza
S.D. Automotive Museum
Pan-American Plaza
Presidents Way
WorldBeat Center
U.S. Naval Medical Center
S.D. Hall of Champions Sports Museum
Municipal Gym
Veterans Museum & Memorial Center
Wieber Ave.
S.D. Air & Space Museum
Starlight Bowl
1 Marston House
2 Cabrillo Bridge
3 San Diego Museum of Man
4 Old Globe Theatre
5 Alcazar Garden
6 Mingei International Museum
7 San Diego Museum of Art
8 Timken Museum of Art
9 Visitors Center
10 Palm Canyon
11 Japanese Friendship Garden Tea Pavilion
12 Spreckels Organ Pavilion
13 House of Pacific Relations International Cottages
14 San Diego Automotive Museum
15 San Diego Air & Space Museum
16 San Diego Hall of Champions Sports Museum
17 Botanical Building & Lily Pond
18 Museum of Photographic Arts
19 San Diego Model Railroad Museum
20 Reuben H. Fleet Science Center
21 San Diego Natural History Museum
22 Spanish Village Art Center
23 Balboa Park Miniature Railroad & Carousel
24 Gardens

Previous page: California's first mission, San Diego de Alcalá, founded by Friar Junípero Serra.

Established in 1868, Balboa Park is the second-oldest city park in the United States. Much of its striking architecture, which now houses a variety of museums, was the product of the 1915–16 Panama–California Exposition and the 1935–36 California Pacific International Exposition. Balboa Park (p 9) is beloved by urbanites for its extensive and mature botanical collection, owing largely to the efforts of Kate Sessions, a horticulturist who devoted her life to transforming the desolate mesas and scrub-filled canyons into the oases they are today. ***Note:*** The park encompasses more than a dozen museums, so try to visit the two or three that most appeal to you. **START: Bus 1, 3, 7, or 120 to Balboa Park.**

❶ ★ Marston House. This elegant Craftsman home is listed on the National Register of Historic Places. *See p 39.*

❷ ★ Cabrillo Bridge. Offering excellent views of downtown, the bridge straddles scenic, sycamore-lined Hwy. 163 and provides a dramatic entrance to the park. Built in 1915 for the Panama–California Exposition, it's patterned after a bridge in Ronda, Spain. Directly ahead are the Museum of Man's distinctive California Tower and the park's main thoroughfare, El Prado. This is the westside entrance to the park; Laurel St. leads directly to the bridge. 🕔 *5 min.*

❸ ★ kids San Diego Museum of Man. This anthropological museum emphasizes the peoples of North and South America; there are also Egyptian mummies and relics and a museum store with great folk art. Historical figures carved on the facade include conquistador Juan Rodríguez Cabrillo, Spanish Kings Charles I and Phillip III, and, at the very top, Father Junípero Serra. Tours to the top of the tile-domed California Tower are available for an extra fee. 🕔 *1 hr.* ☎ *619/239-2001. www.museumofman.org. Admission $13 adults, $10 seniors & active-duty military, $8 students, $6 children 3–12, free for children under 3. Daily 10am–5pm.*

Inside the Museum of Man.

❹ ★★★ Old Globe Theatre. This is actually a three-theater complex that includes the Old Globe, an outdoor stage, and a small theater-in-the-round. Built for the 1935 exposition as a replica of Shakespeare's original theater, the Globe was meant to be demolished after the fair but was saved by a group of dedicated citizens. In 1978, an arsonist destroyed the theater, which was rebuilt into what you see today; the facility also received a sweeping renovation for its 75th anniversary in 2010. 🕔 *10 min.* ☎ *619/234-5623. www.theoldglobe.org. Backstage tours are offered most weekends at 10:30am & cost $5 for adults, $3 for students, seniors & military. Performances are Tues–Sun,*

The Old Globe Theatre.

with weekend matinees. The box office is open Tues–Sun from noon until the end of the last performance. Tickets $29–$102.

5 ★ Alcazar Garden. This formal garden is patterned after the ones surrounding the Alcazar Castle in Seville, Spain. The large tree at the rear is an Indian laurel fig, planted by Kate Sessions when the park was first landscaped. ⏲ *10 min. Free admission. Open 24 hr. but caution should be exercised after dark.*

6 ★★ Mingei International Museum. The Mingei offers changing exhibitions that celebrate folk art, including textiles, costumes, jewelry, toys, pottery, paintings, and sculpture. The gift shop's folk art selection is always irresistible. ⏲ *At least 30 min.* ☎ *619/239-0003. www.mingei.org. Admission $10 adults; $7 seniors, children 6–17, students & military with ID; free for children under 6. Tues–Sun 10am–5pm.*

7 ★ San Diego Museum of Art (SDMA). The exquisite facade was inspired by the famous university building in Salamanca, Spain. The three life-size figures over the scalloped entryway are the Spanish painters Bartolomé Murillo, Francisco de Zurbarán, and Diego Velázquez. The museum holds San Diego's most extensive collection of fine art; major touring exhibitions are presented as well. There's also an ongoing schedule of concerts, films, and lectures, usually themed with a current show. ⏲ *At least 1 hr.* ☎ *619/232-7931. www.sdmart.org. Admission $12 adults, $9 seniors & military, $8 students, $4.50 children 6–17, free for children under 6. Admission to traveling exhibits varies; the Sculpture Garden is always free. Thurs–Sat & Mon–Tues 10am–5pm; Sun noon–5pm (closed Wed).*

Nikigator at the Mingei Museum.

Passport to Balboa Park

If you plan to visit multiple museums in one day, buy the One-Day Explorer pass, which allows admission to five museums in 1 day. It's $45 for adults and $26 for children ages 3 to 12. The Multi-Day Explorer allows entrance to 17 museums and attractions and is valid for 1 week. It's $55 for adults and $29 for children ages 3 to 12. If you plan to spend a day at the zoo as well, purchase the One-Day Zoo Admission with the Multi-Day Pass for $94 for adults and $61 for children. The passports can be purchased at any participating attraction (except the zoo), at the visitor center, or online at www.balboapark.org.

San Diego's booming craft beer scene gets museum-level treatment at ★★ **Panama 66** in SDMA's Sculpture Garden. Several local brews are on tap in the open-air space surrounded by 19th- and 20th-century sculptures, including works from Henry Moore and Alexander Lieberman. Gourmet pub food and a kids' menu including PB&J are on offer until 1 hour before closing. Jazz, salsa, and other bands play most Friday and Saturday nights. ☎ *619/696-1966. Free admission to Sculpture Garden. Mon 11am–4pm, Tues–Fri 11am–10pm, Sat–Sun 10am–10pm. $9–$13.*

8 ★ **Timken Museum of Art.** This small, always-free museum houses a collection of 19th-century American paintings and works by European old masters as well as a worthy display of Russian icons and San Diego's only Rembrandt painting. 🕓 *30 min.* ☎ *619/239-5548. www.timkenmuseum.org. Free admission. Tues–Sat 10am–4:30pm; Sun noon–4:30pm.*

9 **Visitors Center.** Pick up maps, souvenirs, and discount tickets to the museums; guided and self-guided tours begin here, too. In the courtyard behind the Visitors Center, you'll find the beautiful *Woman of Tehuantepec* fountain sculpture by Donal Hord as well as the Prado restaurant (p 10). 🕓 *10 min.* ☎ *619/239-0512. www.balboapark.org. Daily 9:30am–4:30pm.*

10 ★ **Palm Canyon.** Fifty-eight species of palm, plus magnolia trees and a Moreton Bay fig tree, provide a tropical canopy along this short, dead-end walkway. It's secluded, so it's not recommended you venture here after dark. 🕓 *15 min. Free admission. Open 24 hr.*

11 ★ **Japanese Friendship Garden.** A tea pavilion serving sushi, salads, and other Japanese

The San Diego Museum of Art in Balboa Park.

The Timken Museum of Art.

favorites overlooks an 11½-acre (5-hectare) canyon that has been carefully developed to include traditional Japanese elements, including a small meditation garden. ⏲ *15 min.* ☎ *619/232-2721. www.niwa.org. Free admission to teahouse. Admission to the garden $8 adults; $7 seniors, students & military; free for children under 6. Mon–Fri 10am–5pm, Sat–Sun 10am–4:30pm.*

⓬ ★ **Spreckels Organ Pavilion.** The ornate pipe organ was donated to San Diego by brothers John D. and Adolph B. Spreckels, and famed contralto Ernestine Schumann-Heink sang at the December 31, 1914, dedication. Free recitals are performed on one of the largest outdoor organs in the world (its vast structure contains 4,530 pipes) on Sundays at 2pm, with additional concerts and events scheduled in summertime. ⏲ *15 min.* ☎ *619/702-8138. http://spreckelsorgan.org. Free admission.*

Palm Canyon in Balboa Park with 58 species of palm trees.

⓭ **House of Pacific Relations International Cottages.** This cluster of cottages, some from the 1935 Exposition, disseminates information about the culture, traditions, and history of more than 30 countries. Special events are presented by one of the nations every Sunday from 2 to 3pm, March through October. ⏲ *At least 15 min.* ☎ *619/234-0739. www.sdhpr.org. Free admission. Sun noon–4pm. The adjacent United Nations Building houses an international gift shop where you can buy jewelry, toys, books, and UNICEF greeting cards.* ☎ *619/233-5044. Daily 10am–4:30pm.*

⓮ ★ **San Diego Automotive Museum.** Gear-heads and those who appreciate the sculptural beauty of fine design enjoy the displays of Harley-Davidsons and Indian Motorcycles and an exhibit on Steve McQueen's racing career. ⏲ *15 min.* ☎ *619/231-2886. www.sdautomuseum.org. Admission $9 adults, $6 seniors & active military, $5 students, $4 children 6–15, free for children under 6. Daily 10am–5pm (last admission 4:30pm).*

⑮ ★★ kids **San Diego Air & Space Museum.** This kid-pleaser has more than 60 aircraft on display, providing an overview of aeronautical history from the days of hot-air balloons to the space age. 🕓 *1 hr.* ☎ *619/234-8291. www.sandiegoairandspace.org. Admission $20 adults; $17 seniors, students & retired military; $11 children 3–11; free for active military with ID & children under 3. Daily 10am–4:30pm.*

⑯ ★ **San Diego Hall of Champions Sports Museum.** From baseball great Ted Williams to Olympic gold medalist Shaun White, San Diego's best-ever athletes and the sports they played are celebrated at this slick museum. You can try out your play-by-play skills at the two-dozen-plus exhibits, rotating art shows, and interactive stations. 🕓 *1 hr.* ☎ *619/234-2544. www.sdhoc.com. Admission $8 adults; $6 seniors, students & military; $4 children 7–17; free for children under 7. Daily 10am–4:30pm.*

⑰ ★★★ **Botanical Building and Lily Pond.** This serene park within the park is a great retreat on a hot day; ferns, orchids, impatiens, begonias, and other plants—about 2,100 tropical and flowering varieties, plus rotating exhibits—are sheltered here. The graceful 250-foot-long (76m) building, part of the 1915 Panama–California Exposition, is one of the world's largest wood-lath structures. The lily pond out front attracts sun worshippers, painters, and buskers. 🕓 *15 min.* ☎ *619/235-1100. Free admission. Fri–Wed 10am–4pm; closed Thurs & major holidays.*

San Diego Automotive Museum.

⑱ ★★ **Museum of Photographic Arts.** This is one of the few museums in the United States devoted exclusively to the photographic arts, encompassing not only traditional photography but also cinema, video, and digital art. There's also a plush cinema that screens classic films on an ongoing basis and a great bookstore. 🕓 *At*

San Diego Air & Space Museum.

The Botanical Building and lily pond in Balboa Park.

least 30 min. ☎ 619/238-7559. www.mopa.org. Admission $8 adults, $7 seniors, $6 students, free for active military & children under 12 with adult. Tues–Sun 10am–5pm.

⑲ ★ kids **San Diego Model Railroad Museum.** Kids and train buffs will love the scale-model railroads depicting Southern California's transportation history and terrain with an astounding attention to miniature details. ⏲ *30 min. Located in the Casa de Balboa, below the Museum of Photographic Arts. ☎ 619/696-0199. www.sdmrm.org. Admission $9 adults, $7 seniors, $4 students, $5 military, $2 children 6–15, free for children under 5 with adult admission. Tues–Fri 11am–4pm, Sat–Sun 11am–5pm.*

The tornado machine at the Reuben H. Fleet Science Center.

⑳ ★★ kids **Reuben H. Fleet Science Center.** A must-see for kids of any age, this tantalizing collection of interactive exhibits and virtual rides is designed to stimulate the imagination and teach scientific principles. There is also an IMAX dome theater, which is used for planetarium shows the first Wednesday of each month at 7 and 8:15 pm. ⏲ *At least 1 hr. ☎ 619/238-1233. www.rhfleet.org. Fleet Experience admission includes an IMAX film & exhibit galleries: $8.95 adults, seniors & children 3–12 (exhibit gallery can be purchased individually, $20 adults, $18 seniors, $17 kids 3–12); planetarium show: $17 adults, $16 seniors & kids 3–12. Mon–Fri 10am–5pm; Sat–Sun 10am–6pm; later closing times possible.*

㉑ ★★ kids **San Diego Natural History Museum.** Founded in 1874, this is one of the West's oldest scientific institutions, focusing on the flora, fauna, and mineralogy of the region. The museum shows 3-D nature films in its giant-screen theater; exhibits include life-size reproductions of a T-Rex skeleton, a Megaladon shark, and other giants. The museum also presents special exhibitions, free nature hikes, and a full schedule of classes, lectures, and overnight expeditions for both families and adults. ⏲ *At least 1 hr. ☎ 619/232-3821. www.sdnhm.org. Admission $17 adults; $15 seniors; $12 students, kids ages 13–17 & active-duty military; $11 children 3–12; free for children under 3. Two films in the museum's theater are included with admission. Daily 10am–5pm.*

㉒ ★ Spanish Village Art Center. This collection of 37 picture-perfect *casitas* is home to more than 250 artists, specializing in everything from glass blowing to woodcarving. Many of the artists work on-site, allowing you to watch the art-making process. ⏲ *20 min. ☎ 619/233-9050. www.spanishvillageart.com. Free admission. Daily 11am–4pm.*

The Spanish Village Art Center.

The San Diego Natural History Museum.

㉓ ★ kids Balboa Park Miniature Railroad and Carousel. The open-air railroad takes a 3-minute journey through a grove of eucalyptus trees, while the carousel, built in 1910, is one of the last to still offer a ring grab. ⏲ *20 min. Zoo Dr., next to San Diego Zoo entrance. Railroad: ☎ 619/231-1515. www.sandiegozoo.org. Summer daily 11am–6:30pm, Sept–May weekends and holidays only 11am–4:30pm. Carousel: ☎ 619/239-0512. www.balboapark.org. Summer daily 11am–5:30pm, Sept–May weekends & holidays only 11am–5pm. Admission $2 Railroad (free for children under 1), $2 Carousel.*

㉔ ★★ Gardens. Cross Park Boulevard via a pedestrian overpass and you'll find, to your left, a Desert Garden, and to your right, the Inez Grant Parker Memorial Rose Garden, home to some 2,500 roses. (Blooms peak Mar–May.) ⏲ *20 min. www.balboapark.org. Free admission. Open 24 hr. but not recommended after dark.*

San Diego with Kids

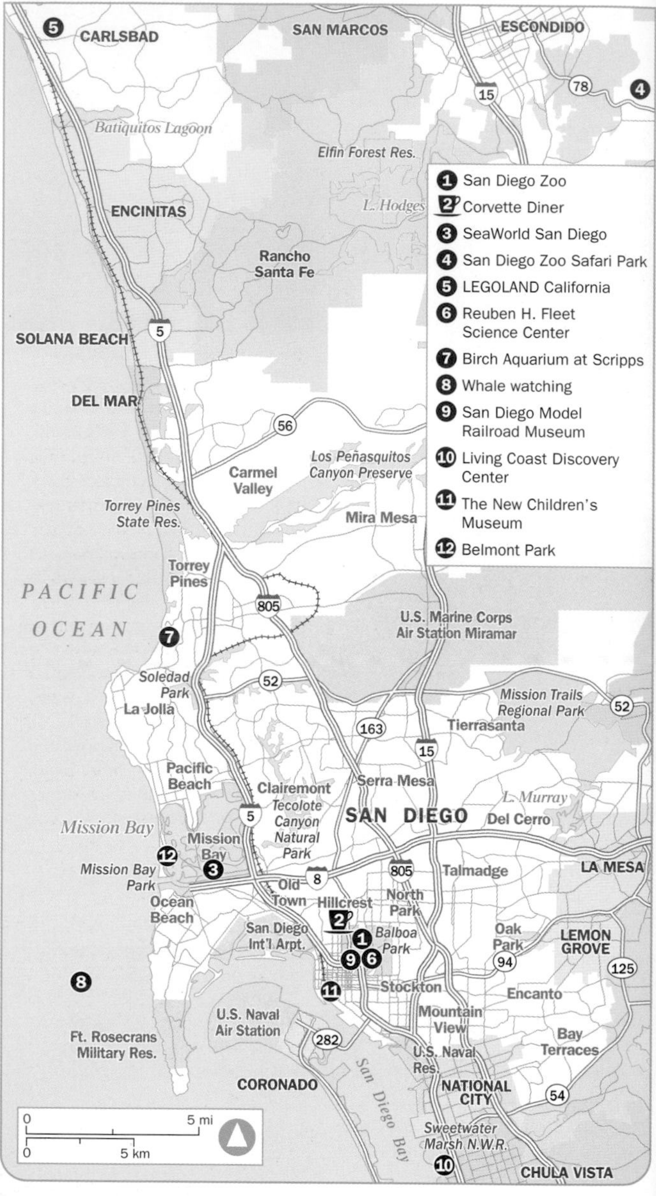
1 San Diego Zoo
2 Corvette Diner
3 SeaWorld San Diego
4 San Diego Zoo Safari Park
5 LEGOLAND California
6 Reuben H. Fleet Science Center
7 Birch Aquarium at Scripps
8 Whale watching
9 San Diego Model Railroad Museum
10 Living Coast Discovery Center
11 The New Children's Museum
12 Belmont Park
CARLSBAD
SAN MARCOS
ESCONDIDO
Batiquitos Lagoon
Elfin Forest Res.
L. Hodges
ENCINITAS
Rancho Santa Fe
SOLANA BEACH
DEL MAR
Carmel Valley
Los Peñasquitos Canyon Preserve
Torrey Pines State Res.
Mira Mesa
Torrey Pines
PACIFIC OCEAN
U.S. Marine Corps Air Station Miramar
Soledad Park
La Jolla
Mission Trails Regional Park
Tierrasanta
Pacific Beach
Clairemont
Serra Mesa
Tecolote Canyon Natural Park
SAN DIEGO
L. Murray
Del Cerro
Mission Bay
Mission Bay Park
Talmadge
LA MESA
Old Town
Hillcrest
North Park
Ocean Beach
San Diego Int'l Arpt.
Balboa Park
Oak Park
LEMON GROVE
Stockton
Encanto
U.S. Naval Air Station
Mountain View
Ft. Rosecrans Military Res.
Bay Terraces
U.S. Naval Res.
CORONADO
San Diego Bay
NATIONAL CITY
Sweetwater Marsh N.W.R.
CHULA VISTA
0 5 mi
0 5 km

In San Diego, activities abound for kids—from toddlers to teens. With its renowned theme parks and zoo, and its kid-friendly museums (where unsuspecting young minds just might learn a thing or two), San Diego more than lives up to its reputation as a family vacation destination. Best of all, these places won't bore the adults in tow either. **START: Bus 7 to the San Diego Zoo in Balboa Park.**

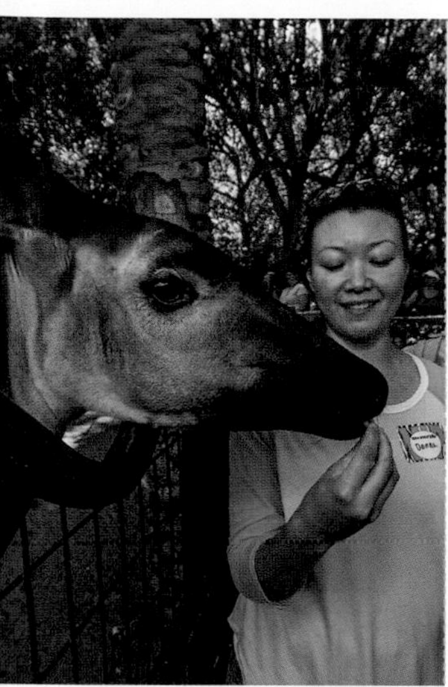

Feeding the animals at the San Diego Zoo.

❶ ★★★ San Diego Zoo. San Diego's world-famous zoo appeals to children of all ages, and the double-decker bus tours bring all the animals into easy view of even the smallest visitors. There's a **Children's Zoo** where kids can feed and pet the animals, and the **Skyfari** aerial tram offers thrills and views over Balboa Park to the sea. *See p 17.*

Get a taste of the rockin' 1950s at the **❷ Corvette Diner,** where the jukebox is loud and the gum-snapping waitresses slide into your booth to take your order. The restaurant has several themed rooms and an arcade with everything from air hockey to Guitar Hero. *2965 Historic Decatur Rd. (in Liberty Station, off Rosecrans St.). ☎ 619/542-1476. www.cohnrestaurants.com. $9–$15 (kids' plates $7.95).*

❸ ★ SeaWorld San Diego. Crowd-pleasing shows and rides highlight this marine-life theme park, made infamous in the 2013 documentary *Blackfish,* about the dangers and consequences of keeping killer whales in captivity. The iconic **Shamu** orca whale show took a big PR hit and will be replaced in 2017. Other shows—starring dolphins, sea lions, household pets, and (in summer) human acrobats—run several times throughout the day. SeaWorld's real strengths, though, are in the simulated marine environments, including **Wild Arctic** (with beluga whales, walruses, and polar bears), **Manatee Rescue,** the **Shark Encounter,** and—everyone's favorite—the **Penguin Encounter.** *At least 3 hr. 500 SeaWorld Dr.*

Orca whale show at SeaWorld.

Admission Discounts

San Diego's three main animal attractions offer combo tickets that can save you some cash. If you plan to visit both the zoo and Safari Park, a 2-Visit Pass is $90 for adults, $70 for children 3 to 11; passes are valid for 1 year and can be used twice at the same attraction if you choose. A 3-for-1 pass gives you unlimited passes to the zoo, Safari Park, and SeaWorld for 7 days from first use; the cost is $165 for adults, $135 for children ages 3 to 9. Passes are available at the participating parks and on their websites.

Other value options include the **Southern California CityPass** (☎ 888/330-5008; www.citypass.com), which covers SeaWorld, LEGOLAND, and Disneyland Resorts. Passes are $329 for adults and $294 for kids ages 3 to 9 (a savings of about 30 percent), valid for 14 days. You can add the San Diego Zoo or Safari Park for $38 for adults, $30 for kids ages 3 to 9. **Go San Diego Card** (☎ 866/628-9032; www.gosandiegocard.com) offers unlimited general admission to more than 50 Southern California attractions, including the zoo and LEGOLAND (SeaWorld is available only on multi-day passes). One-day packages start at $84 for adults and $79 for children (ages 3–12).

☎ 800/257-4268 or 619/226-3901. www.seaworld.com. Admission starts at $69 adults & children ages 3–9, free for children under 3. Web specials available. Hours vary seasonally, but always at least daily 10am–5pm; most weekends & during summer 9am–11pm. Parking starts at $16. Bus: 8/9.

Feeding giraffes at the San Diego Zoo Safari Park.

4 ★★★ San Diego Zoo Safari Park. Originally a breeding facility for the San Diego Zoo, the 1,800-acre (728-hectare) Safari Park's animal collection represents some 430 different species. Many of the animals roam freely in vast enclosures, allowing giraffes to interact with antelopes, much as they would in Africa. Although the San Diego Zoo may be "world famous," it's the Safari Park that many visitors celebrate as their favorite. Roar & Snore sleepovers, which are held year-round (except Dec and Jan) on most Fridays and Saturdays—with extended dates in summer—let you camp out next to the animal compound (reservations required). 🕒 *At least 3 hr. 15500 San Pasqual Valley Rd. ☎ 760/747-8702. www.sdzsafaripark.org. Admission $50 adults, $40 children 3–11, free for children under 3 & active-duty military (U.S. & foreign). Daily*

9am–4pm (grounds close at 5pm); extended hours during summer & Festival of Lights (2 weekends in Dec). Parking $12. Bus: 386 (Mon–Sat). The park is 34 miles (55km) north of downtown San Diego in a rural setting, making a car almost a necessity.

5 ★ LEGOLAND California. This theme park in Carlsbad, 40 minutes north of downtown San Diego, offers a full day of entertainment for families. There are more than 50 rides, shows, and attractions, including hands-on interactive displays; scale models of international landmarks (such as the Eiffel Tower), constructed of LEGO bricks; and a water park with slides and pools. LEGOLAND is geared toward children ages 2 to 12, with just enough of a thrill-ride component that preteens will be amused; however, most teenagers will find this place a bit of a snooze. A sister attraction, Sea Life Aquarium, is next door, displaying live fish in giant tanks. *At least 3 hr. 1 Legoland Dr. ☎ 877/534-6526 or 760/918-5346. www.legoland.com or www.sealifeus.com. LEGOLAND $67 adults, $57 seniors & children 3–12, free for children under 3; water park additional $10 per person. Sea Life $19 adults, $16 seniors, $12 children; discounted 1- or 2-day park-hopper tickets available. July–Aug daily 10am–8pm, June daily 10am–5 or 6pm, off-season Thurs–Mon 10am–5 or 6pm. Closed Tues–Wed Sept–May, but open daily during winter & spring vacation periods. Parking $12. Bus: 321. From San Diego, you'll need a car.*

Excited about entering LEGOLAND.

6 ★★ Reuben H. Fleet Science Center. With its hands-on exhibits, motion simulator rides, and an IMAX theater, this science funhouse draws kids like magnets. *See p 26.*

The Birch Aquarium at Scripps.

Gray whale spotting in San Diego Bay.

7 ★★ Birch Aquarium at Scripps. This beautiful facility is both an aquarium and a museum, operated as the interpretive arm of the world-famous Scripps Institution of Oceanography. The aquarium affords close-up views of marine life from the Pacific Northwest and California coasts, Mexico's Sea of Cortez, and the tropical seas, all presented in more than 60 tanks; the giant kelp forest and moon jellyfish are particularly impressive. The outdoor demonstration tide pool also offers amazing coastal views and hosts a summer evening concert series. *90 min. 2300 Expedition Way. ☎ 858/534-3474. www.aquarium.ucsd.edu. Admission $17 adults, $13 seniors, $11–$12 college students, $14 teens 13–17, $13 children 3–12, free for children under 3. Daily 9am–5pm; special hours for events. Free parking. Bus: 30.*

A barn owl at the Living Coast Discovery Center.

8 ★★ Whale Watching. The easiest (and cheapest) way to observe the migration of the Pacific gray whales every mid-December to mid-March is to head to Cabrillo National Monument (p 13), where you'll find a glassed-in observatory and educational whale exhibits. Better yet, head to sea—the variety of options includes kayaks and large ships with lots of amenities. *La Jolla Kayak (☎ 858/459-1114; www.lajollakayak.com) leads guided kayak tours in search of passing whales. It's about a 1-mile (1.6km) paddle that departs daily at 10am & noon from La Jolla Shores. $59. Embarcadero-based companies offering expeditions include Hornblower Cruises (☎ 888/467-6256 or 619/686-8715; www.hornblower.com) & Flagship Cruises (☎ 800/442-7847 or 619/234-4111; www.flagshipsd.com). Trips are 3 or 3½ hr.; fares run $40–$45 for adults, with discounts for seniors, military & kids.*

9 ★ San Diego Model Railroad Museum. This 27,000-square-foot (2,508-sq.-m) space has four permanent scale-model railroad dioramas, along with interactive multimedia displays, to fire the imagination of train lovers of all ages. *See p 26.*

10 ★★ Living Coast Discovery Center. Formerly called the Chula Vista Nature Center, this wonderful, interactive nature center is about 15 minutes south of downtown. It highlights the plants and animals native to San Diego Bay and the surrounding wetlands, featuring exhibits of sea turtles, stingrays, and small sharks in kid-level open tanks, along with raptors and sea birds in aviaries. *At least 1 hr. 1000 Gunpowder Point Dr. ☎ 619/409-5900. www.theliving coast.org. $14 adults; $9 seniors, students & kids ages 4–17; free for children under 4. Daily 10am–5pm. The (free) parking lot is located away from the center & a shuttle bus ferries guests btw. the two points every 10–15 min. (last shuttle at 4pm). Trolley: Blue Line to Bayfront/E St. Call ☎ 619/409-5900 for center shuttle transportation from trolley stop.*

⓫ ★ The New Children's Museum. This state-of-the-art facility opened in 2008 and features local artists' ever-changing pieces that can be climbed on, touched, or interacted with (they just might intrigue the adults in tow as well). The downtown space also offers lots of arts-based classes and good old-fashioned play areas; it appeals mostly to the under-13 set. *1 hr. 200 W. Island Ave. (at Front St.). ☎ 619/233-8792. www.thinkplay create.org. Admission $12 adults & children, $8 seniors & military, free for children under 1. Mon, Wed, Thurs, Sat 10am–4pm; Fri 9:30am–4pm; Sun noon–4pm. Parking $10. Bus: 3, 11, 120, or 992. Trolley: Orange Line to Convention Center.*

Scribble board at the New Children's Museum.

A roller-coaster ride at Belmont Park in Mission Beach.

⓬ ★★ Belmont Park. This seaside amusement park on the Mission Beach boardwalk first opened in 1925 as a means to promote the then scarcely populated coastal areas. There are plenty of carnival-style rides, but the star attractions are the Giant Dipper roller coaster and the Plunge, a huge indoor pool that was closed for renovations at press time. Both are Roaring '20s originals. The park has been through several incarnations and now includes wave machines, a zip line, a rock-climbing wall, and a miniature golf course along with several restaurants and snack stands. *2 hr. 3190 Mission Blvd. (at W. Mission Bay Dr.). ☎ 858/488-1549. www.belmontpark.com. Rides are $3–$6 each; unlimited-ride wristbands are $26 (over 50 in./127cm) & $16 (under 50 in./127cm); wave rides start at $20 per hour, with a one-time registration fee of $10. Daily 11am–10pm (weekend & summer hours later; closed Mon–Thurs Jan–Feb). Bus: 8/9.*

Historic San Diego

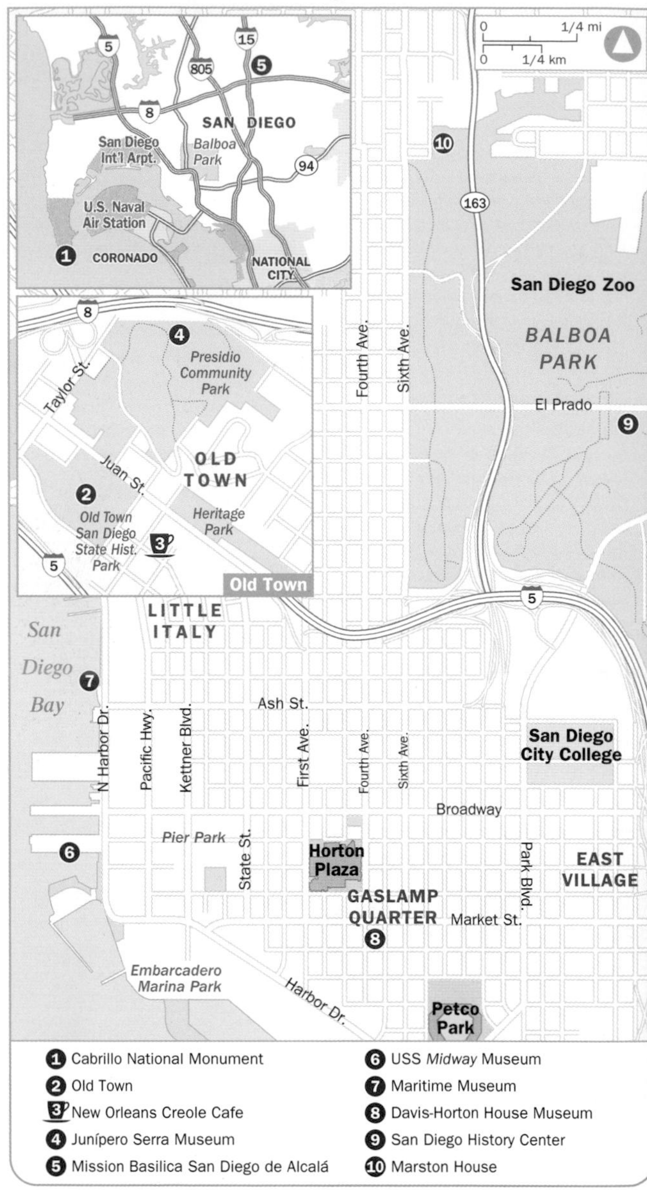

1 Cabrillo National Monument
2 Old Town
3 New Orleans Creole Cafe
4 Junípero Serra Museum
5 Mission Basilica San Diego de Alcalá
6 USS *Midway* Museum
7 Maritime Museum
8 Davis-Horton House Museum
9 San Diego History Center
10 Marston House

San Diego is where California began. Conquistador Juan Rodríguez Cabrillo first claimed the region in the name of Spain in 1542, but it would be more than 220 years before Spain sent an occupying force to colonize Alta California. In 1769, soldiers and missionaries, including Father Junípero Serra, set up camp on Presidio Hill overlooking what is now Old Town, making it the first European settlement in California. San Diego would eventually grow into a Wild West boomtown, complete with such characters as the famed lawman Wyatt Earp. And even from the earliest days of the 20th century, the U.S. military coveted San Diego's strategic geographic location, making it the bastion of military heritage it remains today. If you like to bolster your trips with a little history, San Diego is an excellent choice with lots to offer. **START: Bus 84.**

1 ★★★ kids Cabrillo National Monument. From the park's location high atop Point Loma, you can overlook San Diego Bay and see the spot where Juan Cabrillo came ashore and met with some very concerned Kumeyaay Indians in 1542. There are also museum installations describing the point's long military history; the cemetery you pass on the way into the park is Fort Rosecrans National Cemetery, a military graveyard since the 1870s. *See p 13.*

The Cabrillo National Monument.

2 ★ Old Town. The flags of Spain, Mexico, and the United States flew in succession over the dusty pueblo of San Diego, a rough-and-tumble outpost of frontier settlers. History comes alive daily in Old Town State Historic Park (p 9), where you can wander the original town square, lined with reconstructed and original buildings re-creating the era from 1821 to 1872. The structures now serve as museums, shops, and restaurants. Directly south of the park, along San Diego Avenue, are more curio stores and dining options as well as the Whaley House Museum, which attracts attention far and wide for its reputation of being certifiably haunted. A little farther down the street is El Campo Santo, the town's original cemetery. A block east of the Whaley House is Heritage Park, a collection of seven gorgeously restored Victorian buildings, including Southern California's first synagogue. *Whaley House: ⏲ 30 min. 2476 San Diego Ave. ☎ 619/297-7511. www.whaleyhouse.org. Admission before 5pm $10 adults, $6 seniors & children 6–12; admission after 5pm $13 adults, $8 seniors & children. Free for children under 6, though admission is not recommended for kids under 6 in the*

Whaley House Museum.

evening hours. May–Sept daily 10am–9:30pm; Oct–Apr Sun–Tues 10am–4:30pm, Thurs–Sat 10am–9:30pm. Heritage Park: ⏲ 20 min. 2454 Heritage Park Row (corner of Juan & Harney sts.). ☎ 858/565-3600. www.sandiegocounty.gov/parks/heritage.html. Free admission. Daily sunrise to sunset. Trolley: Blue or Green Line to Old Town.

When you're seated on the lovely patio of the small 3 **New Orleans Creole Café,** amid the shade trees of the Whaley House complex, you won't mind a little geographical incongruity one bit. You'll happily enjoy your po' boy, gumbo, or muffuletta while the throngs line up elsewhere for mediocre Mexican food. *2476 A San Diego Ave. (behind Whaley House gift shop). ☎ 619/542-1698. www.neworleanscreolecafe.com. $12–$22.*

Junípero Serra Museum.

4 ★ Junípero Serra Museum. Perched on a hill above Old Town, this Spanish Mission–style structure is located where, in 1769, the first mission, first presidio, and first non-Native settlement on the West Coast of the United States were founded. This is the "Plymouth Rock of the Pacific Coast." The museum's exhibits introduce visitors to the Native American, Spanish, and Mexican people who first called this place home; on display are their belongings, from cannons to cookware. Built in 1929, the stately building offers great views from its 70-foot (21m) tower. Presidio Park, which was established around the museum, is a nice place for a picnic and has extensive walking trails. The museum is often closed for special events; call or check the online calendar before visiting. ⏲ *1 hr. 2727 Presidio Dr.*

☎ 619/232-6203. www.sandiego history.org. Admission $6 adults; $4 seniors, students & military; $3 children 6–17; free for children under 6. Sat–Sun 10am–4pm. Trolley: Blue or Green Line to Old Town.

❺ ★ Mission Basilica San Diego de Alcalá. This was the first link in a chain of 21 missions founded by Spanish missionary Junípero Serra. In 1774, the mission was moved from Old Town to its present site for agricultural reasons and to separate the indigenous converts from the fortress that included the original building. The mission was sacked by the local tribe a year after it was built, leading Father Serra to reconstruct it using 5- to 7-foot-thick (1.5–2.1m) adobe walls and clay tile roofs, rendering it harder to burn. Mass is said daily in this active Catholic parish. ***Note:*** In the North County city of Oceanside, you can also visit **Mission San Luis Rey de Francia** (4050 Mission Ave.; ☎ 760/757-3651; www.sanluisrey.org). Known as the "King of the Missions," it's California's largest, founded in 1798. *🕓 30 min. 10818 San Diego Mission Rd. ☎ 619/281-8449. www.mission sandiego.com. Admission $5 adults, $2 seniors & students, $1 children under 12. Free Sun & for daily masses. Daily 9am–4:45pm; mass Mon–Sat 7am & 5:30pm; Sun 7, 8, 10, 11am, noon & 5:30pm. Trolley: Green Line to Mission San Diego.*

Old Town San Diego.

❻ ★ USS *Midway* Museum. The USS *Midway* had a 47-year military history that began 1 week after the Japanese surrender of World War II in 1945. The carrier is now moored at the Embarcadero and has become the world's largest floating naval-aviation museum. A self-guided audio tour takes visitors to several levels of the ship, telling the story of life on board. The highlight is climbing up the superstructure to the bridge and gazing down

Plane on the deck of USS Midway *Museum.*

Spooks & Splashes

Those who want to take a walk on the supernatural side can stroll through Old Town with "ghost hunter" **Michael Brown** (☎ 619/972-3900; www.oldtownsmosthaunted.com). He leads tours in search of real paranormal activity Thursday through Sunday at 9pm; tickets are $19 adults, $10 children 6 to 12, and free for kids 5 and under. An 11pm tour is available by reservation for $39 per person. **Haunted San Diego Tours** (☎ 619/255-6170; www.hauntedsandiegotours.com) features costumed storytellers spinning supernatural yarns aboard the "ghost bus" as you visit some of the city's most mysterious sites. Tours run Thursday through Monday at 7pm. Tickets are $35 (it's not recommended for children under 10).

The 90-minute amphibious **SEAL (Sea and Land Adventures) tour** (☎ 619/298-8687; www.sealtours.com) departs from Seaport Village and motors along the Embarcadero before splashing into San Diego Bay. The narrated tour gives you the maritime and military history of San Diego from the right perspective. Trips are scheduled daily, with at least three trips each day and more on weekends. The cost is $39 for adults and $19 for kids 4 to 12 ($1 for children 3 and under).

on the 1,001-foot-long (305m) flight deck, with various aircraft poised for duty. In 2014, the museum debuted a fascinating multimedia show on the Battle of the Midway. ***Note:*** Be prepared to climb many stairs and ladders. ⏲ *1 hr. 910 Harbor Dr. (at Navy Pier). ☎ 619/544-9600. www.midway.org. Admission $20 adults, $17 seniors, $15 students, $10 retired military & children 6–12, free for children under 6 & active-duty military. Daily 10am–5pm. Bus: 2 or 992. Trolley: Orange or Blue Line to America Plaza.*

7 ★★ kids Maritime Museum. This flotilla of classic ships is led by the full-rigged merchant vessel *Star of India* (1863), a National Historic Landmark and the world's oldest iron merchant ship still afloat. The collection also includes the HMS *Surprise*, a painstakingly accurate reproduction of an 18th-century Royal Navy Frigate, which played a supporting role to Russell Crowe in the film *Master and Commander*, and a 300-foot-long (91m) Cold War–era B-39 Soviet attack submarine. You can board and tour each vessel. ⏲ *90 min. 1492 N. Harbor Dr. ☎ 619/234-9153. www.sdmaritime.org. Admission $16 adults; $13 seniors over 62, students 13–17 & active-duty military; $8 children 3–12; free for children under 6. Daily 9am–8pm (until 9pm in summer). Bus: Numerous routes, including 2 or 992. Trolley: Blue Line to County Center/Little Italy.*

8 ★ Davis-Horton House Museum. Shipped by boat to San Diego in 1850 from Portland, Maine, this is the oldest structure in the Gaslamp Quarter. It is a well-preserved example of a prefabricated "saltbox" family home and has remained structurally unchanged for more than 150 years, although it originally stood at another location. A museum on the first and second floors documents life in "New Town" and profiles some of the city's early movers and shakers. The Gaslamp Quarter Historical Foundation also makes its home here, and it has a nice gift store in the basement. *30 min. 410 Island Ave. (at Fourth Ave.). 619/233-4692. www.gaslampquarter.org. Admission $10 adults, $8 seniors, $5 students. Tues–Sat 10am–5pm, Sun noon–4pm. The Historical Foundation offers walking tours of the neighborhood Sat at 11am; cost is $20, $15 seniors & active military, $10 students. Bus: 3, 11, or 120. Trolley: Gaslamp Quarter or Convention Center.*

9 ★ San Diego History Center. Operated by the San Diego Historical Society, this Balboa Park museum offers permanent and changing exhibits on topics related to the history of the region. Many of the museum's photographs depict Balboa Park and the growth of the city. Books and other items relating to San Diego history are available in the gift shop, and the research library downstairs is open Monday through Friday (9:30am–1pm). *45 min. 1649 El Prado, in Casa del Balboa. 619/232-6203. www.sandiegohistory.org. Admission $10 adults; $8 seniors, students & military; $6 children 6–17; free for children under 6. Daily 10am–5pm. Bus: 7.*

10 ★ Marston House. Noted San Diego architects Irving Gill and William Hebbard designed this Craftsman house in 1905 for George Marston, a local businessman and philanthropist. Listed on the National Register of Historic Places, the home's interior is furnished with decor from the Arts and Crafts period, including Roycroft, Stickley, and Limbert pieces, as well as art pottery. The house is open for tours that start every half-hour. *45 min. 619/297-9327. www.sohosandiego.org. Admission $15 adults, $12 seniors, $7 children 6–12, free for kids under 6. Fri–Mon 10am–5pm. Bus: 3 or 120.*

The Marston House.

The Best Golf Courses

Balboa Park Municipal Golf Course 4
Coronado Municipal Golf Course 5
Park Hyatt Aviara Golf Club 1
Riverwalk Golf Club 3
Torrey Pines Golf Course 2
CARLSBAD
Batiquitos Lagoon
Elfin Forest Res.
L. Hodges
ENCINITAS
Rancho Santa Fe
Rancho Bernardo
SOLANA BEACH
POWAY
DEL MAR
Los Peñasquitos Canyon Preserve
Carmel Valley
Mira Mesa
Miramar Res.
Torrey Pines State Res.
Torrey Pines
PACIFIC OCEAN
U.S. Marine Corps Air Station Miramar
Soledad Park
La Jolla
Mission Trails Regional Park
Tierrasanta
Pacific Beach
Clairemont
Serra Mesa
Tecolote Canyon Natural Park
SAN DIEGO
L. Murray
Del Cerro
Mission Bay
Mission Bay Park
Talmadge
LA MESA
Old Town
Ocean Beach
Hillcrest
North Park
San Diego Int'l Arpt.
Balboa Park
Oak Park
LEMON GROVE
Stockton
Encanto
U.S. Naval Air Station
Mountain View
Ft. Rosecrans Military Res.
Bay Terraces
U.S. Naval Res.
CORONADO
NATIONAL CITY
San Diego Bay
Sweetwater Marsh N.W.R.
CHULA VISTA
0 5 mi
0 5 km

With its mild year-round climate and nearly 100 courses, half of them public, San Diego County is an ideal destination for golfers. This selection includes acclaimed courses for hardcore aficionados and easily accessed greens for casual duffers. All take advantage of San Diego's diverse terrain, from canyons and mesas to estuaries and ocean. For a full list of San Diego courses, check out the San Diego Golf Pages (www.golfsd.com). **San Diego Golf Reservations** (☎ 858/456-8373; www.sandiegogolf.com) can arrange tee times for you at the premier courses. START: **Bus 2.**

Balboa Park Municipal Golf Course. Surrounded by the beauty of Balboa Park, this 18-hole course features fairways sprinkled with eucalyptus leaves and distractingly nice views of the San Diego skyline. It's convenient and affordable—the perfect choice for visitors who want to work some golf into their vacation rather than the other way around. *2600 Golf Course Dr. (off Pershing Dr. or 26th St. in the southeast corner of the park). ☎ 619/570-1234 (automated reservation system) or 619/239-1660 (pro shop). www.balboagc.com. Nonresident fees $40 weekdays, $50 weekends; twilight rate $24 weekdays, $30 weekends; cart rental $15–$30; club rental $25–$50. Reservations are suggested at least a week in advance; first-come, first-served tee times offered from 6:30–7am. Bus: 2, exit at C & 26th sts., head north into the park.*

Coronado Municipal Golf Course. The postcard vistas will test your powers of concentration at this 18-hole, par-72 course overlooking Glorietta Bay, the Coronado Bridge, and the downtown San Diego skyline. There's also a coffee shop, pro shop, and driving range on site. Half of the daily tee times are awarded via a day-of-play lottery (6–8:59am); the rest can be obtained by calling ☎ 619/435-3121 up to 2 days out, or ☎ 619/435-3121, ext. 1, 3 to 14 days prior ($16 per person fee). If you don't win the lottery, you can still add your name to a stand-by list and step in for no-shows. *2000 Visalia Row. ☎ 619/435-3121. www.golfcoronado.com. Greens fees $35 weekdays, $40 weekends & holidays; cart fees $18 per person. Greens fees for twilight play $20 weekdays, $22 weekends; cart rates $11 per person.*

Park Hyatt Aviara Golf Club in Carlsbad.

Club rental $50 ($30 twilight rate). Bus: 901, exit at Pomona Ave. & Glorietta Pl.

★★ **Park Hyatt Aviara Golf Club.** In Carlsbad (40 min. north of downtown San Diego), Aviara was designed by Arnold Palmer and is uniquely landscaped to incorporate natural elements that blend in neatly with the protected Batiquitos Lagoon nearby. The course is 7,007 yards (6,407m) from the championship tees, laid out over rolling hillsides with plenty of bunker and water challenges (casual golfers may be frustrated). Practice areas are available for putting, chipping, sand play, and driving, and the pro shop and clubhouse are fully equipped. *7447 Batiquitos Dr. ☎ 760/603-6900. www.parkaviara.hyatt.com. Greens fees Mon–Thurs $215 (including mandatory cart); Fri–Sun $235; afternoon rates start at 1:30pm in winter, 3pm in summer ($140 weekdays, $145 weekends); club rental $85. Coaster: Carlsbad Village Station; cab it from there.*

★ **Riverwalk Golf Club.** Redesigned by Ted Robinson and Ted Robinson Jr., these links wandering along the Mission Valley floor are the most convenient courses for anyone staying downtown or near the beaches. Riverwalk sports a slick, upscale clubhouse; four lakes with waterfalls (in play on 13 of the 27 holes); open, undulating fairways; and trolley tracks on which a bright red trolley speeds through now and then without proving too distracting. *1150 Fashion Valley Rd. ☎ 619/296-4563. www.riverwalkgc.com. Nonresident greens fees, including cart, $89 Mon–Fri, $99 Sat–Sun; senior, twilight & bargain evening rates available; club rental $30–$55. Trolley: Green Line to Fashion Valley Transit Center.*

Torrey Pines Golf Course.

★★★ **Torrey Pines Golf Course.** These two gorgeous, municipal 18-hole championship courses, on the coast between La Jolla and Del Mar, are only 20 minutes from downtown San Diego. Home of the Farmers Insurance Open (formerly the Buick Invitational), and the setting for a memorable U.S. Open in 2008, Torrey Pines is second only to Pebble Beach as California's top golf destination. On a bluff overlooking the ocean, the north course is picturesque and has the signature hole (no. 6), but the south course is more challenging and has more sea-facing play. *11480 Torrey Pines Rd. ☎ 877/581-7171 (option 3 for automated reservations 8–90 days in advance; $43 booking fee) or 800/985-4653 for the pro shop & lessons. www.torreypinesgolfcourse.com. Greens fees on the south course $183 Mon–Thurs, $229 Fri–Sun; on the north course $100 Mon–Thurs, $125 Fri–Sun; twilight & senior rates available; cart rental $40; club rental $69. First-come, first-served tee times available from sun-up to 7:30am. Single golfers also stand a good chance of getting on the course if they just turn up & get on the waiting list for a threesome. Lessons assure you a spot on the course. Bus: 101.*

3 The Best Neighborhood Walks

Gaslamp Quarter

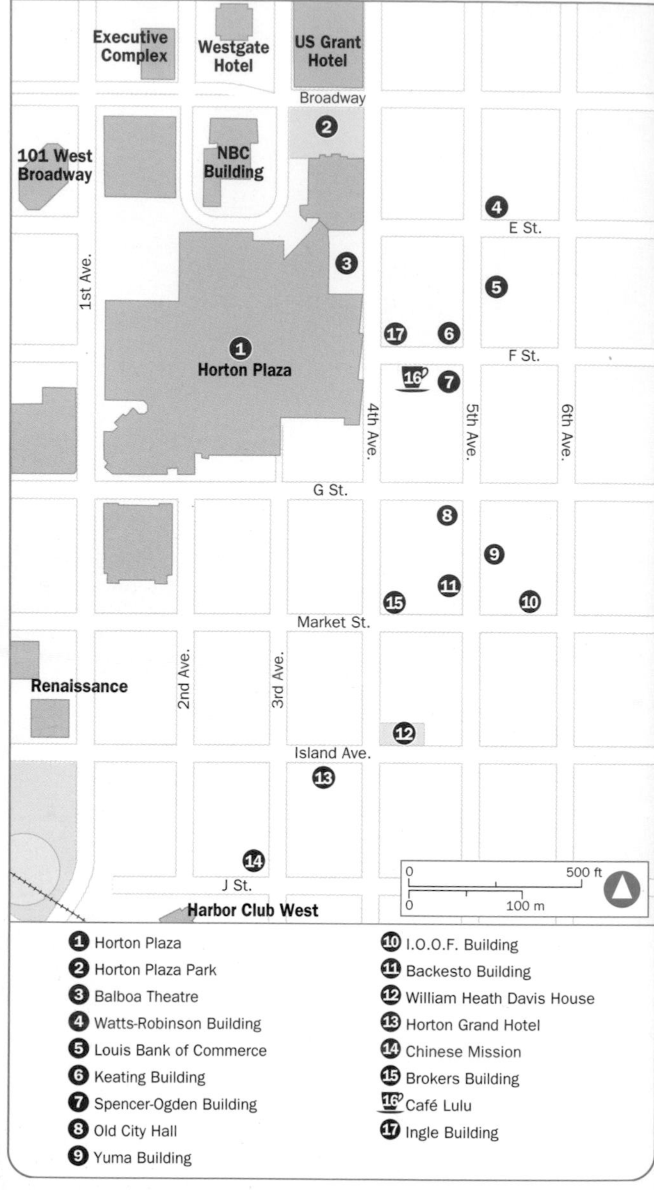

Previous page: Colorado House in Old Town San Diego.

A **National Historic District covering some 16 city blocks,** the Gaslamp Quarter features many Victorian-style commercial buildings built between the Civil War and World War I. The father of modern San Diego, Alonzo Horton, purchased 1,000 acres (405 hectares) of muddy, bayfront land for $260 in 1867 and ignited a real-estate boom. Horton's "New Town" is today's Gaslamp Quarter, featuring a proliferation of restaurants, shops, clubs, and hotels that make its 1880s heyday look downright deserted. The Gaslamp Quarter is bound by Fourth Avenue to the west, Sixth Avenue to the east, Broadway to the north, and L Street and the waterfront to the south. It's all very walkable thanks to Horton's business savvy—he wanted to maximize his land sales, so he laid out small blocks (creating more desirable corner lots) with no alleys. **START: Any downtown bus to Horton Plaza; Blue or Orange Line trolley to Civic Center.**

❶ ★ **Horton Plaza.** A colorful conglomeration of shops, eateries, and fanciful architecture, Horton Plaza spearheaded the revitalization of downtown when it opened in 1985. The ground floor is home to the Jessop Street Clock, designed by Joseph Jessop Sr. and built primarily by Claude D. Ledger. It stood outside Jessop's Jewelry Store on Fifth Avenue from 1907 until being moved to Horton Plaza in 1985 and has reportedly stopped only three times in its history: once after being hit by a team of horses, once after an earthquake, and again on the day in 1935 when Ledger died. *Bound by Broadway, First & Fourth aves. & G St.* ☎ *619/239-8180. www.westfield.com/hortonplaza.*

❷ ★ **Horton Plaza Park.** This small park in front of Horton Plaza has been expanded and completely redesigned. Its centerpiece 1910 fountain with bronze medallions of San Diego's "founding fathers"—Juan Rodríguez Cabrillo, Father Junípero Serra, and Alonzo Horton—was designed by architect Irving Gill. New in 2016 are three pavilions sheltering coffee, ice cream, and snack outlets, along with a discount ticket booth. *Corner of Fourth Ave. & Broadway.*

❸ ★★★ **Balboa Theatre.** After years of sitting dormant and decrepit, this Spanish Renaissance–style theater has been restored to its 1920s glory. The tile dome, striking tile work in the foyer, and two

Gaslamp Quarter.

Horton Plaza.

20-foot-high (6m) ornamental waterfalls inside are all in prime condition and serve as a dramatic backdrop for concerts and appearances by varied artists. A state-of-the-art cinema system was added in 2016, and four to six films are featured each month. *868 Fourth Ave. (southwest corner of Fourth Ave. & E St.). ☎ 619/570-1100 or 619/615-4000. www.sdbalboa.org.*

4 ★ Watts-Robinson Building. Built in 1913 in a Chicago School of Architecture style, this was one of San Diego's first skyscrapers. It once housed 70 jewelers and is now a boutique hotel (**Gaslamp Plaza Suites;** see p 137). Take a minute to look inside at the marble wainscoting, tile floors, ornate ceiling, and brass ornamentation. *903 Fifth Ave. (northeast corner of Fifth Ave. & E St.).*

5 ★★ Louis Bank of Commerce. Built in 1888, this iconic building was the first in San Diego made of granite. It once housed the city's first ice cream parlor; an oyster bar frequented by Wyatt Earp (of OK Corral shootout fame); and, upstairs, the Golden Poppy Hotel, a brothel run by a fortune teller, Madame Coara. After a fire in 1904, the original towers of the building were removed, and the iron eagles perched atop them disappeared. A 2002 renovation installed a new pair of eagles, cast at the same English foundry as the originals. *835 Fifth Ave.*

6 ★ Keating Building. A San Diego landmark dating from 1890, this structure was nicknamed the "marriage building." It was developed by businessman George Keating, who died halfway through construction; his wife, Fannie, finished the project, changing some of the design along the way. She had her husband's name engraved in the top cornice as a tribute to him. Originally heralded as one of the city's most prestigious office buildings, it featured such conveniences as steam heat and a wire-cage elevator. A sleek boutique hotel is now ensconced here (**the Keating;** see p 140). *432 F St. (northwest corner of Fifth Ave. & F St.).*

7 ★ Spencer-Ogden Building. Built in 1874, this is one of the oldest buildings in the Gaslamp Quarter—and it's lucky to still be

Balboa Theatre.

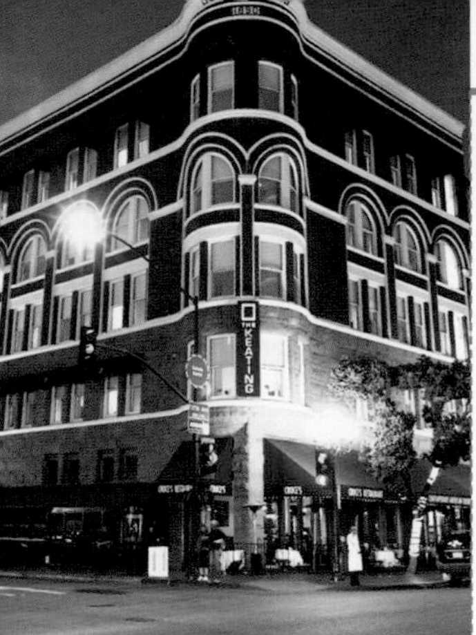

Keating Building.

standing. It escaped major damage after an explosion in 1887 caused by a druggist who was making fireworks. Other tenants over the years included real estate agents, an import business, a home-furnishing business, and a "Painless Parker" dental office. Edgar Parker owned a chain of dental offices and legally changed his name to "Painless" to avoid claims of false advertising. *770 Fifth Ave.*

8 ★ Old City Hall. Also dating from 1874, when it was a bank, this Florentine Italianate building features 16-foot (5m) ceilings, 12-foot (4m) windows framed with brick arches, antique columns, and a wrought-iron cage elevator. Notice that the windows on each floor are different. (The top two stories were added in 1887, when it became the city's public library.) The entire city government filled this building in 1900, with the police department on the first floor and the council chambers on the fourth. Incredibly, this beauty was completely encased in stucco in the 1950s in an attempt at modernization. It was restored in the 1980s. *664 Fifth Ave. (southwest corner of Fifth Ave. & G St.).*

9 ★★ Yuma Building. The striking edifice was built in 1888 and was one of the first brick buildings downtown. The brothel at the Yuma was the first to be closed during the infamous 1912 cleanup of the area. In the end, 138 women (and no men) were arrested. They were given a choice: Join the Door of Hope charity and reform or take a one-way train ride to Los Angeles. Of these women, 136 went to Los Angeles (many were back within days); 1 woman was pronounced insane; and the last became San Diego's first telephone operator. *631 Fifth Ave.*

10 ★ I.O.O.F. Building. Finally finished in 1882 after 9 years of construction, this handsome building served as a joint lodge for the Masons and Odd Fellows. Gaslamp lore has it that while watching a parade from the balcony, King Kalakaua, Hawaii's last reigning king, caught cold and died shortly thereafter in San Francisco in 1891. *526 Market St.*

11 Backesto Building. Built in 1873, this classical revival and Victorian corner building was expanded to its present size and height over

Yuma Building.

Touring the Town

Old Town Trolley Tours offers an easy way to get an overview of the city. These vehicles, gussied up like old-time trolleys, do a 30-mile (48km) circular route, and you can hop off at any one of 11 stops, explore at leisure, and reboard when you please (the trolleys run every half-hour). Stops include Old Town, the Gaslamp Quarter and downtown area, Coronado, the San Diego Zoo, and Balboa Park. You can begin wherever you want, but you must purchase tickets before boarding (most stops have a ticket kiosk). This narrated ride costs $39 for adults ($19 for kids 4–12, free for children 3 and under) for one complete circuit; the route by itself takes about 2 hours. The trolleys operate daily from 8:50am to 5pm in winter and from 9am to 6pm in summer (☎ 619/298-8687; www.historictours.com).

Seeing the city via Old Town Trolley Tours.

its first 15 years. It housed the neighborhood's first grocer and dry goods store and was the original home of San Diego Hardware, an iconic downtown business that moved to the 'burbs when 21st-century rents proved prohibitive. At the turn of the 20th century, this part of the Gaslamp was known as the Stingaree, the city's notorious red-light district. Gambling, opium dens, and wild saloons were all part of the mix. ***617 Fifth Ave. (northwest corner of Fifth Ave. & Market St.).***

⑫ ★ Davis-Horton House. Downtown's oldest surviving structure, this prefabricated lumber home was shipped to San Diego around Cape Horn from New England in 1850. Alonzo Horton lived in the house in 1867, at its original location at the corner of Market and State streets. Around 1873, it was moved to 11th Avenue and K Street, where it served as the county hospital. It was relocated to this site in 1984 and completely refurbished. The entire house, now a museum and educational gift shop, and the small park next to it are open to the public (see p 38). The Gaslamp Quarter Historical Foundation is also headquartered here. *410 Island Ave. (at Fourth Ave.).* ☎ *619/233-4692. www.gaslampquarter.org.*

⑬ ★ **Horton Grand Hotel.** Two hotels, built in 1886, were moved here—very gently—from other sites and then renovated and connected by an atrium; the original Grand Horton is to your left, and the Brooklyn Hotel is to your right. Now it's all one: the Horton Grand Hotel. The life-size papier-mâché horse (Sunshine), in the sitting area near reception, stood in front of the Brooklyn Hotel when the ground floor was a saddlery. Wyatt Earp lived upstairs at the Brooklyn for most of his 7 years in San Diego. In the Palace Bar, look for the portrait of Ida Bailey, a local madam whose establishment, the Canary Cottage, once stood nearby. *311 Island Ave. (southwest corner of Island & Fourth aves.).* *See p 139.*

⑭ ★ **Chinese Mission.** Originally on First Avenue, this charming brick building built in 1927 was a place where Chinese immigrants (primarily men) could learn English and find employment. Religious instruction and living quarters were also provided. The building was rescued from demolition and moved to its present location, where it now contains the San Diego Chinese Historical Museum. There's also a gift shop and a small garden. ⏲ *20 min. 404 Third Ave. (at J St.).* ☎ *619/338-9888. www.sdchm.org. Admission $5, free for children under 12. Tues–Sat 10:30am–4pm; Sun noon–4pm.*

⑮ **Brokers Building.** Constructed in 1889, this building has 16-foot (5m) wood-beam ceilings and cast-iron columns. In recent years, it was converted to artists' lofts, with the ground floor dedicated to the downtown branch of the Hooters chain. Due to the failure of many previous ventures here as well as a fire and a structural collapse, this was thought of as a "cursed corner." *402 Market St. (northeast corner of Fourth Ave. & Market St.).*

It has a hip, bohemian vibe (hookah pipes are available), but if you're straight-arrow conservative, don't be put off— ⑯ **Café LuLu** is an inclusive place. Ostensibly a coffee bar, the cafe also serves sweets and has a full bar; it stays open late, too. *419 F St. (near Fourth Ave.).* ☎ *619/238-0111. Sun–Thurs 11am–1am; Fri–Sat 11am–3am. $3.50–$8.*

⑰ ★ **Ingle Building.** It dates from 1906 and is now home to the Hard Rock Cafe. The mural on the F Street side of the building depicts a group of deceased rock stars (including Hendrix, Lennon, Joplin, and Elvis, of course) lounging at sidewalk tables. Stained-glass windows from the original Golden Lion Tavern (1907–32) front Fourth Avenue. Inside, the restaurant's stained-glass ceiling was taken from the Elks Club in Stockton, California, and much of the floor is original. *801 Fourth Ave. (northeast corner of Fourth Ave. & F St.).*

Old Town

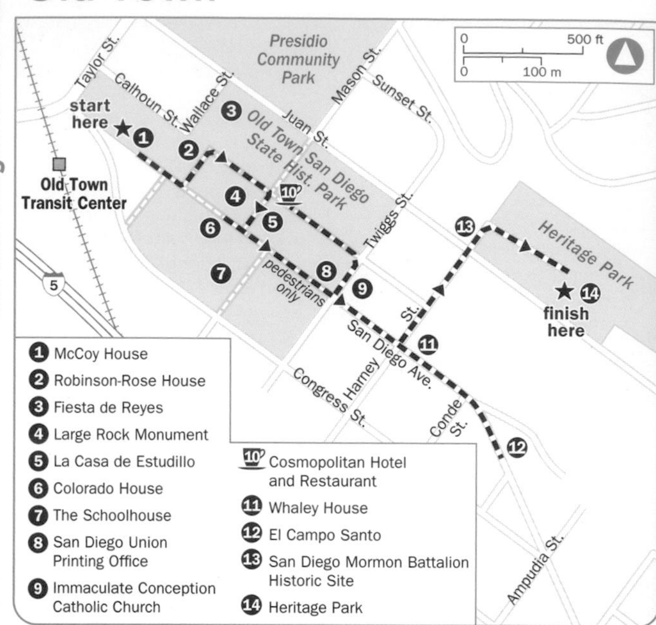

San Diego's Mexican and Spanish colonial history is vividly evident in Old Town. A visit here will transport you to an era of village greens and one-room schoolhouses, a time when *vaqueros* and whalers, outlaws and officers, *Californios* and Yankees all mingled—sometimes uneasily—in this then-tiny pueblo. When you stroll through Old Town State Historic Park, you don't have to look hard or very far to see a glimmer of yesteryear. This free park is just part of the Old Town experience, though. The compact neighborhood is home to other historic sites as well as lots of shopping and dining, much of it themed to California's frontier past. **START: Blue or Green Line trolley to Old Town Transit Center.**

❶ **McCoy House.** The interpretive center for Old Town State Historic Park (see p 9) is a historically accurate replication of the home of James McCoy, San Diego's larger-than-life lawman/legislator. With exhibits, artifacts, and visitor information, the house gives a great overview of life in San Diego from 1821 to 1872. ⏲ *30 min. Wallace & Calhoun sts. (northwest corner of the park).*

❷ **Robinson-Rose House.** Built in 1853 as a family home, the park visitor center was also once a newspaper and railroad office. Here you'll see a large model of Old Town the way it looked prior to 1872. ⏲ *15 min.*

House in Old Town San Diego State Historic Park.

❸ **Fiesta de Reyes.** Colorful shops and restaurants spill into a flower-filled courtyard where costumed employees and weekend entertainment create an early-California atmosphere. ⏱ *30 min. Juan St. (btw. Wallace & Mason sts.). ☎ 619/297-3100. www.fiestadereyes.com.*

❹ **Large Rock Monument.** This site commemorates the first U.S. flag flown in Southern California, hoisted here on July 29, 1846.

❺ ★ **La Casa de Estudillo.** An original adobe building from 1827, this U-shaped house has covered walkways and an open central patio. The walls are 3- to 5-feet-thick (1 to 1.5m), holding up the heavy beams and tiles and insulating against summer heat (in those days, the thicker the walls, the wealthier the family).

Fiesta de Reyes.

❻ **Colorado House.** Built in 1851, it was destroyed by fire in 1872, as were most buildings on this side of the park. The museum features an original Wells Fargo stagecoach, numerous displays of the overland-express business, and a video presentation. ⏱ *15 min.*

❼ ★ **The Schoolhouse.** An original building dating from 1865, this school was commissioned by San Diego's first mayor, Joshua Bean, brother of the notorious "hanging judge" Roy Bean. Mary Chase Walker, the first teacher, ventured here from the East when she was 38 years old. She enjoyed the salary but hated the fleas, mosquitoes, and truancy; after a year, she resigned to marry the president of the school board.

❽ **San Diego Union Building.** This house arrived in Old Town after being prefabricated in Maine in 1851 and shipped around the Horn (it has a distinctly New England–style appearance). Inside you'll see the original hand press

Bedroom in La Casa de Estudillo.

used to print the *San Diego Union,* first published out of this building in 1868.

❾ **Immaculate Conception Catholic Church.** The cornerstone was laid in 1868, making it the first church built in California that was not part of the Mission system. With the movement of the community to New Town in 1872, it lost its parishioners and wasn't dedicated until 1919. *2540 San Diego Ave. (at Twiggs St., which divides the park from the rest of Old Town).* ☎ *619/295-4141. www.ic-sandiego.org.*

Share some tasty guacamole and chips or dine on creative versions of Mexican classics in Old Town's grandest mansion, built in the late 1820s for the Bandini family. The best tables at 10 **Cosmopolitan Hotel and Restaurant** are located in the original courtyard. *2660 Calhoun St.* ☎ *619/297-1874. www.oldtowncosmopolitan.com. Mon–Fri 11am–9pm; Sat–Sun 10am–9pm. $9–$18.*

⓫ **Whaley House.** The first two-story brick structure in Southern California, it was built between 1856 and 1857. The house is said to be haunted by several ghosts, including that of Yankee Jim Robinson, who was hanged on the site in 1852. The house is beautifully furnished with period pieces. ⏱ *30 min.* *See p 35.*

⓬ **El Campo Santo.** San Diego's first cemetery, established in 1850, is the final resting place for, among others, the unfortunate Yankee Jim Robinson (see above). Small brass markers along the path mark the remains of some of San Diego's earliest citizens. *2 short blocks south of the Whaley House on the east side of San Diego Ave.*

Handset press in the San Diego Union Printing Office.

The 1865 schoolhouse on Mason Street (see p 51).

⑬ ★★ kids San Diego Mormon Battalion Historic Site. Multimedia exhibits describe the 2,000-mile (3,200km) march from Iowa to San Diego undertaken by 5,000 Mormon men and women to join the U.S. Army in the mid–19th century. Costumed docents describe the pioneer lifestyle and offer hands-on activities, including panning for gold. *⏲ 45 min. 2510 Juan St. ☎ 619/298-3317. www.lds.org/locations/historical-sites. Free admission. Daily 9am–9pm.*

⑭ Heritage Park. Seven original 19th-century buildings are in this 8-acre (3.2-hectare) park; each was saved from destruction and moved here. Among the highlights are the Sherman-Gilbert House (1887), with its distinctive widow's walk, and the classic revival Temple Beth Israel, dating from 1889. The temple and the Senlis Cottage housing the park office and restrooms are the only buildings open to the public. *2454 Heritage Park Row (corner of Juan & Harney sts.). See p 35.*

Historic Victorian homes in Heritage Park.

Embarcadero

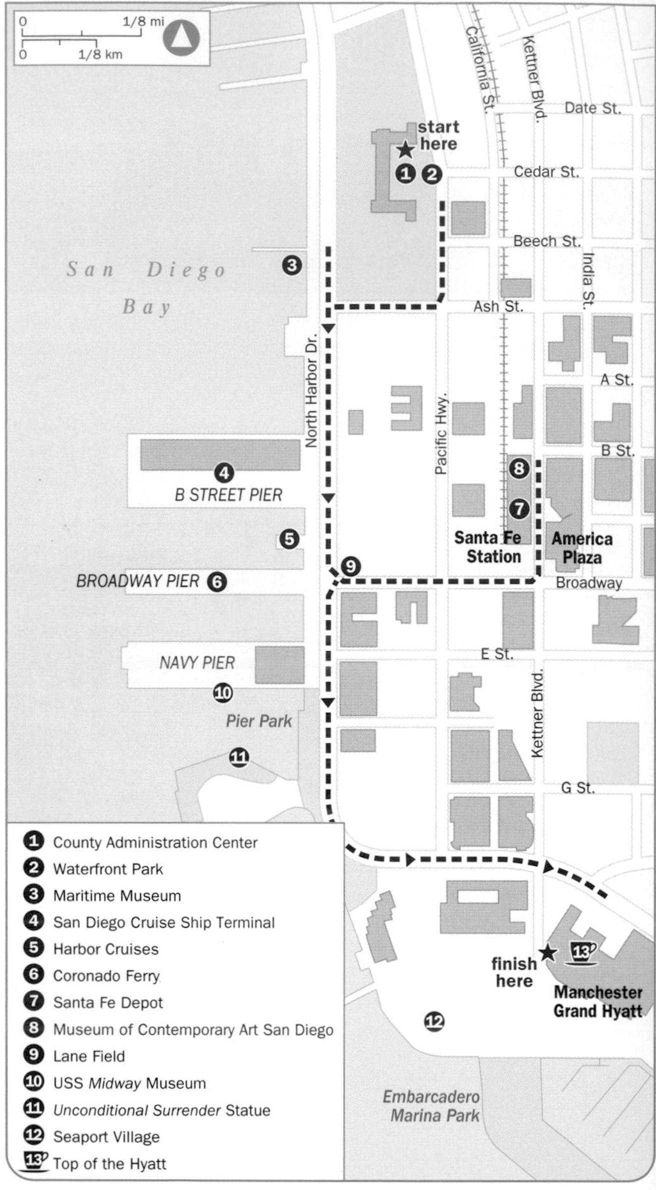
0 1/8 mi
0 1/8 km
California St.
Kettner Blvd.
Date St.
start here
Cedar St.
Beech St.
India St.
San Diego Bay
Ash St.
North Harbor Dr.
Pacific Hwy.
A St.
B St.
B STREET PIER
Santa Fe Station
America Plaza
BROADWAY PIER
Broadway
E St.
NAVY PIER
Pier Park
Kettner Blvd.
G St.
finish here
Manchester Grand Hyatt
Embarcadero Marina Park
1 County Administration Center
2 Waterfront Park
3 Maritime Museum
4 San Diego Cruise Ship Terminal
5 Harbor Cruises
6 Coronado Ferry
7 Santa Fe Depot
8 Museum of Contemporary Art San Diego
9 Lane Field
10 USS *Midway* Museum
11 *Unconditional Surrender* Statue
12 Seaport Village
13 Top of the Hyatt

Upon seeing San Diego Bay in 1602, the second European visitor to the area, Sebastián Vizcaíno, declared it to be "a port which must be the best to be found in all the South Sea." A walk along the waterfront, known as the Embarcadero, may convince you as well. The bay is filled with yachts, cruise ships, sailboats, U.S. Navy vessels, tour boats, and the occasional kayak. Harbor Drive edging the waterfront is constantly changing, with condos in new glass towers facing the bay and entrepreneurs vying for rights to any available commercial space. START: **Blue Line trolley to County Center/Little Italy.**

❶ County Administration Center. Built in 1936 with funds from the Works Progress Administration, the center was dedicated in 1938 by President Franklin D. Roosevelt. This Art Deco beauty is one of San Diego's most graceful buildings and is listed on the National Register of Historic Places. The waterfront side is presided over by the dignified 23-foot-high (7m) granite statue, *Guardian of Water,* created by San Diego's most notable sculptor, Donal Hord. A cafeteria with great harbor views is on the fourth floor. *1600 Pacific Hwy.* ☎ *619/531-5197. Mon–Fri 8am–5pm.*

❷ ★★★ kids Waterfront Park. Just when it seemed all the land along the bay would be gobbled up, this 12-acre (5-hectare) wonderland opened beside and behind the county building. Facilities include a large playground, lots of grassy areas for picnicking and playing, and, perhaps best of all, an underground parking lot (entrance on Ash Street). Kids can't resist racing through the shallow pool in an 830-foot-long fountain with 31 jets shooting water high toward the sky; adults have been known to dangle their toes in the water as well. Trees and gardens have become more established since the park opened in 2014, but it's still best to use plenty of sunscreen and wear a hat for shade. Bring snacks and drinks. *1600 Pacific Hwy.* ☎ *619/232-7275. Daily 6am–10pm; fountain jets run from 11am–7pm.*

❸ ★★ kids Maritime Museum. Not a building but a collection of ships, the main attraction is the magnificent *Star of India,* built in 1863. The vessel, whose billowing sails are a familiar sight along Harbor Drive, once carried cargo to India, transported immigrants to New Zealand, and braved the Arctic ice in Alaska to work in the salmon industry. Another component of the museum is the 1898 ferry *Berkeley,* which operated between San Francisco and Oakland. In service through 1958, it

Lord Hornblower Cruise in San Diego Bay.

Coronado Ferry.

carried survivors to safety 24 hours a day for 4 days after the 1906 San Francisco earthquake. You can also check out the HMS *Surprise*, which had a star turn in the film *Master and Commander;* a Soviet-era B-39 attack submarine; the *Californian*, a replica of a 19th-century revenue cutter; *Medea*, a 1904 steam yacht; and *Pilot*, which served as San Diego Bay's official pilot boat for 82 years. *See p 38.*

❹ **San Diego Cruise Ship Terminal.** Located on the B Street Pier, it has a large nautical clock at the entrance. The flag-decorated terminal's interior is light and airy; you'll also find a snack bar, gift shop, and restrooms.

❺ ★ **Harbor Cruises.** Hornblower Cruises and San Diego Harbor Excursions run daily 1- and 2-hour sightseeing cruises around the bay, departing from near the Broadway Pier. Choose from a variety of vessels, everything from antique yachts to three-deck behemoths, and both companies also offer evening dinner/dance cruises as well as weekend champagne brunch packages. Ticket booths are right along the waterfront. *Hornblower Cruises: 970 Harbor Dr. ☎ 888/467-6256 or 619/686-8715. www.hornblower.com. Harbor tours $24–$29 per person. San Diego Harbor Excursions: 990 Harbor Dr. ☎ 800/442-7847 or 619/234-4111. www.sdhe.com. Harbor tours $24–$29 ($2 off for seniors & military, half price for children 4–12). Dinner cruises start at $60 adults, $36 children; brunch cruise $65 adults, $39 children.*

❻ **Coronado Ferry.** This pedestrian-only ferry makes hourly trips between San Diego and Coronado. Buy tickets from the Harbor Excursion booth—a one-way trip is 15 minutes. *Sun–Thurs on the hour from 9am–9pm, Fri–Sat until 10pm. Return trips from the Ferry Landing in Coronado to the Broadway Pier are Sun–Thurs every hour on the half-hour from 9:30am–9:30pm, Fri–Sat until 10:30pm. $4.75 each way.*

❼ ★ **Santa Fe Depot.** Also known as Union Station, this railroad station was built in 1915 and provides one of the city's best examples of Spanish colonial revival style. Check out the vaulted ceiling, wooden benches, and walls covered in striking green-and-gold tiles. A scale model of the aircraft carrier USS *Midway* is also on display. *West end of Broadway, btw. India St. & Kettner Blvd.*

❽ ★★★ **Museum of Contemporary Art San Diego (MCASD).** What was once the train station's baggage building has been transformed into a dynamic space for this cutting-edge art museum. Designed by the same architect responsible for the Warhol museum in Pittsburgh and the Picasso museum in Spain, this is one of the city's cultural flagships, featuring permanent, site-specific work by such artists as Richard Serra and Jenny Holzer. Changing exhibitions are scheduled at both this space and MCASD's original downtown annex across the street. ⏲ *1 hr. 1100 & 1001 Kettner Blvd.*

(btw. B St. & Broadway). ☎ 858/454-3541. www.mcasd.org. Admission $10 adults, $5 seniors & military, free for anyone 26 & under; free admission 3rd Thurs 5–7pm; paid ticket good for admission to MCASD La Jolla within 7 days. Thurs–Tues 11am–5pm; 3rd Thurs 11am–7pm.

9 ★ Lane Field. This valuable corner lot, home of the Pacific Coast League Padres from 1936 to 1957, was the subject of endless negotiations for decades. Underused as a parking lot, it is now the site of a Residence Inn by Marriott and a SpringHill Suites, which both opened in 2016. Another high-rise tower at the south end of the lot is under development. *900 W. Broadway at Harbor Dr.*

10 USS *Midway* Museum. Decommissioned in 1991, the USS *Midway* saw 47 years of service, stretching from the end of World War II to Desert Storm, where it acted as the flagship for that operation. This aircraft carrier is now a floating naval museum, telling the story of life on board during its missions. *See p 37.*

11 *Unconditional Surrender* Statue. Kitsch on a giant scale. This 25-foot (7.6m), full-color statue re-creates an iconic American image: Alfred Eisenstaedt's 1945 photo of a sailor and nurse in passionate embrace following the news of Japan's surrender to end World War II. Nearby is a salute to another American icon, Bob Hope. Featuring a cast of 15 bronze statues, this installation depicts the comedian entertaining the troops. *750 N. Harbor Dr.*

View of the bay from the Manchester Grand Hyatt.

Seaport Village.

12 kids Seaport Village. This 14-acre (5.6-hectare) outdoor shopping center has more than 50 stores and restaurants, coupled with an unbeatable bay-front location. Kids love the classic carousel—Charles Looff of Coney Island carved the animals out of poplar in 1895; live entertainment is also often scheduled on weekends. *849 W. Harbor Dr. (at Kettner Blvd.). ☎ 619/235-4014. www.seaportvillage.com. Daily 10am–9pm; restaurants have extended hours.*

There's no better place in San Diego for a sunset than the 13 **★★ Top of the Hyatt,** a 40th-floor lounge with sweeping views of the city and harbor. It's in the eastern tower of the Manchester Grand Hyatt and opens at 3pm daily. *1 Market Pl. ☎ 619/232-1234. $5–$15.*

La Jolla

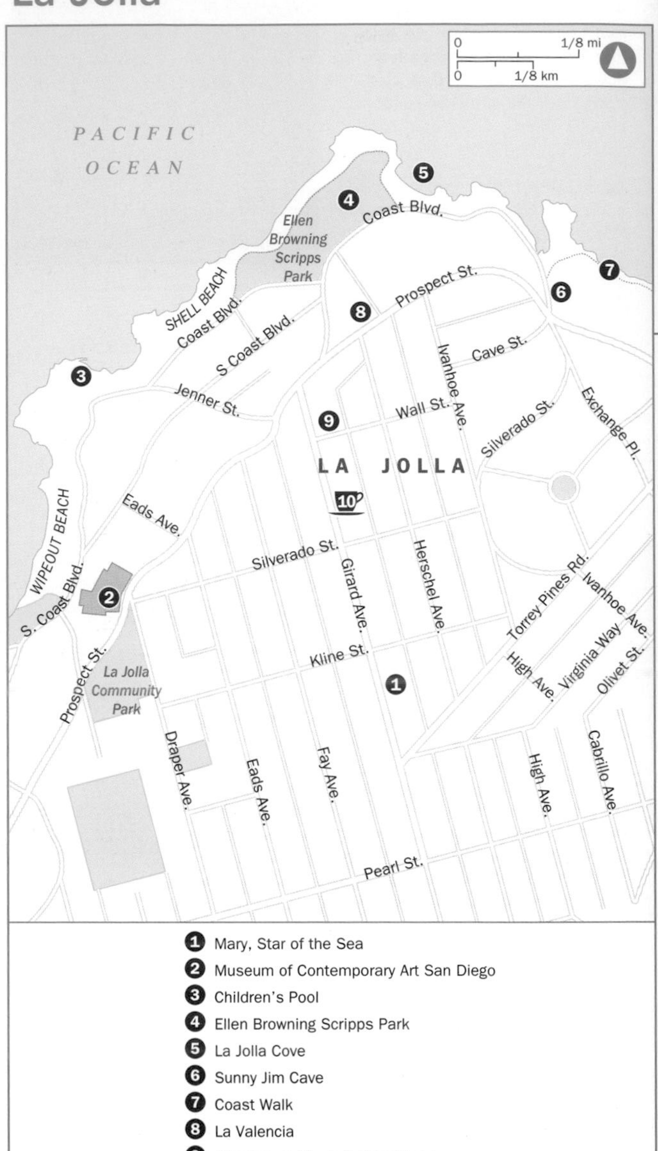

1 Mary, Star of the Sea
2 Museum of Contemporary Art San Diego
3 Children's Pool
4 Ellen Browning Scripps Park
5 La Jolla Cove
6 Sunny Jim Cave
7 Coast Walk
8 La Valencia
9 Athenaeum Music & Arts Library
10 Girard Gourmet

La Jolla is Southern California's Riviera. This seaside community of about 40,000 is home to an inordinate number of wealthy folk who could probably live anywhere. They choose La Jolla for good reason—it features a gorgeous coastline, outstanding restaurants, and a slew of upscale boutiques and galleries. The heart of La Jolla is referred to as the Village, roughly delineated by Pearl Street to the south, Prospect Street to the north, Torrey Pines Road to the east, and the rugged coast to the west; this picturesque neighborhood is an ideal place to simply stroll about. It's undetermined whether "La Jolla" (pronounced la-HOY-ya) is misspelled Spanish for "the jewel" or an indigenous word for "cave," but once you see it, you'll likely go with the first definition. **START: Bus route 30 to Silverado St. and Girard Ave.**

❶ ★ Mary, Star of the Sea. Dedicated in 1937, this beautiful little Mission-style Catholic church was designed by noted San Diego architect Carleton Winslow Sr. Above the entrance, a striking mosaic re-creates the original fresco painted there by Mexican artist Alfredo Ramos Martínez. An influential art instructor in Mexico, Martínez's students included Rufino Tamayo and David Alfaro Siqueiros. Inside the church, accomplished Polish artist John De Rosen painted the unique mural above the altar. It depicts the Virgin Mary on a crescent moon, presiding over a storm-tossed sea. *15 min. 7669 Girard Ave. 858/454-2631. www.marystarlajolla.org. Daily services.*

❷ ★★★ Museum of Contemporary Art San Diego (MCASD). Focusing on work produced since 1950, this museum's holdings include noteworthy examples of minimalism, light and space work, conceptualism, installation, and site-specific art (the outside sculptures were designed specifically for this location). MCASD also offers lectures, cutting-edge films, and special events on an ongoing basis; the bookstore is a great place for contemporary gifts, and the cafe is a pleasant stop before or after your visit. The museum is on a bluff overlooking the Pacific Ocean, and the views from the galleries are gorgeous. The original building on the site, designed by Irving Gill in 1916, was the residence of Ellen Browning Scripps. *90 min. 700 Prospect St. 858/454-3541. www.mcasd.org. Admission $10 adults; $5 seniors, students & military; free for ages 25 & under; free 3rd Thurs of the month 5–7pm; paid ticket good for admission to MCASD downtown within 7 days. Thurs–Tues 11am–5pm; 3rd Thurs 11am–7pm.*

The Museum of Contemporary Art San Diego in La Jolla.

3 ★★ kids Children's Pool. A seawall protects this pocket of sand—originally intended as a calm swimming bay for children but serving since 1994 as home for a colony of harbor seals; on an average day, you'll spot dozens lolling in the sun. After much heated debate (and even acts of civil disobedience), people were allowed to swim here again—to the displeasure of many. Although it is possible to now go in the water at the Children's Pool, keep in mind those are federally protected *wild* animals, and it is illegal to approach them or harass them in any way. The water here can also have high levels of bacteria, so content yourself with viewing the animals from a safe distance. Also note that volunteers, with speed dials set to "lifeguard," keep watch to make sure no one bothers the colony. *15 min.*

4 ★★ Ellen Browning Scripps Park. This park and the bluffside walkway that courses through it afford some of California's finest coastal scenery. There's plenty of soft grass where you can toss a Frisbee, have a picnic, or just laze. A series of rustic wooden shelters—popular among seagulls, pigeons, and pedestrians—overlooks La Jolla's shapely curves. The La Jolla Cove Bridge Club—a Works Project Administration structure dating to 1939, where card games still take place—must be one of the world's most view-enhanced card rooms and can be booked as an utterly romantic wedding venue. *30 min. La Jolla Cove Bridge Club. ☎ 858/459-7000. www.lajollacovebridgeclub.org. Games Sun, Wed, Fri noon–3:30pm.*

La Jolla Cove.

5 ★★★ kids La Jolla Cove. These protected calm waters, celebrated as the clearest along the coast, attract snorkelers, scuba divers, and beach lovers. The small sandy beach gets cramped during the summer, but the cove's "look but don't touch" policy safeguards the bright orange Garibaldi, California's state marine fish, plus other sea life, including abalone, octopus, and lobster. The unique Underwater Park stretches from here to the northern end of Torrey Pines State Reserve and incorporates kelp forests, artificial reefs, two deep canyons, and tidal pools. *30 min.*

6 kids Sunny Jim Cave. The only one of La Jolla's seven sea caves accessible by land, the Sunny Jim Cave is reached by a narrow, often slippery, staircase in the Cave Store. (Sunny Jim was a cartoon character created in 1902 for a cereal advertising campaign, and the cave opening resembles his profile.) Part art gallery, part antiques store, this cliff-top shop also rents snorkel equipment in summer and sells gear year-round. The passageway with 145 steps was dug through the rock in 1902–03. *20 min. 1325 Cave St. (just off Prospect St.). ☎ 858/459-0746. www.cavestore.com. Admission $5 adults, $3 kids 3–16, free for 2 & under. Daily 10am–4:30pm.*

La Valencia Hotel on the cliffs of La Jolla.

❼ ★★ **Coast Walk.** As you face the ocean, continue past the Cave Store. You'll find two paths; one leads to a fabulous wood-platform overlook, the other continues along the bluffs. It's a cool little trail, affording expansive views of the coast. You can exit at a stairway that leads back to Prospect Street (before you come to the white wooden bridge) and circle back into town. If you continue along the trail, it will put you on Torrey Pines Road, an extra 10- to 15-minute walk back to the village. 🕓 *30 min.*

❽ ★★★ **La Valencia.** Within its bougainvillea-draped walls and wrought-iron garden gates, this bastion of gentility resurrects a golden age, when such celebrities as Greta Garbo and Charlie Chaplin vacationed here. The bluff-top hotel, which looks much like a Mediterranean villa, has been the centerpiece of La Jolla since opening in 1926. Among the several lounges and restaurants, some with incredible vistas, that can be enjoyed by nonguests, the Café La Rue has a Parisian sidewalk bistro vibe (see p 15). 🕓 *15 min. 1132 Prospect St. (at Herschel Ave.).* ☎ *800/451-0772 or 858/454-0771. www.lavalencia.com.*

❾ ★★ **Athenaeum Music & Arts Library.** One of only 16 nonprofit, membership libraries in the U.S., the Athenaeum hosts art exhibits, jazz and classical concerts, lectures, and special events open to the general public. Visitors can browse through the vast collection of books, music, and more, but only members can take something out. Founded in 1899, the library has expanded into adjacent buildings, including one built by Balboa Park architect William Templeton Johnson. 🕓 *30 min. 1008 Wall St. (at Girard Ave.).* ☎ *858/454-5872. www.ljathenaeum.org. Gallery exhibits are free. Tues, Thurs–Sat 10am–5:30pm; Wed 10am–8:30pm.*

With its small bakery and restaurant, 10 ★ **Girard Gourmet** always draws a crowd for its cookies, quiches, soups, salads, and deli sandwiches (the eight-grain bread is a must). The Belgian proprietor also whips up heartier fare, like lamb stew and duck à l'orange, and charming special occasion cookies from Valentine hearts to Halloween ghosts. It's the perfect place to gather your goods for a picnic. *7837 Girard Ave.* ☎ *858/454-3325. www.girardgourmet.com. Mon–Sat 7am–8pm; Sun 7am–7pm. $2–$22.*

Hillcrest

1. Hillcrest Sign
2. *"Fossils Exposed"*
3. *"The Loading Dock"*
4. John Wear Memorial
5. Mamá Testa Taqueria
6. Marston Addition Canyon
7. Marston House
8. Seventh Avenue
9. Wednesday Club
10. Design Center
11. Brass Rail
12. Guild Theater

Centrally located, brimming with popular restaurants and boutiques, Hillcrest is one of San Diego's most vibrant neighborhoods, thanks in no small part to its role as the heart of the local gay and lesbian community. In the 1920s, Hillcrest was the city's first self-contained suburb, making it a desirable address for bankers and businessmen, who built their mansions here. Despite the cachet of being close to Balboa Park (home of the San Diego Zoo and numerous museums), the area fell into neglect in the 1960s. By the late 1970s, however, legions of preservation-minded residents began restoring Hillcrest, and the community is once again among San Diego's best places to live, work, and play.

START: **Bus route 1, 3, or 120 to Fifth and University aves.**

❶ **Hillcrest Sign.** Donated to the community in 1940 by a group of local businesswomen, this Art Deco Hillcrest landmark stretches 21 feet (6.5m) across University Avenue, utilizing 240 feet (73m) of pink neon lighting. It went dark for some time but was taken down and refurbished in 1983. Its relighting in August 1984 was the genesis of Hillcrest's annual street fair. Also of note, on the north side of University, is the neon sign for Jimmy Wong's Golden Dragon, a holdover from 1955 (the restaurant itself is defunct). *Corner of University & Fifth aves.*

❷ ***Fossils Exposed.*** You can go on a bit of a scavenger hunt as you walk the neighborhood, searching for artist Doron Rosenthal's *Fossils Exposed.* This 1998 public art project features 150 granite markers randomly embedded into the sidewalk along University Avenue, from First Avenue to Park Boulevard. The 4½-inch (11cm) pieces are stylized representations of actual plant and animal fossils that would be found in this region.

❸ ***The Loading Dock.*** This detailed, *trompe l'oeil* mural was painted by artist Linda Churchill in 1999 on the west side of the Ace Hardware building. *Corner of University & 10th aves.*

❹ **John Wear Memorial.** On December 13, 1991, 17-year-old John Wear was accosted and

Hillcrest's Art Deco landmark sign.

stabbed to death as he walked down the street with two friends, because his assailants believed he was gay. This small plaque in the sidewalk is dedicated to his memory and to the ending of all hate crimes. *1029 University Ave.*

5 ★★ **Mamá Testa Taqueria** features a nearly overwhelming selection of tacos—soft, rolled, or hard shell—featuring recipes from all over Mexico. Fans believe you won't find better tacos anywhere, on either side of the border. *1417A University Ave. ☎ 619/298-8226. www.mamatestataqueria.com. Mon–Thurs 11:30am–9pm; Fri–Sat 11:30am–11pm; Sun noon–8pm. $5–$9.*

6 ★ **Marston Addition Canyon.** Turn south down Vermont Street from University Avenue and head through part of residential Hillcrest. At the corner of Cypress Street, you'll come to the trailhead for this open-space oasis in the heart of the city. Follow the (usually) dry creek bed toward the sound of the ocean—actually it's the traffic on Hwy. 163. Take the footbridge over the freeway and head up the paved path into Balboa Park proper. *20 min. Note: This is a very isolated part of the park. It's not recommended you attempt this after dark. If you are doing this walk in the evening, retrace your steps back to University & Sixth aves. & resume the tour there.*

7 ★ **Marston House.** Built in 1905, this gorgeous Craftsman mansion designed by William Hebbard and Irving Gill was the home of one of San Diego's most prominent families. It's now a museum sitting on 5 beautifully landscaped acres (2 hectares), and the interior is filled with decor and furniture from the Arts and Crafts period. *See p 39.*

8 ★ **Seventh Avenue.** Architecture buffs should continue on down Seventh Avenue for a concentrated dose of classic design. The 10 other houses on this short, shady street represent more brilliant work from architects Irving Gill and William Hebbard, who created the Marston House, as well as prominent San Diego architects Richard Requa and Frank Mead. All the homes were constructed between 1905 and 1913 in what was known as Crittenden's Addition, which dates back to 1887. **Note:**

Marston House.

These are all private residences, so keep to the sidewalk. ***3500 block of Seventh Ave.***

❾ **Wednesday Club.** With the encouragement of architect Irving Gill, Hazel Waterman pursued a career in architecture following the death of her husband, who was the son of California governor Robert Waterman. With her only formal architectural education coming via a correspondence course, Gill hired her on, and she helped with three of the houses on Seventh Avenue (see above). She moved on to design this structure in 1911, clearly influenced by Gill. ***540 Ivy Lane (Sixth Ave. & Ivy Lane).***

❿ **Design Center.** Fans of contemporary design will appreciate this building by architect Lloyd Ruocco, San Diego's leading post-war modernist. Built in 1949, the structure served as Ruocco's office and as the location of his wife Ilse's interior decorating business and showroom. Fittingly, the space has been used by a succession of architectural and design firms ever since. ***3611 Fifth Ave.***

⓫ **Brass Rail.** This is San Diego's oldest gay bar—it's been in the neighborhood since 1963 (although it was originally on the other side of the street and prior to that had been downtown). It's been in this spot since 1973. ***3796 Fifth Ave. (at Robinson St.). ☎ 619/298-2233. www.thebrassrailsd.com.***

⓬ **Guild Theater.** A series of failed enterprises has occupied what was once a beautiful, Spanish Revival–style movie house that first opened in 1913. Renamed the Guild in the late 1950s, the plug was finally pulled on it in 1997. A tragic event for many locals, the Guild was completely destroyed—what you see is a re-creation of the facade based on the original design. ***3835 Fifth Ave.***

Coronado

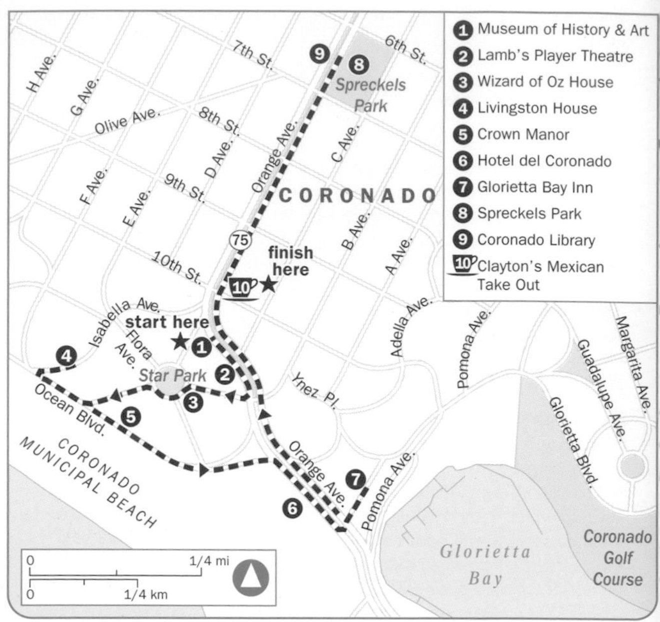

You may be tempted to think of Coronado as an island (you do cross the San Diego–Coronado Bay Bridge to get to it from downtown), but it's actually on a peninsula connected to the mainland by a narrow sand spit, the Silver Strand. It's a wealthy, self-contained community inhabited by lots of retired Navy brass and young families who live on quiet, tree-lined streets. The northern portion of Coronado is home to a U.S. Naval base, in use since World War I; the rest of the area has a history as an elite village with plenty of big, beautiful homes. Shops and restaurants line the main street, Orange Avenue, recognized by the National Main Street Center as one of the country's most romantic streets. You'll also find several ritzy resorts, including the landmark Hotel del Coronado, which fronts one of the area's finest beaches. START: **Bus route 901.**

1 ★ Museum of History and Art. This museum displays archival materials about the development of Coronado and also offers tourist information. Exhibits include photographs of the Hotel del Coronado in its infancy, the old ferries, Tent City (a seaside campground for middle-income vacationers from 1900 to 1939), and notable residents and visitors. Other memorabilia include army uniforms, old postcards, and even recorded music. You'll also learn about the island's military aviation history during World Wars I and II. ⏲ *30 min. 1100 Orange Ave.* ☎ *619/435-7242. www.coronadohistory.org. Admission is free, although there is a suggested donation of $5 adults, $3 seniors. Mon–Fri 9am–5pm; Sat–Sun 10am–5pm.*

2 ★ Lamb's Players Theatre. This acclaimed troupe is one of the few professional theaters in the country with a year-round resident company. The intimate theater space is in the Spreckels Building, a neoclassical structure designed by Harrison Albright, who also created the Organ Pavilion in Balboa Park and the downtown Spreckels Theater. *1142 Orange Ave.* ☎ *619/437-6000. www.lambsplayers.org.*

3 Wizard of Oz House. Author L. Frank Baum was a frequent visitor to Coronado, where he wrote several of his beloved *Wizard of Oz* books. It's believed he even patterned elements of the Emerald City after the architecture of the Hotel del Coronado. Baum occupied this colonial revival home, known as the Lemeche-Meade House, in the early 1900s. ***Note:*** This is a private home. *1101 Star Park Circle.*

Lamb's Players Theatre.

Coronado Museum of History and Art.

4 ★★ Livingston House. Also known as the Baby Del, this spectacular Queen Anne Revival home was built in 1887, 6 months before the Hotel Del. It's believed the house was a training ground for carpenters who would work on the Del and, indeed, might have been designed by the Del's architects, working under a pseudonym. The house is privately owned. *1144 Isabella Ave.*

5 ★★ Crown Manor. San Diego's all-star architectural team of William Hebbard and Irving Gill created the original designs for this amazing 27-bedroom, oceanfront estate in 1902. Also known as the Richards-Dupee Mansion, this private home covers 20,000 square feet (1,858 sq. m) and was commissioned by Bartlett Richards, a Nebraska cattle baron. Richards ran afoul of the law for questionable land schemes in his home state and died while in federal custody in 1911. He was elected to the National Cowboy Hall of Fame in 1970. *1015 Ocean Blvd.*

6 ★★★ Hotel del Coronado. San Diego's romantic Hotel del Coronado is an unmistakable landmark with a colorful past. When it opened in 1888, it was among the first buildings rigged with Thomas Edison's new invention, electric light (its electrical power plant supplied the entire city of Coronado until 1922). Author L. Frank Baum, a frequent guest, designed the dining room's original crown-shaped chandeliers. The hotel has also played host to royalty and celebrities—Edward, Prince of Wales (later King Edward VIII and then Duke of Windsor), caused a sensation with his visit in 1920, and of course, Marilyn Monroe, Tony Curtis, and Jack Lemmon famously frolicked here in the film *Some Like It Hot*. *See p 139.*

7 ★★ Glorietta Bay Inn. The Spreckels Mansion is now known as the Glorietta Bay Inn, a delightful small hotel. It was designed by John Spreckels's go-to architect, Harrison Albright, and built in 1908. Spreckels, along with his family and money, abandoned San Francisco after the 1906 earthquake and set up shop in San Diego. The sugar magnate was particularly involved with Coronado, where he became the sole owner of the Hotel Del. The Glorietta Bay Inn's 1950s motel-style annexes are lamentable, but the home's glory is still very much in evidence in the original guest rooms and public spaces. *1630 Glorietta Blvd.* ☎ *800/283-9383 or 619/435-3101. www.gloriettabayinn.com.*

Aerial view of Hotel del Coronado.

8 ★★ Spreckels Park. The founding fathers of Coronado were land speculators who purchased the peninsula—mostly inhabited by jackrabbits—for $110,000 in 1885. Their intent from the beginning was to create a resort community. J. D. Spreckels donated this 8-acre park facing Orange Avenue in 1909, and it has remained the community's gathering point. Art shows, book sales, and garden shows are often held here on weekends, and summer band concerts are a hometown tradition. The park is jammed during major events, including the Fourth of July parade, an extravaganza befitting Coronado's military history. *975 C Ave.*

9 ★★ Coronado Library. J. D. Spreckels commissioned architect Harrison Albright to design a classical revival Grecian temple for the growing community's library in 1909. The library's significant works of art include two fresco murals painted by Alfredo Ramos Martinez for the La Avenida Cafe in 1938 and rescued and restored when the cafe fell into ruins in the 1990s. The library's parklike grounds include a rose garden and 60-foot-high star pine trees. Second Hand Prose, a used bookstore stocked with current bestsellers and other books, is on D Avenue, right behind the library. For hours, check the store's website at coronadofol.org. *640 Orange Ave.* ☎ *619/522-7390. www.coronado.ca.us/library. Mon–Thurs 10am–9pm; Fri–Sat 10am–6pm; Sun 1–5pm.*

The no-frills, walk-in-closet-sized **10 Clayton's Mexican Take Out** lacks any pretense of charm, which, of course, is its charm. No eating on the premises. *1107 10th St. (at Orange Ave., behind Clayton's Coffee Shop).* ☎ *619/437-8811. Daily 11am–7pm. Cash only. $3–$8.* ●

4 The Best Shopping

Shopping **Best Bets**

Best **Jewelry That Doubles as Art**
★★★ Taboo Studio *1615½ W. Lewis St. (p 79)*

Best **Sexy Beachwear**
★★ Sauvage *1025 Prospect St. (p 77)*

Best **Stylin' Chapeau**
★★ Village Hat Shop *3821 4th Ave. (p 77)*

Best **Spot for Local Artists**
★ Spanish Village Art Center *1770 Village Place (p 75)*

Best **Place to Find Dr. Seuss on the Loose**
★★ Chuck Jones Gallery *232 Fifth Ave. (p 74)*

Best **Place for Mid-Century Modernists**
★★★ Boomerang for Modern *2475 Kettner Blvd. (p 79)* and ★★★ Mid-Century *3795 Park Blvd. (p 79)*

Best **Fashions for Moms-to-Be**
★★ Mabel's *136 S. Cedros Ave. (p 74)*

Best **Denim**
★★ G-Star Raw *470 Fifth Ave. (p 77)*

Best **Zen-ful Gifts**
★★ Vitreum *619 W. Fir St. (p 78)*

Previous page: Sauvage in La Jolla.

Best **Stuff from out of Africa**
★★ Africa and Beyond *1250 Prospect St. (p 74)*

Best **Place to Buy a Trilobite**
★★ Dinosaur Gallery *1327 Camino del Mar (p 77)*

Best **Beeswax**
★★ Knorr Candle Shop *14906 Villa de la Valle (p 78)*

Best **Funky Bookstore**
★★ D.G. Wills Books *7461 Girard Ave. (p 75)*

Best **Place for Rare Vinyl**
★★★ Folk Arts Rare Records *2881 Adams Ave. (p 79)*

Best **Place for Surfer Girls and Boys**
★★ Quiksilver/Roxy *1111 Prospect St. (p 73)*

Best **South-of-the-Border Treasures**
★★★ Bazaar del Mundo *4133 Taylor St. (p 77)*

Best **Shopping Center for Fashionistas**
★★ Fashion Valley Center *7007 Friars Rd. (p 80)*

Best **Shopping Center for Fashionistas Looking for Discounts**
★★★ Carlsbad Premium Outlets *5600 Paseo del Norte (p 80)*

Downtown Shopping

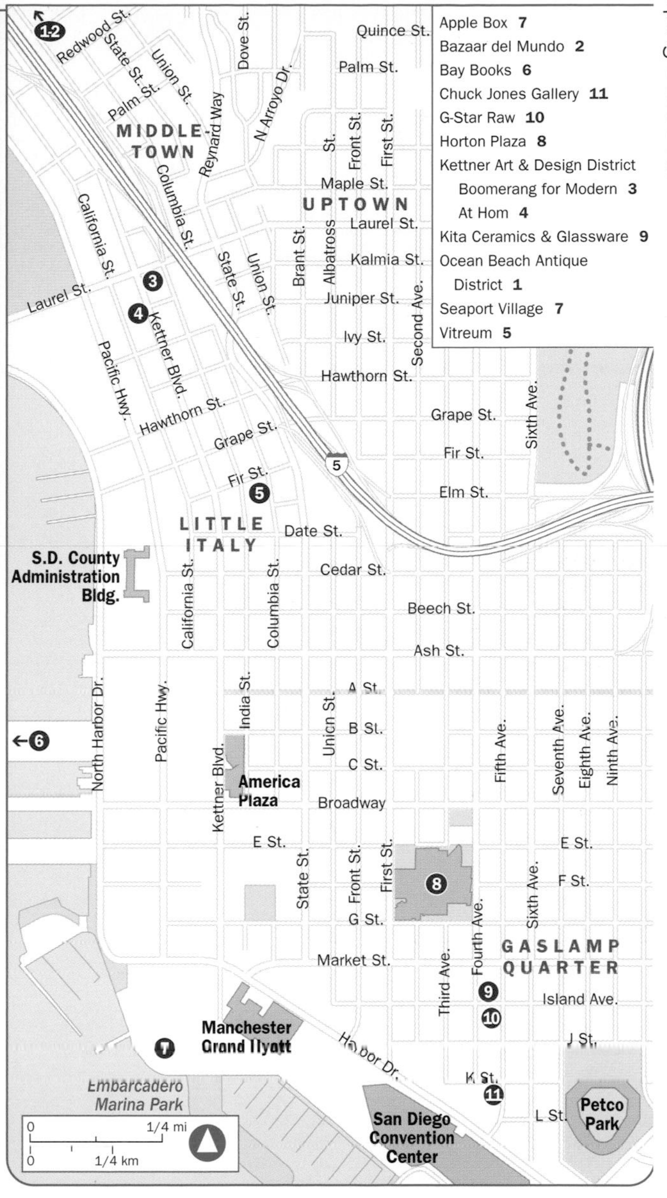
Apple Box 7
Bazaar del Mundo 2
Bay Books 6
Chuck Jones Gallery 11
G-Star Raw 10
Horton Plaza 8
Kettner Art & Design District
Boomerang for Modern 3
At Hom 4
Kita Ceramics & Glassware 9
Ocean Beach Antique District 1
Seaport Village 7
Vitreum 5
MIDDLE-TOWN
UPTOWN
LITTLE ITALY
GASLAMP QUARTER
S.D. County Administration Bldg.
America Plaza
Manchester Grand Hyatt
Embarcadero Marina Park
San Diego Convention Center
Petco Park
Redwood St.
State St.
Union St.
Palm St.
Reynard Way
Dove St.
N Arroyo Dr.
Quince St.
Front St.
First St.
Maple St.
Laurel St.
Kalmia St.
Juniper St.
Ivy St.
Hawthorn St.
Second Ave.
Brant St.
Albatross St.
Columbia St.
California St.
Kettner Blvd.
Pacific Hwy.
Grape St.
Fir St.
Elm St.
Sixth Ave.
Date St.
Cedar St.
Beech St.
Ash St.
A St.
B St.
C St.
Broadway
India St.
North Harbor Dr.
Fifth Ave.
Seventh Ave.
Eighth Ave.
Ninth Ave.
E St.
F St.
G St.
Market St.
Third Ave.
Fourth Ave.
Island Ave.
J St.
K St.
L St.
Harbor Dr.
5
0 1/4 mi
0 1/4 km

Hillcrest Shopping

La Jolla Shopping

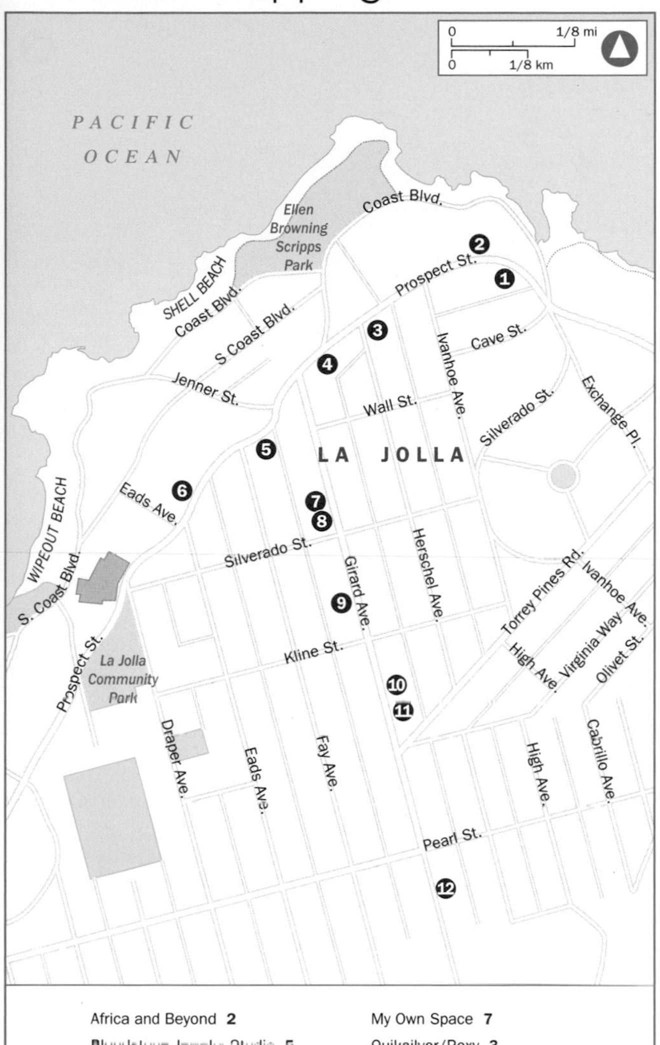

Africa and Beyond **2**	My Own Space **7**
Blondstone Jewelry Studio **5**	Quiksilver/Roxy **3**
D.G. Wills Books **12**	Quint Contemporary Art **9**
Emilia Castillo **1**	Sauvage **4**
Joseph Bellows Gallery **10**	Tasende Gallery **6**
Laura Gambucci **11**	Warwick's **8**

North County Shopping

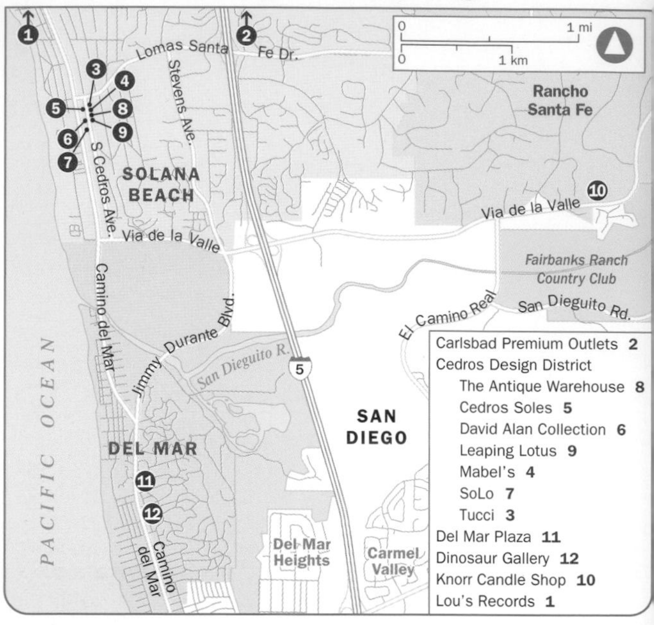

Shopping A to Z

Antiques & Collectibles

★ Ocean Beach Antique District OCEAN BEACH San Diego's greatest concentration of antiques stores are found along the main drag of Ocean Beach. There are mall-style shops featuring dozens of dealers under one roof and tiny specialty boutiques. *4800 block of Newport Ave. (at Sunset Cliffs Blvd.). www.antiquesinsandiego.com. AE, DISC, MC, V. Bus: 35 or 923. Map p 71.*

Art

★★ Africa and Beyond LA JOLLA A collection of contemporary and traditional African sculpture, textiles, jewelry, and furnishings. *1250 Prospect St. (east of Ivanhoe Ave.). ☎ 800/422-3742 or 858/454-9983. www.africaandbeyond.com. AE, DISC, MC, V. Bus: 30. Map p 73*

★★ Chuck Jones Gallery GASLAMP QUARTER Animation cels by the likes of Dr. Seuss and Chuck Jones, the creator of Bugs Bunny and Daffy Duck, as well as classic Hollywood glamour photography. *232 Fifth Ave. (at K St.). ☎ 619/294-9880. www.chuckjones.com. AE, DC, DISC, MC, V. Trolley: Gaslamp Quarter. Map p 71.*

★★★ Joseph Bellows Gallery LA JOLLA Devotees of photography will want to check out this gallery, which showcases both

Ian and Julie Allen offer a collection of jewelry and furnishings at Africa and Beyond.

contemporary and vintage work. *7661 Girard Ave. (btw. Kline St. & Torrey Pines Rd.).* ☎ *858/456-5620. www.josephbellows.com. AE, DISC, MC, V. Bus: 30. Map p 73.*

★★★ **Quint Contemporary Art** LA JOLLA Perhaps the city's finest contemporary art gallery, the Quint has resided in 10 places over its 3 decades and now has a 3,000-square-foot (278 sq. m) space in tony La Jolla. *7547 Girard Ave.* ☎ *858/454-3409. www.quintgallery.com. AE, MC, V. Bus: 30. Map p 73.*

★ **Spanish Village Art Center** BALBOA PARK A collection of 37 casitas provides a home for some 250 artists working in everything from origami to glass. You can watch live as the artists do their thing. *1770 Village Place (in Balboa Park).* ☎ *619/233-9050. www.spanishvillageart.com. Most studios accept MC, V. Bus: 7. Map p 72.*

★★ **Tasende Gallery** LA JOLLA With its modern architecture and serene environs, this museum-like sculpture gallery provides a calm respite from the commercial hubbub nearby. *820 Prospect St. (at Jenner St.).* ☎ *858/454-3691. www.tasendegallery.com. No credit cards. Bus: 30. Map p 73.*

Books

★★ **Bay Books** CORONADO A superb collection of international magazines hints at the breadth of offerings at this independent shop, whose customers appreciate meeting Newt Gingrich, "Sully" Sullenberger, and other thought-provoking authors. *1029 Orange Ave. (btw. 10th St. & C Ave.).* ☎ *619/435-0070. www.baybookscoronado.com. AE, DISC, MC, V. Bus: 901 or 904. Map p 71.*

★★ **D.G. Wills Books** LA JOLLA This charmingly musty shop has books stacked to its wood rafters. If you're looking for something scholarly, offbeat, or esoteric, this is the place for you. *7461 Girard Ave. (at Pearl St.).* ☎ *858/456-1800.*

Artist opening at Chuck Jones Gallery.

Photographic prints in Joseph Bellows Gallery.

www.dgwillsbooks.com. AE, DISC, MC, V. Bus: 30. Map p 73.

★★★ **Warwick's** LA JOLLA This family-run business has been here since the 1930s. It's a browser's delight with more than 40,000 titles in stock; authors also come in for readings several times a week at this pet-friendly spot. An outlet at the San Diego airport makes waiting for flights a pleasure. *7812 Girard Ave. (between Wall & Silverado sts.). ☎ 858/454-0347. www.warwicks.com. AE, DC, DISC, MC, V. Bus: 30. Map p 73.*

Children: Fashion & Toys

★ kids **Apple Box** EMBARCADERO Specializing in wooden toys, you'll find everything from puzzles and pull toys to rocking horses and toy chests. A second location is in Old Town (2611 San Diego Ave., #3; ☎ 619/542-1867). *Seaport Village, 837 W. Harbor Dr., Ste. C (at Kettner Blvd.). ☎ 619/230-1818. www.appleboxtoys.com. AE, DISC, MC, V. Trolley: Orange Line to Seaport Village. Map p 71.*

Artist show at the Quint Gallery.

★★ **Mabel's** SOLANA BEACH Hip fashions and gifts for infants and style-conscious moms-to-be. *136 S. Cedros Ave. (south of Lomas Santa Fe Dr.). ☎ 858/794-0066. AE, DISC, MC, V. Bus: 101. Coaster: Solana Beach. Map p 74.*

★★ kids **Quiksilver/Roxy** LA JOLLA Teens and tweens will love the surf and skate gear at this conjoined boys/girls shop in the heart of La Jolla village. *1111 Prospect St. (at Herschel Ave.). ☎ 858/459-1267. www.quiksilver.com. AE, DISC, MC, V. Bus: 30. Map p 73.*

Fashion

★★ **Cedros Soles** SOLANA BEACH Just try to resist the fabulous shoes for women here; there's also a great selection of handbags and other accessories. *143 S. Cedros Ave., Ste. L (south of Lomas Santa Fe Dr.). ☎ 858/794-9911. www.cedrossoles.com. AE, DISC, MC, V. Bus: 101. Coaster: Solana Beach. Map p 74.*

★★ **G-Star Raw** GASLAMP QUARTER This international chain has a cool San Diego boutique, selling Euro-style denim. *470 Fifth Ave. (btw. Island Ave. & J St.). ☎ 619/238-7088. www.g-star.com. AE, DISC, MC, V. Bus: 992. Trolley: Gaslamp Quarter. Map p 71.*

★★★ **Laura Gambucci** LA JOLLA Bucking the conservative La Jolla trend, this women's boutique features unique, contemporary styles and sexy shoes and handbags. *7655 Girard Ave., Ste. A (btw. Kline St. & Torrey Pines Rd.). ☎ 858/551-0214. www.lauragambucci.com. AE, DISC, MC, V. Bus: 30. Map p 73.*

★★ **Sauvage** LA JOLLA Hit the sand in style with some fabulous beach and swimwear from this local line. This sleek, chic boutique has a selection for the guys, too. *1025 Prospect St. (btw. Girard & Herschel aves.). ☎ 858/729-0015. www.sauvagewear.com. AE, DISC, MC, V. Bus: 30. Map p 73.*

★ **Tucci** SOLANA BEACH This boutique is chic and sophisticated, offering contemporary, international designs in a comfortably mod space. *130 S. Cedros Ave., Ste. 140 (south of Lomas Santa Fe Dr.).*

Spanish Village Art Center.

The Roxy store in La Jolla.

☎ 858/259-8589. www.tucciboutique.com. AE, MC, V. Bus: 101. Coaster: Solana Beach. Map p 74.

★★ **Village Hat Shop** HILLCREST The range of hats for hipsters, fashion plates, and sun-phobics entices fans of this decades-old family business. There's a second location at Seaport Village (853 W. Harbor Dr.; ☎ 619/233-7236). *3821 Fourth Ave. (btw. Robinson & University aves.). ☎ 619/683-5533. www.villagehatshop.com. AE, MC, V. Bus: 1, 3, 10, 11, or 120. Map p 72.*

Gifts

★★★ **Bazaar del Mundo** OLD TOWN This cluster of shops packed with clothing, furnishings, and all sorts of amazing folk art from throughout Latin America is especially festive around Day of the Dead and Christmas. *4133 Taylor St. (at Sunset St.). ☎ 619/296-3161. www.bazaardelmundo.com. AE, MC, V. Bus: 7, 8, 10, 35. Trolley: Blue, Orange & Green Lines. Map p 71.*

★★ kids **Dinosaur Gallery** DEL MAR Own a piece of (pre)history—fossils, gems and minerals, and amber jewelry. Models,

Sauvage Boutique.

puzzles, and more for the kids, too. *1327 Camino Del Mar (btw. 13th & 14th sts.).* ☎ *858/794-4855. AE, MC, V. Bus: 101. Map p 74.*

★★ Kita Ceramics & Glassware GASLAMP QUARTER *Objets d'art* from Italy, Japan, and San Diego, including Murano glass jewelry and lighting, pottery, and home accessories. *517 Fourth Ave., Ste. 101 (at Island Ave.).* ☎ *619/239-2600. www.kitaceramicsglass.com. AE, MC, V. Bus: 992. Trolley: Convention Center. Map p 71.*

★★ Knorr Candle Shop DEL MAR This family-run business has been making beeswax candles here since 1928; it's one of the largest candle stores in the country. *14906 Via de la Valle (east of El Camino Real).* ☎ *858/755-2051. www.knorrcandleshop.com. AE, DISC, MC, V. Bus: 308. Map p 74.*

★★ Vitreum LITTLE ITALY The artfully Zen display of vases, incense burners, and decorative items is worth a jaunt to this pretty cottage. *619 W. Fir St. (btw. Columbia & India sts.).* ☎ *619/237-9810. www.vitreum-us.com. MC, V. Bus: 83. Trolley: County Cntr/Little Italy Map p 71.*

Home Decor

★★★ Cedros Design District SOLANA BEACH More than two-dozen chic and eclectic shops. Highlights include the **Antique Warehouse** (212 S. Cedros Ave.; ☎ 858/755-5156; DISC, MC, V); **David Alan Collection** (241 S. Cedros Ave.; ☎ 858/481-8044; www.thedavidalancollection.com; AE, DISC, MC, V); **Leaping Lotus** (240 S. Cedros Ave.; ☎ 858/720-8283; www.leapinglotus.com; AE, MC, V); and **SoLo** (309 S. Cedros Ave.; ☎ 858/794-9016; www.solocedros.com; AE, DISC, MC, V).

Bazaar del Mundo.

A Farmers Market operates on Sunday afternoons. *Primarily the 100 & 200 blocks of S. Cedros Ave. (south of Lomas Santa Fe Dr.). www.cedrosavenue.com. Bus: 101. Coaster: Solana Beach. Map p 74.*

★★ **Emilia Castillo** LA JOLLA From her studio in Taxco, Mexico, Emilia Castillo produces fantastic, one-of-a-kind silver, gold, and porcelain home decor and jewelry. *1273 Prospect St. (east of Ivanhoe Ave.). ☎ 858/551-9600. www.emiliacastillolajolla.com. AE, DISC, MC, V. Bus: 30. Map p 73.*

★★ **Kettner Art & Design District** LITTLE ITALY A conglomeration of cool stores and art galleries highlight this appealing neighborhood. Standouts include **Boomerang for Modern** (2475 Kettner Blvd.; ☎ 619/239-2040; www.boomerangformodern.com; AE, DISC, MC, V); and **At Hom** (2310 Kettner Blvd.; ☎ 619/744-9974; www.at-hom.com; AE, MC, V). *Kettner Blvd. & India St. btw. Laurel & Date sts. Bus: 83. Trolley: County Cntr/Little Italy. Map p 71.*

★★★ **Mid-Century** HILLCREST Way-cool pottery, light fixtures, cocktail accessories, furniture, and more from the 1940s, '50s, and '60s. *3795 Park Blvd. ☎ 619/295-4832. www.midcenturystore.com. AE, DISC, MC, V. Bus: 7. Map p 72.*

★★ **My Own Space** LA JOLLA Modern and minimalist furniture and accessories (with a touch of whimsy) highlight this sleek boutique. *7840 Girard Ave. (btw. Silverado & Wall sts.). ☎ 858/459-0099. www.mosmyownspace.com. AE, V. Bus: 30. Map p 73.*

Jewelry

★★ **Blondstone Jewelry Studio** OCEAN BEACH Creative jewelry designs, including unique rings, pendants, earrings, and bracelets

Kita Ceramics.

incorporating seashells and tumbled sea-glass "mermaid tears." There's a second location in La Jolla (925 Prospect St.; ☎ 858/456-1994). *4931 Newport Ave. (btw. Cable & Bacon sts.). ☎ 619/223-2563. www.blondstone.com. AE, MC, V. Bus: 35. Map p 73.*

★★★ **Taboo Studio** MISSION HILLS The jewelry here is more than just simple ornamentation; these pieces are works of art created by nationally and internationally known jewelry artists. *1615½ W. Lewis St. (btw. Stephens St. & Palmetto Way). ☎ 619/692-0099. www.taboostudio.com. AE, DISC, MC, V. Bus: 83. Map p 72.*

Music

★★★ **Folk Arts Rare Records** NORMAL HEIGHTS Nirvana for serious collectors of jazz, folk, blues, and country music. A huge selection of 78s and other rarities; if you don't have a turntable, the store also can create custom recordings on CD. *3072 El Cajon Blvd. (btw. Ohio & Illinois sts.). ☎ 619/282-7833. www.folkartsrarerecords.com. MC, V. Bus: 2. Map p 72.*

★★★ **Lou's Records** ENCINITAS A mind-blowing spot for anyone seriously into music or movies. A compound of buildings dedicated to new and imported CDs, used CDs and vinyl, as well as DVDs. *434 N. Coast Hwy. 101 (btw. El Portal St. & North Ct.).* ☎ *888/568-7732 or 760/753-1382. www.lousrecords.com. AE, DISC, MC, V. Bus: 101. Map p 74.*

Shopping Centers

★★★ **Carlsbad Premium Outlets** CARLSBAD Some of the biggest names in fashion and retail are elbow to elbow at this smart and handsome outlet mall featuring some 90 stores. It has a fine-dining component, too. *5600 Paseo del Norte (adjacent to I-5).* ☎ *888/790-7467 or 760/804-9045 www.premiumoutlets.com. Bus: 101. Map p 74.*

★★★ **Del Mar Plaza** DEL MAR With its ocean-view terraces, fountains, destination restaurants, and open-air wine bar, this might be the nicest mall you've ever seen. There are more than 30 shops and eateries. *1555 Camino Del Mar (at 15th St.).* ☎ *858/847-2284. www.delmarplaza.com. Bus: 101. Map p 74.*

Carlsbad Premium Outlets.

★★ **Fashion Valley Center** MISSION VALLEY This upscale shopping center features Nordstrom and Neiman Marcus department stores, as well as more than 200 specialty shops and an 18-screen movie theater. *7007 Friars Rd. (btw. Hwy. 163 & Fashion Valley Rd.).* ☎ *619/688-9113. www.simon.com. Bus: 6, 14, 20, 25, 41, 120, or 928. Trolley: Blue or Green Line to Fashion Valley. Map p 72.*

★★ **Horton Plaza** GASLAMP QUARTER This colorful shopping center has more than 130 specialty shops, a performing arts venue, a 14-screen cinema, two major department stores, and a variety of restaurants and short-order eateries. *324 Horton Plaza (bounded by Broadway, 1st & 4th aves. & G St.).* ☎ *619/239-8180. www.westfield.com/hortonplaza. Bus: 2, 3, 5, 7, 11, 15, 20, 30, 50, 120, 150, 210, 850, 860, 901, 923, 929, or 992. Trolley: Blue or Orange Line to Civic Center. Map p 71.*

★ **Mission Valley Center** MISSION VALLEY This old-fashioned outdoor mall has budget-minded offerings like Nordstrom Rack outlet store and Target, plus a 20-screen theater and 150 other stores and places to eat. *1640 Camino del Rio N. (alongside I-8 at Mission Center Rd.).* ☎ *619/296-6375. www.westfield.com/missionvalley. Bus: 6 or 14. Trolley: Green Line to Mission Valley Center. Map p 72.*

★ kids **Seaport Village** EMBARCADERO This 14-acre (5.5-hectare) bayfront outdoor mall provides an idyllic setting that visitors love. Many of the more than 50 shops are of the Southern California cutesy variety, but the atmosphere is pleasant, and there are a few gems. *849 W. Harbor Dr. (at Kettner Blvd.).* ☎ *619/235-4014. www.seaportvillage.com. Trolley: Orange Line to Seaport Village. Map p 71.* ●

5 The Best of **San Diego Outdoors**

The Best **Beaches**

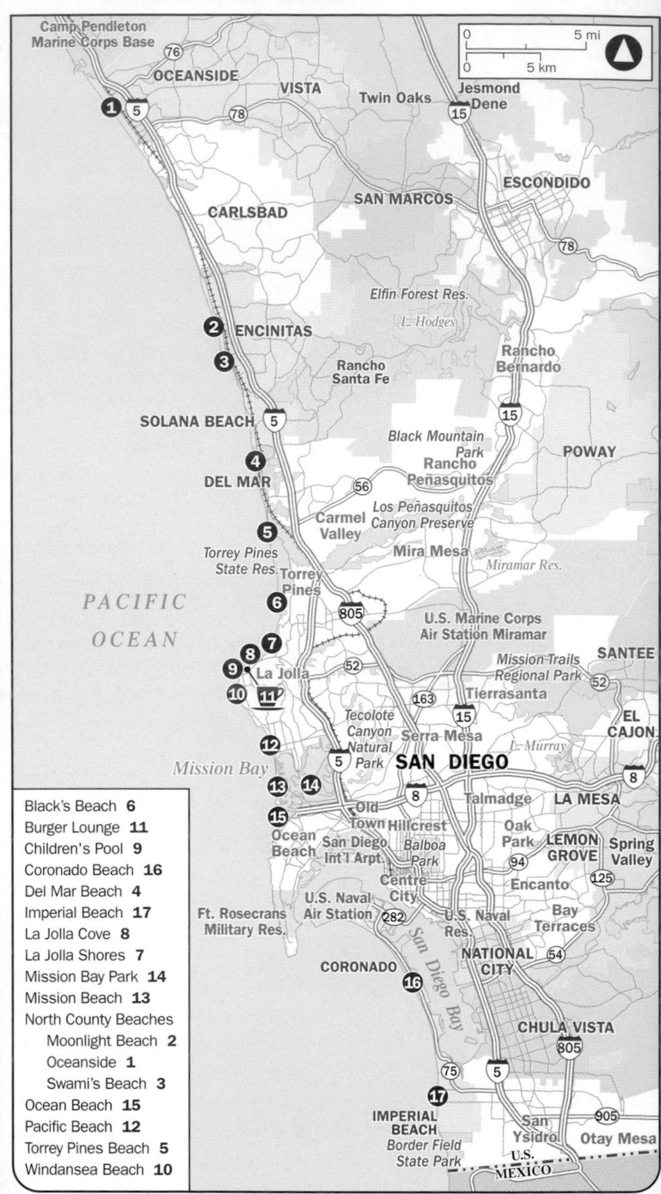
Black's Beach 6
Burger Lounge 11
Children's Pool 9
Coronado Beach 16
Del Mar Beach 4
Imperial Beach 17
La Jolla Cove 8
La Jolla Shores 7
Mission Bay Park 14
Mission Beach 13
North County Beaches
Moonlight Beach 2
Oceanside 1
Swami's Beach 3
Ocean Beach 15
Pacific Beach 12
Torrey Pines Beach 5
Windansea Beach 10
0 5 mi
0 5 km
Camp Pendleton Marine Corps Base
OCEANSIDE
VISTA
Twin Oaks
Jesmond Dene
ESCONDIDO
SAN MARCOS
CARLSBAD
Elfin Forest Res.
L. Hodges
ENCINITAS
Rancho Santa Fe
Rancho Bernardo
SOLANA BEACH
Black Mountain Park
POWAY
Rancho Peñasquitos
DEL MAR
Los Peñasquitos Canyon Preserve
Carmel Valley
Mira Mesa
Miramar Res.
Torrey Pines State Res.
Torrey Pines
PACIFIC OCEAN
U.S. Marine Corps Air Station Miramar
SANTEE
Mission Trails Regional Park
La Jolla
Tierrasanta
EL CAJON
Tecolote Canyon Natural Park
Serra Mesa
L. Murray
SAN DIEGO
Mission Bay
Talmadge
LA MESA
Old Town
Hillcrest
Oak Park
LEMON GROVE
Spring Valley
Ocean Beach
San Diego Int'l Arpt.
Balboa Park
Centre City
Encanto
U.S. Naval Air Station
Ft. Rosecrans Military Res.
U.S. Naval Res.
Bay Terraces
San Diego Bay
NATIONAL CITY
CORONADO
CHULA VISTA
IMPERIAL BEACH
Border Field State Park
San Ysidro
Otay Mesa
U.S.
MEXICO

Previous page: Windansea Beach in San Diego.

San Diego County is blessed with 70 miles (113km) of sandy coastline and more than 30 individual beaches. Even in winter and spring, when water temperatures drop into the 50s, the beaches are great places to walk, jog, and surf. In summer, when water temps crawl to the high 60s, the beaches teem with locals and visitors alike, the bikinis come out, pecs are flexed, and parking is nearly nonexistent. You must hit the popular spots early on weekend mornings or spend the day cruising for a legal parking place. ***Tip:*** The coast is often socked in with chill fog, called June Gloom, in early summer. The best beach weather usually arrives in August and September.

★★ **Black's Beach.** Located at the base of steep, 300-foot-high (91m) cliffs, this 2-mile-long (3km) beach is out of the way and not easy to reach, but it draws scores with its secluded beauty and good swimming and surfing conditions—the graceful spectacle of paragliders launching from the cliffs above adds to the show. It's an unofficial nude beach, though technically nude sunbathing is illegal. Citations are rarely issued—lifeguards will either ignore it or just ask you to cover up. (Tickets will be written if you disregard their request.) There are no facilities here. *Bus: 101 to the Torrey Pines Gliderport; hike down the trail. You can also walk to Black's from beaches south (La Jolla Shores) or north (Torrey Pines).*

The 1 ★ **Burger Lounge** is a fast-food joint—La Jolla style. This sleek and modern burger spot has plenty of panache—it's casual but fashionable, serving grass-fed, organic beef burgers, as well as hand-cut fries and salads. Milkshakes, wine, and beer are also on the short menu. This California chain has eight other locations in the San Diego area. *1101 Wall St. (at Herschel Ave.). ☎ 858/456-0196. www.burgerlounge.com. Sun–Thurs 10:30am–9pm, Fri–Sat 10:30am–10pm. $8.*

★★ kids **Children's Pool.** Think clothing-optional Black's Beach is the city's most controversial sun-sea-sand situation? Think again—the Children's Pool is currently home to the biggest man-vs.-beast struggle since *Moby Dick*. A seawall shields this pocket of sand, originally intended as a calm swimming bay for children, but since 1994, when an offshore rock outcrop was designated as a protected mammal reserve, the beach has been cordoned off for the resident harbor seal population. The water can be foul, but swimming has been reinstated here—under the watchful eye of seal-loving volunteers. Most people just come to observe the

Black's Beach.

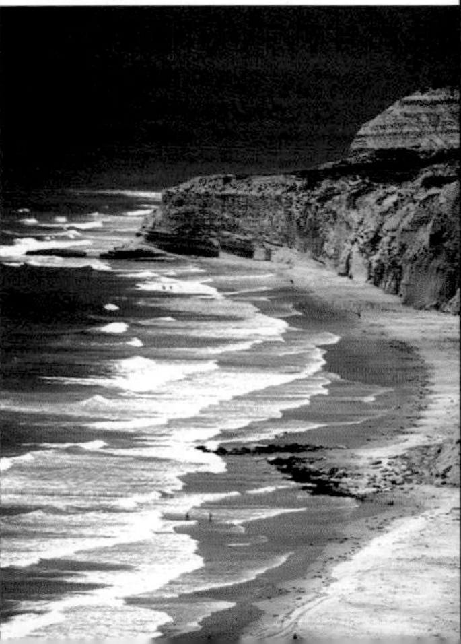

Sea lions loll on the beach at the Children's Pool.

colony. *See p 60. Bus: 30 to Girard Ave. & Silverado St. Walk 2 blocks down Girard Ave., cross Prospect St. to Ocean Lane.*

★★★ kids Coronado Beach. Lovely, wide, and sparkling, this beach is conducive to strolling and lingering, especially in the late afternoon. At the north end, you can watch fighter jets flying in formation from the Naval base, while just south is the pretty section fronting Ocean Boulevard and the Hotel del Coronado. Waves are gentle here, so the beach draws many families—and their dogs, which are allowed off-leash at the most northwesterly end. South of the Hotel Del, the beach becomes the beautiful, often deserted Silver Strand. The southern section closest to the hotel belongs to the U.S. Navy and is off-limits to civilians. The islands visible from here, Los Coronados, are 18 miles (29km) away and belong to Mexico. *Bus: 901 or 904 to the Hotel Del Coronado.*

★★ kids Del Mar Beach. The Del Mar Thoroughbred Club's slogan, as famously sung by DMTC founder Bing Crosby, is "where turf meets the surf." This town beach represents the "surf" portion of that phrase. It's a long stretch of sand backed by grassy cliffs and a playground area; several restaurants offer dining right alongside the beach. Del Mar is about 15 miles (24km) north of downtown San Diego. *Bus: 101.*

★ Imperial Beach. A half-hour south of downtown San Diego by car or trolley, and only a few minutes from the Mexican border, Imperial Beach is popular with surfers and local youth, who can be somewhat territorial about "their" beach in summer. I.B., as it's known, has 3 miles (5km) of surf breaks plus a guarded "swimmers only" stretch; check with lifeguards before getting wet, though, since sewage runoff from nearby rivers can sometimes foul the water. I.B. also plays host to the annual U.S. Open Sandcastle Competition in late July, with world-class sand creations ranging from nautical scenes to dinosaurs. *Trolley: Blue Line to Palm Ave., transfer to Bus 933/934.*

★★★ kids La Jolla Cove. The tropical-hued waters of La Jolla Cove represent San Diego at its

Coronado Beach.

Del Mar Beach.

most picture-perfect, though reality has its drawbacks. Seals and seagulls have claimed the rocks above the water, creating an odiferous ambience. Battles rage over dealing with the problem. Still, as part of the San Diego–La Jolla Underwater Ecological Reserve, the Cove is a perfect place to snorkel and dive. If the small beach gets a little too crowded, classy, grassy Ellen Browning Scripps Park (see p 60) on the bluff above it provides a great alternative. ***See p 60. Bus: 30. Walking directions same as previous.***

★★★ kids **La Jolla Shores.** The wide, flat mile of sand at La Jolla Shores is popular with joggers, swimmers, kayakers, novice scuba divers, and beginning body- and board-surfers, as well as families. Weekend crowds can be enormous, quickly occupying both the sand and the metered parking spaces in the lot. There are restrooms, showers, and picnic areas here, as well as palm-lined Kellogg Park across the street. ***Bus: 30 to La Jolla Shores Dr. & Avenida de la Playa. Walk 5 blocks down Avenida de la Playa.***

★★ kids **Mission Bay Park.** This 4,600-acre (1,862-hectare) aquatic playground contains 27 miles (43km) of bayfront, picnic areas, children's playgrounds, and paths for biking, in-line skating, and jogging. The bay lends itself to windsurfing, sailing, water-skiing, and all forms of personal watercraft. There are dozens of access points; one of the most popular is off I-5 at Clairemont Drive. Also accessed from this spot is Fiesta Island, where the annual softball-cum-beach party spectacle known as the Over the Line Tournament is held to raucous enthusiasm in July; a 4-mile (6.5km) road loops around the island. Vacation Island, in the center of the bay, is home to Paradise Point Resort (see p 143) and Ski Beach. Parts of the bay have been subject to closure over the years due to high levels of bacteria, so check for posted warnings. Personally, I'd rather sail on Mission Bay than swim in it. ***Bus: 8/9 or 30. See p 96.***

★ **Mission Beach.** While Mission Bay Park is a body of saltwater surrounded by land and bridges, Mission Beach is actually a beach on the Pacific Ocean. Always popular,

Paddleboarding at Mission Bay Park.

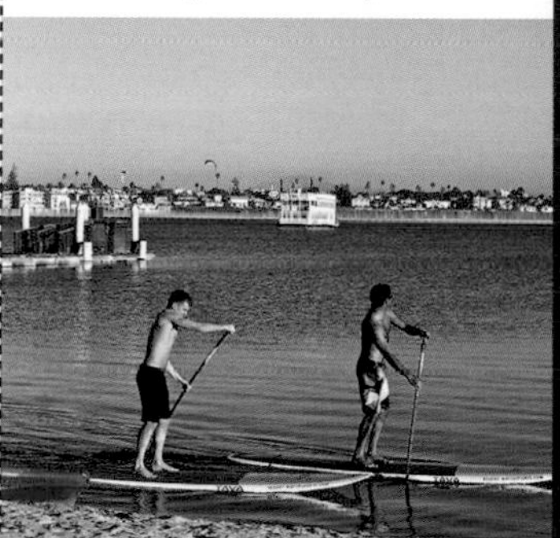

the sands and wide cement boardwalk sizzle with activity and great people-watching in summer; at the southern end, several volleyball games are almost always underway. The long beach and path extend from the rock jetty at the Mission Bay Channel north to Belmont Park amusement center and its Giant Dipper roller coaster (see p 33) and on to Pacific Beach Drive. Parking is often tough, with your best bets being the public lots at Belmont Park or at the south end of West Mission Bay Drive. Busy Mission Boulevard is the centerline of a 2-block-wide isthmus that separates the ocean and Mission Bay; it stretches a mile north to Pacific Beach. *Bus: 8/9 to Mission Beach.*

★★ **Ocean Beach.** The northern end of Ocean Beach Park, officially known as Dog Beach, is one of only a few in the county where your pooch can roam and frolic with other people's pets. The beach extends south from here in areas designated for swimming and surfing to the half-mile-long O.B. Pier, where surfers congregate at the surf break by the pier's pilings and anglers dangle their lines from the railings above. Rip currents can be strong here and sometimes discourage swimmers from venturing beyond waist depth (check with the lifeguard stations). Facilities at the beach include restrooms, showers, picnic tables, volleyball courts, and several parking lots. ***Bus: 35 or 923 to Newport Ave.***

★★ **Pacific Beach.** There's always action here, particularly along the extension of the paved Mission Beach boardwalk called Ocean Front Walk. It runs along Ocean Boulevard (just west of Mission Blvd.) to the pier. Surfing is popular year-round here, in marked sections, and the beach is well staffed with lifeguards. You're on your own to find street parking. Pacific Beach is also the home of Tourmaline Surfing Park, a half-mile (.8km) north of the pier, where the sport's old guard gathers to surf waters where swimmers are prohibited; reach it via Tourmaline Street, off Mission Boulevard. *Bus 8/9.*

★★★ **Torrey Pines Beach.** Combining a visit to Torrey Pines State Reserve with a day at the beach below the park makes for the quintessential San Diego outdoor experience. It's rarely

Never too young to learn to surf at Mission Beach.

North County Beaches

Those inclined to venture farther north in San Diego County won't be disappointed. The Pacific Coast Highway leads to inviting beaches, such as these in Encinitas: peaceful ★★★ **Swami's Beach** for surfing and ★★ **Moonlight Beach,** popular with families and volleyball buffs. Farthest north is ★★ **Oceanside,** which has one of the West Coast's longest wooden piers, wide sandy beaches, and several popular surfing areas. To reach these beaches by mass transit, take bus #101 or the Encinitas or Oceanside Coaster.

overcrowded, though you need to be aware of high tide (when most of the sand gets a bath). In almost any weather, it's a great beach for walking. ***Note:*** At this and any other bluff-side beach, never sit at the bottom of the cliffs. The hillsides are unstable and could collapse. *Bus: 101.*

★★ **Windansea Beach.** The fabled locale of Tom Wolfe's *Pump House Gang,* Windansea is legendary to this day among California's surf elite and remains one of San Diego's prettiest strands. This is not a good beach for swimming or diving, so come to surf (no novices, please), watch surfers, or soak in the camaraderie and party atmosphere. Windansea has no facilities, and street parking is first-come, first-served. *Bus: 30 to Nautilus St.*

Ocean Beach Pier at sunset.

Cabrillo National Monument

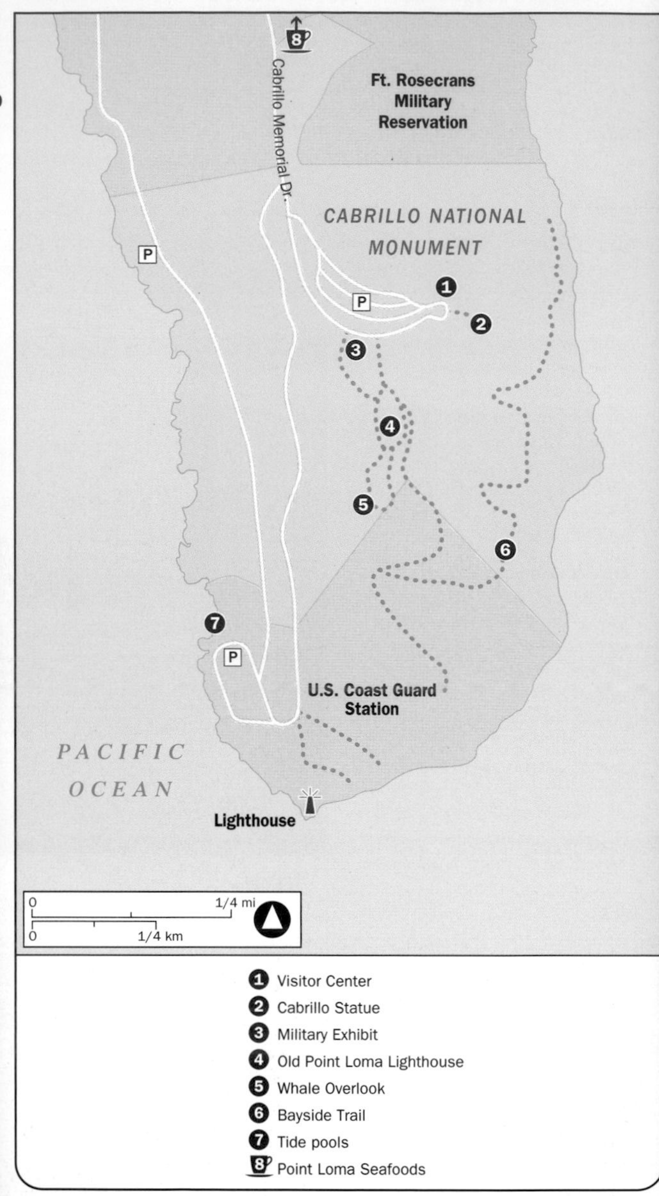
Cabrillo Memorial Dr.
Ft. Rosecrans Military Reservation
CABRILLO NATIONAL MONUMENT
P
U.S. Coast Guard Station
PACIFIC OCEAN
Lighthouse
0
1/4 mi
0
1/4 km
1 Visitor Center
2 Cabrillo Statue
3 Military Exhibit
4 Old Point Loma Lighthouse
5 Whale Overlook
6 Bayside Trail
7 Tide pools
8 Point Loma Seafoods

"On this day, Thursday, September 28, 1542, we discovered a port, closed and very good." When Juan Rodríguez Cabrillo led his three galleons into that sheltered harbor some 475 years ago, he became the first European to set eyes on what would become the West Coast of the United States. Point Loma, the spit of land that protected Cabrillo and his flotilla from an oncoming storm, is now the site of Cabrillo National Monument, a 160-acre (65-hectare) national park that is rich not only in history, but in natural wonders as well. **START: Bus route 84.**

❶ ★★ **Visitor Center.** Start your tour amid the center's numerous publications on San Diego history, marine life, and the age of exploration in the 16th century, and its glassed-in observation area offering stellar panoramas, including views of the actual spot where Cabrillo's party came ashore. The park's auditorium has ongoing screenings of films about Cabrillo's journey, whale migration, and more; a small museum features interactive exhibits about the conquistador and Spain's far-flung empire. Declared a national monument in 1913 by President Woodrow Wilson, the park is also the site of special events, including a re-enactment of Cabrillo's landing every late September/early October, and whale-related festivities every winter. *See p 13.*

Cabrillo National Monument.

❷ ★★ **Cabrillo Statue.** This 15-foot (4.5m) statue portrays Cabrillo looking steadfast and resolute; he doesn't seem to be much

The view of downtown San Diego from Cabrillo National Monument.

The Old Point Loma Lighthouse.

enjoying the 360-degree view from his privileged position. The flesh-and-blood Cabrillo was Portuguese (actual name, João Rodrigues Cabrilho), and as a soldier serving Spain, he made a name for himself as a crossbowman during Hernán Cortés' siege of Tenochtitlán (now Mexico City) and also participated in the conquest of Guatemala. His adventuring would come to an end several months after his visit to San Diego when he died from an injury suffered in a skirmish with Chumash Indians on one of Southern California's Channel Islands.

❸ **Military Exhibit.** Point Loma's strategic importance has long been recognized, and the area was established as a military reserve in 1852. Long-range gun batteries bristled from this plateau during both World Wars, and their remnants are still here. In a small building once used as an army radio station, there is an exhibit documenting San Diego's 19th Coast Artillery and the war hysteria that gripped the city after the attack on Pearl Harbor.

❹ ★★ **Old Point Loma Lighthouse.** This lighthouse had a relatively short lifespan (from 1855 to 1891), its seemingly perfect location compromised by low clouds and fog that often rendered the sweeping beam of light useless. The New Point Loma Lighthouse, situated nearby at sea level, has been in continuous operation since 1891. An interactive exhibit details what life was like for the keepers who lived here in the 19th century, far from the relative comforts of Old Town; the lighthouse itself is filled with period furnishings.

❺ ★ **Whale Overlook.** From this sheltered space, you can spot Pacific gray whales as they make their amazing, 10,000-mile (16,093km) journey from the Bering Sea to the warm lagoons of Mexico's Sea of Cortez, and back again, every mid-December through mid-March. These 40-ton (36T), 50-foot (15m) behemoths (with calves in tow on the return trip) are making the longest migration of any mammal. The overlook is outfitted with recorded information and

Paddleboarding in Point Loma.

Explore the tide pools at low tide, or just go for the views.

high-powered telescopes; if you don't manage to see a whale, you can still have your picture taken with the scaled-down whale sculpture nearby.

❻ ★★ **Bayside Trail.** This trail meanders through a coastal sage ecosystem that has all but disappeared from Southern California. The hiking is easy—the trail is only 2.5 miles (4km) roundtrip—but the bay views are spectacular, and there are informative signs posted along the way, identifying and explaining the local flora and fauna. Audio stations providing historical details in six different languages are located at various sites throughout the park, as well, and rangers and docents often present a variety of talks and guided walks.

❼ ★★ kids **Tide Pools.** Cabrillo National Monument has the only federally protected tide pools on the Southern California mainland. This rocky, intertidal ecosystem hosts a variety of sea life, including crabs, starfish, octopi, and anemones. For the best tide pooling, call ahead (☎ 619/557-5450) to find out when low tide is happening, otherwise there may not be much to see—other than the awe-inspiring cliffs and ocean vistas. Exercise caution when exploring tide pools, the rocks are slippery; do not handle the animals; and expect to get a little bit wet.

There are no food facilities at Cabrillo National Monument so consider stopping by the deli-style seafood market 8 ★★★ **Point Loma Seafoods** before or after visiting the park. This San Diego institution is usually chaos, especially around lunchtime, but this is the place for fresh-off-the-boat fish served in platters, sandwiches, sushi, and soups. *2805 Emerson St. (at Scott St.).* ☎ *619/223-1109. www.pointlomaseafoods.com. Mon–Sat 9am–7pm, Sun 10am–7pm. $8–$16.*

The Best **Hiking**

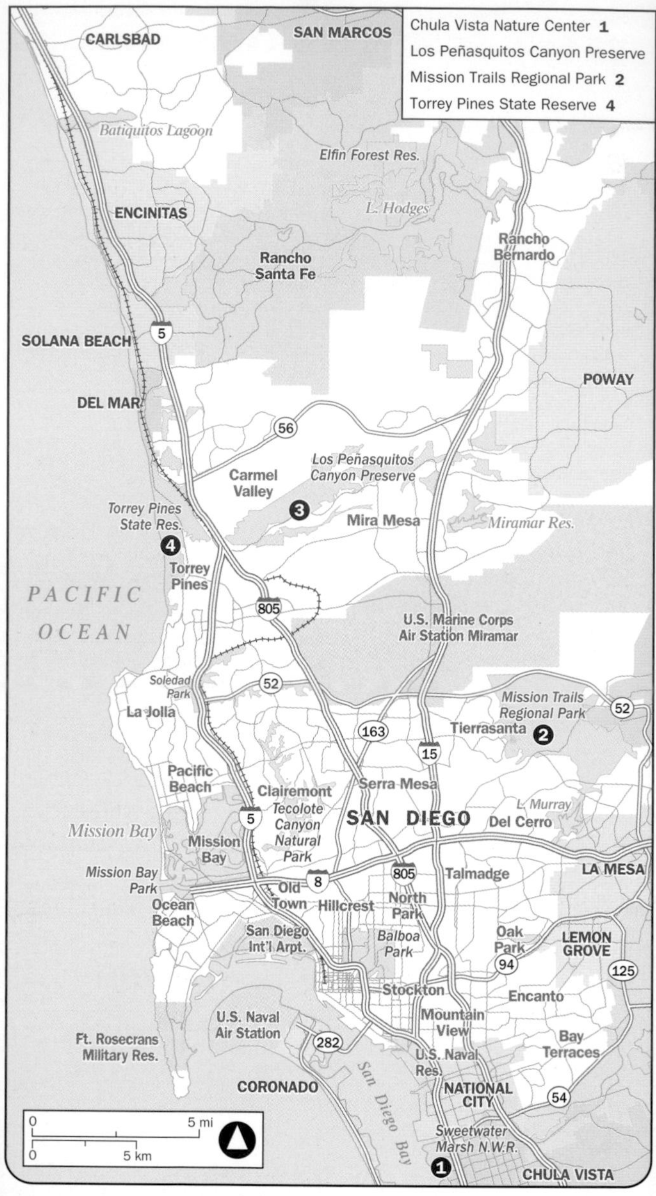

Even from downtown, you don't have to venture far to discover San Diego's wild side. Whether you're looking for solitude along an oak-shaded trail or want to spot an endangered species in its natural habitat, you'll find nearby open-space preserves and parks that will satisfy any outdoor enthusiast. **START: Bus 101 to Torrey Pines State Reserve.**

❶ ★★★ Torrey Pines State Natural Reserve. One of San Diego's most treasured spots, this reserve is home to the country's rarest pine, the Torrey pine, which grows only here and on an island off the coast of Santa Barbara. The 1,750-acre (708-hectare) reserve was established in 1921, from a gift by Ellen Browning Scripps, and encompasses dramatic 300-foot-high (91m), water-carved sandstone bluffs, the beach below them, and a lagoon immediately north. Of the six different trails, none is longer than 1.5 miles (2km), and the aptly named Beach Trail provides access to the ocean; pick up a trail map at the small visitor center, built in the traditional adobe style of the Hopi Indians. Interpretive nature walks are held weekends and holidays at 10am and 2pm. *Hwy. 101 (btw. La Jolla & Del Mar). ☎ 858/755-2063. www.torreypine.org. There are no restrooms or facilities for food or drinks inside the park; you can bring a picnic lunch, but you have to eat it on the beach (restrooms are available on the beach as well)—food & drink (other than water) are not allowed in the upper portion of the reserve. Admission $10–$15 per car. Daily 7:15am–sunset. Bus: 101.*

❷ ★★ Mission Trails Regional Park. This is one of the nation's largest urban parks, a 7,220-acre (2,921-hectare) spread that includes abundant bird life, two lakes, a picturesque stretch of the San Diego River, the remains of the Old Mission Dam (probably the first irrigation project in the West), and 1,592-foot (485m) Cowles Mountain, the summit of which reveals outstanding views over much of the county. There are trails up to 4 miles (6.5km) in length—including a 1.5-mile (2.5km) interpretive trail—some of which are designated for mountain bike use. *1 Father Junípero Serra Trail. ☎ 619/668-3281. www.mtrp.org. Free admission. Daily sunrise to sundown (visitor center 9am–5pm, closed major holidays). Bus: 115 to Jackson Dr. & Navajo Rd., then 1.4 miles (2.25km) to the West Gate.*

Torrey Pines.

Mission Trails Regional Park.

❸ ★★ kids Living Coast Discovery Center. This interpretive center set in the Sweetwater Marsh National Wildlife Refuge is just a 15-minute drive from downtown San Diego. There is a 1.5-mile (2.5km) loop trail through coastal wetlands where more than 220 different species of birds have been identified. The trail also features a photo blind and posted information on the flora and fauna. *See p 32.*

❹ ★★ Los Peñasquitos Canyon Preserve. Stretching for nearly 7 miles (11km), this 4,000-acre (1,619-hectare) preserve is an oasis amid the suburbia that surrounds it. The area was part of the first Mexican land grant in San Diego, and the historic Santa Maria de los Peñasquitos adobe ranch home (1823) still stands at the east end of the park (tours are Sat at 11am and Sun at 1pm). Along the trail are beautiful stands of oak and sycamore; there's also a waterfall that flows year-round. *12020 Black Mountain Rd. ☎ 858/484-7504. www.sandiego.gov/park-and-recreation. Free admission. Daily 8am–sunset. Bus: 210 to Mira Mesa Blvd. & Black Mountain Rd., 1.3 miles (2k) farther north on Black Mountain Rd.*

Relaxing in Los Peñasquitos Canyon Preserve.

Farther Afield

Those in search of a wilderness experience will find ample room to roam in 650,000-acre (263,045-hectare) ★★★ **Anza-Borrego Desert State Park,** California's largest state park, or 26,000-acre (10,522-hectare) ★★ **Cuyamaca Rancho State Park.** Both are less than a 2-hour drive away from downtown San Diego.

The terrain at Anza-Borrego incorporates dry lakebeds, sandstone canyons, granite mountains, palm groves fed by year-round springs, and more than 600 kinds of desert plants. The best time to come is in spring, when wildflowers burst into bloom, transforming the desert into a brilliant palette of pink, lavender, red, orange, and yellow; for up-to-date info on blooms call ☎ 760/767-4684. Your first stop here should be the architecturally striking visitor center (☎ 760/767-4205 or 760/767-5311; www.parks.ca.gov)—in addition to a small museum, it offers information, maps, and audiovisual presentations; an interpreted loop trail is also on site. The visitor center is open daily October through May from 9am to 5pm; June through September, weekends and holidays only, from 9am to 5pm.

Cuyamaca Rancho State Park is about 15 miles (24km) south of the historic mountain town of Julian (see p 150). Though badly burned in an epic firestorm in 2003, Cuyamaca has recovered nicely. The most popular hikes are to 5,700-foot (1,737m) Stonewall Peak (2 miles/3km) and 6,500-foot (1,981m) Cuyamaca Peak (3.5 miles/5.5km)—both offer spectacular vistas. Trailheads for each are at Paso Picacho campground. Five miles (8km) south of that campground is Green Valley campground, where you'll find cool natural pools in which to splash (day use of campgrounds is $8 per vehicle; overnight is $30). The park is reached via Highway 79, 5 miles (8km) north of Interstate 8. For more information, call ☎ 760/765-0755, or go to www.parks.ca.gov.

Mission Bay Park

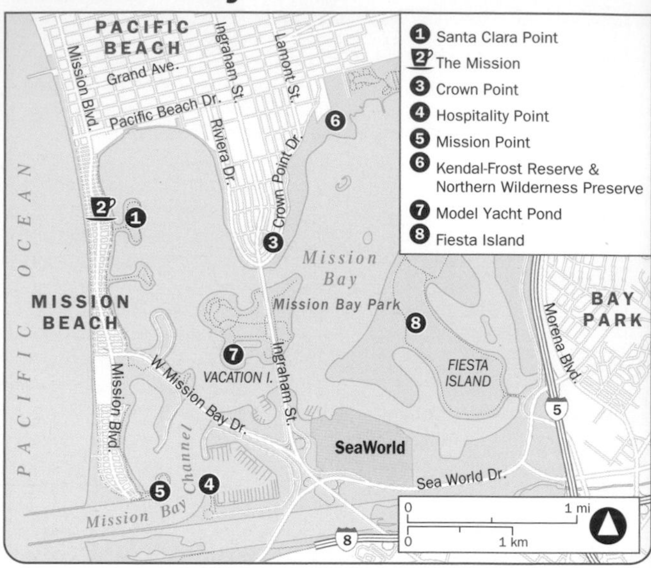

Originally known as False Bay, this swampy marshland was transformed in the 1940s into Mission Bay Park. This vast outdoor playground encompasses more than 4,200 acres (1,700 hectares)—about half of it water, half of it land—with 27 miles (43km) of shoreline, several sandy beaches, grassy parks, wildlife preserves, boat docks and launches (with rental facilities), basketball courts, and an extensive system of pathways. Locals and visitors flock to Mission Bay for everything from kite flying to powerboating, and the vast lawns are packed with extended family and friend gatherings most summer weekends. START: **Bus 8/9 to Santa Clara Pl.**

---

1 ★★ kids Santa Clara Point. Recreation centers don't get any cooler than this city-run facility. Surrounded by the bay, it features tennis courts, a softball field, lighted basketball courts, a playground, and a weight room. At Mission Bay Sportcenter, you can rent sailboats, catamarans, pedal boats, sailboards, kayaks, WaveRunners, motorboats, or surfboards. *Recreation Center, 1008 Santa Clara Pl. ☎ 858/581-9928. www.sandiego.gov. Mon, Wed, Fri 11am–7pm, Tues & Thurs 11am–7:30pm, Sat 10am–3pm, closed Sun. Mission Bay Sportcenter, 1010 Santa Clara Pl. ☎ 858/488-1004; www.missionbaysportcenter.com. Daily 10am–5pm. Bus: 8/9.*

The menu at **2** ★ **The Mission** features all-day breakfasts, from traditional pancakes to nouvelle egg dishes to burritos and quesadillas. At lunch, the menu expands for sandwiches, salads, and a few Chino-Latino items like ginger-sesame chicken tacos. *3795 Mission Blvd. (at San Jose Place). ☎ 858/488-9060. www.themissionsd.com. Daily 7am–3pm. $7–$11.*

3 ★ kids **Crown Point.** You'll find everything you need here for a day of outdoor recreation: large grassy expanses, a white-sand beach, picnic tables, fire rings, barbecue grills, basketball courts, and a boat launch. There are also restrooms and showers. *Crown Point Dr. (there are several large parking lots off this street). Daily 4am–2am, but parking lots close at 10pm. As with all city beaches, smoking, alcohol, & glass containers are prohibited. Bus: 8/9.*

4 ★ **Hospitality Point.** At the confluence of the Mission Bay Channel and the San Diego River, this popular spot lacks a beach, but draws visitors with its ocean, bay, and channel views. The walking and bike path will take you alongside the Flood Control Channel, which doubles as the Southern Wildlife Preserve. The preserve is a sanctuary for more than 100 different species of birds migrating along the Pacific Flyway. Look for herons, egrets, osprey, and the endangered California least tern. *South end of Quivira Rd. Bus: 8/9 to Dana Landing at W. Mission Bay Dr., then less than a mile on Quivira Rd. to the point.*

5 ★ kids **Mission Point.** For those who want to combine an ocean and bay experience, Mission Point will do the trick. At the southern end of Mission Boulevard, this grass-and-sand recreation area is just a short walk from the Mission Beach jetty and the Pacific. Mission Point offers fire rings, picnic tables, a children's playground, and restrooms with showers. This is a swimming area, but there is no lifeguard on duty. *Bayside Lane. Daily 4am–10pm. Free parking available in lots until 10pm. Bus 8/9 to Mission Blvd. at W. Mission Bay Dr., then about a mile south.*

6 ★★★ **Kendall-Frost Reserve and Northern Wilderness Preserve.** Due to its fragile nature, most of this 40-acre (16-hectare) area is off limits to the public. You can get close to it, though, via the pathway that

Mission Bay Park.

Biking at Mission Bay Park.

extends north from Crown Point (see above) or by kayak. This saltwater marsh provides sanctuary to a wide variety of birds: avocets to vireos, coots to loons. Two endangered, non-migratory species, the light-footed clapper rail and Belding's savannah sparrow, even live out their entire lives within this small ecosystem. Like many of the estimated 15 million people who flock to Mission Bay Park every year, the clapper rail takes advantage of the bay's calm waters—it builds a floating nest among the stands of cordgrass.

7 ★ kids Model Yacht Pond. Sailboats and powerboats are ubiquitous features on Mission Bay, but many people are unaware of the flotilla that plies the waters of the Model Yacht Pond in the middle of Vacation Island. Just about any weekend you can find hobbyists with sophisticated, radio-controlled crafts competing or just having fun. Some models are amazingly detailed replicas of historic ships like Spanish galleons or World War II battleships; others are ferocious little hydroplanes capable of speeds in excess of 60 mph (97kmph). *Bus: 8/9 to W. Vacation Rd.*

8 Fiesta Island. This rather barren island at the eastern edge of the bay is often used for events like the Over the Line softball tournament in July and cycling time trials and races. The east side of the island is a popular launching point for watercraft, and there is a water-ski area (permits required). There is a 4-mile (6.5km) road that loops around the island, and fire rings are situated throughout. Picnics are not permitted; there are no restrooms. *Daily 6am–10pm. Bus: 105 to Sea-World Dr.* ●

Mission Point.

6 The Best Dining

Dining Best Bets

Best **Business Lunch**
★ Dobson's Bar & Restaurant $$–$$$ *956 Broadway Circle (p 108)*

Best **Regional Mexican Food**
★★★ El Agave Tequileria $$–$$$ *2304 San Diego Ave. (p 108)*

Best **Breakfast with a View**
★ Brockton Villa $–$$ *1235 Coast Blvd. (p 106)*

Best **Lunch with a View**
★★★ Bertrand at Mister A's $$$$ *2550 Fifth Ave. (p 105)*

Best **Dinner with a View**
★★★ Georges California Modern $$$$ *1250 Prospect St. (p 109)*

Best **Ocean View Anytime**
★★ Wonderland $$–$$$ *5083 Santa Monica Ave. (p 112)*

Best **Use of Local Product (Sea)**
★★★ The Fish Market/Top of the Market $$–$$$$ *750 N. Harbor Dr. (p 109)*

Best **Use of Local Product (Land)**
★★ Whisknladle $$ *1044 Wall St. (p 112)*

Best **Baja-California Cuisine**
★★★ Bracero $$$$ *1490 Kettner St. (p 105)*

Best **Modern American Cuisine**
★★★ Market Restaurant + Bar $$$ *3702 Via de la Valle (p 110)*

Best **Steak**
★★★ Cowboy Star $$–$$$$ *650 10th Ave. (p 107)*

Best **Pan-Asian Cuisine**
★★★ Saffron Noodles and Saté $$–$$$ *3731-B India St. (p 111)*

Best **Pizza**
★★ Bronx Pizza $–$$ *111 Washington St. (p 106)*

Best **Desserts**
★★★ Extraordinary Desserts $ *2929 Fifth Ave. and 1430 Union St. (p 108)*

Best **Bistro**
★★ Cafe Chloe $$–$$$ *721 Ninth Ave. (p 106)*

Best **Picnic Fare**
★★ Bread & Cie $ *350 University Ave. (p 105)*

Most **Romantic Dining Room**
★★★ The Marine Room $$$$ *2000 Spindrift Dr. (p 110)*

Best **Sushi**
★★★ Sushi Ota $$ *4529 Mission Bay Dr. (p 111)*

Best **Place for Hipster Foodies**
★★★ Cucina Urbana $$ *505 Laurel St. (p 108)*

Best **Late-Night Dining**
Brian's 24 Restaurant Bar & Grill $$ *828 Sixth Ave. (p 106)*

Previous page: View of San Diego from Island Prime.

Downtown Dining

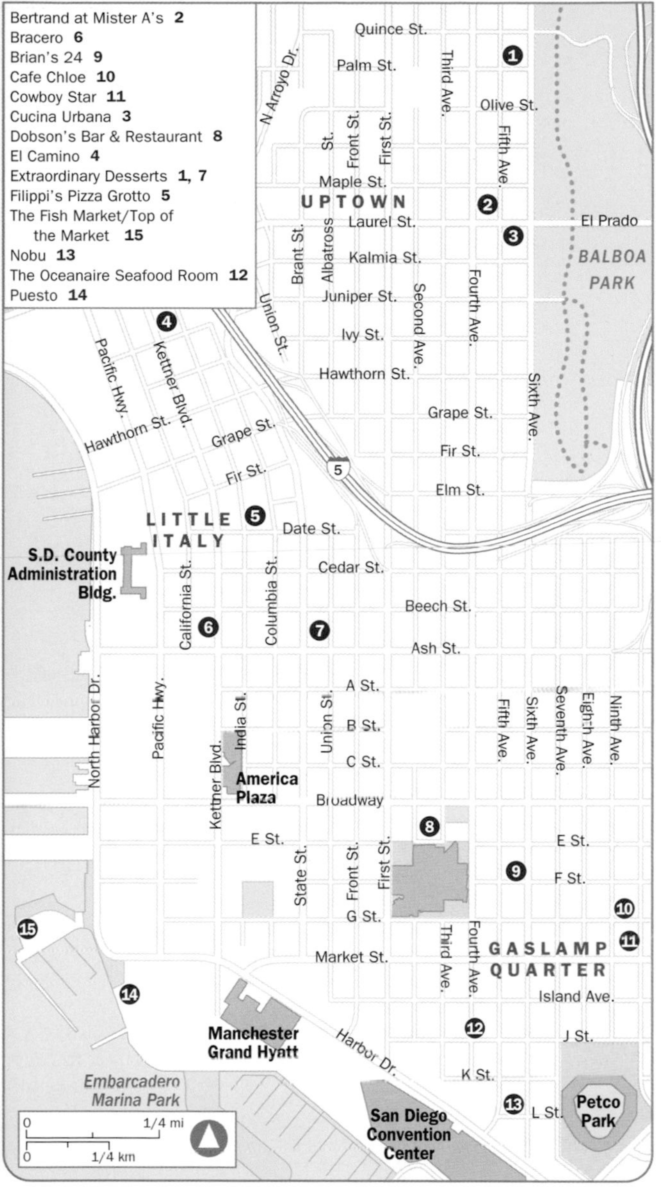
Bertrand at Mister A's 2
Bracero 6
Brian's 24 9
Cafe Chloe 10
Cowboy Star 11
Cucina Urbana 3
Dobson's Bar & Restaurant 8
El Camino 4
Extraordinary Desserts 1, 7
Filippi's Pizza Grotto 5
The Fish Market/Top of the Market 15
Nobu 13
The Oceanaire Seafood Room 12
Puesto 14
Quince St.
Palm St.
N Arroyo Dr.
Third Ave.
Olive St.
Fifth Ave.
St.
Front St.
First St.
Maple St.
UPTOWN
Laurel St.
El Prado
Brant St.
Albatross
Kalmia St.
BALBOA PARK
Juniper St.
Second Ave.
Fourth Ave.
Union St.
Ivy St.
Hawthorn St.
Pacific Hwy.
Kettner Blvd.
Sixth Ave.
Grape St.
Hawthorn St.
Grape St.
Fir St.
Fir St.
5
Elm St.
LITTLE ITALY
Date St.
S.D. County Administration Bldg.
California St.
Columbia St.
Cedar St.
Beech St.
Ash St.
A St.
North Harbor Dr.
Pacific Hwy.
India St.
Union St.
B St.
C St.
Fifth Ave.
Sixth Ave.
Seventh Ave.
Eighth Ave.
Ninth Ave.
Kettner Blvd.
America Plaza
Broadway
E St.
State St.
Front St.
First St.
E St.
F St.
G St.
Third Ave.
Fourth Ave.
GASLAMP QUARTER
Market St.
Island Ave.
Manchester Grand Hyatt
Harbor Dr.
J St.
K St.
Embarcadero Marina Park
L St.
Petco Park
San Diego Convention Center
0
1/4 mi
0
1/4 km

Hillcrest & Old Town Dining

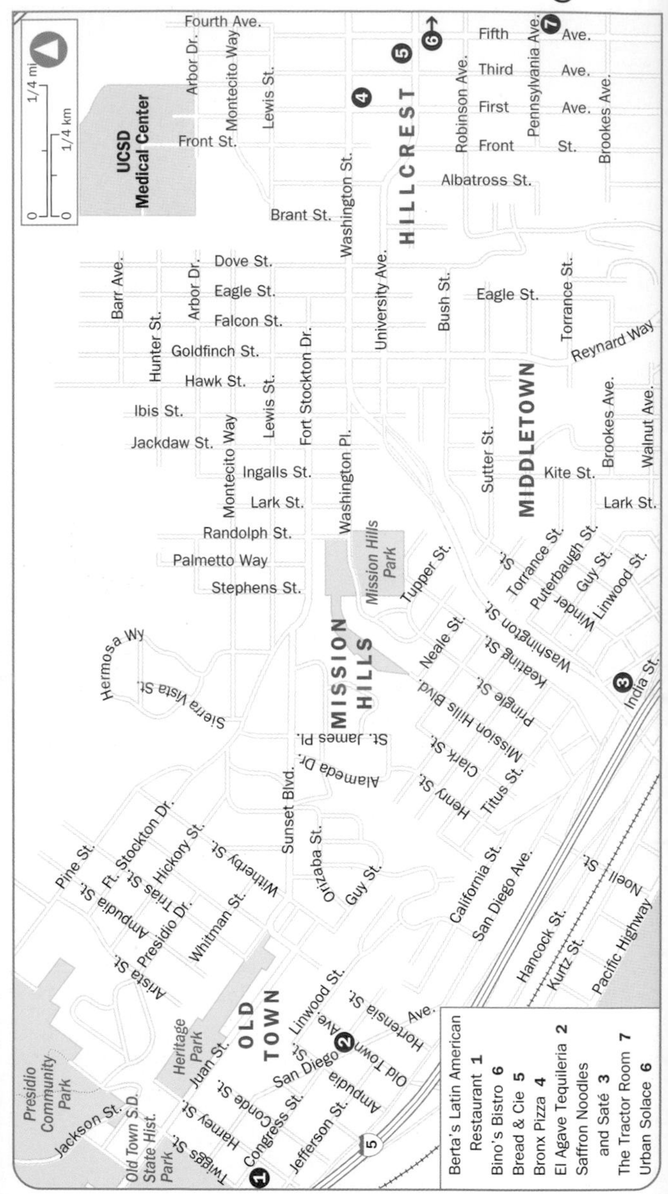
1/4 mi
1/4 km
0
0
UCSD Medical Center
HILLCREST
MIDDLETOWN
MISSION HILLS
OLD TOWN
Mission Hills Park
Heritage Park
Presidio Community Park
Old Town S.D. State Hist. Park
Fourth Ave.
Fifth Ave.
Third Ave.
First Ave.
Front St.
Albatross St.
Brant St.
Washington St.
University Ave.
Robinson Ave.
Pennsylvania Ave.
Brookes Ave.
Arbor Dr.
Montecito Way
Lewis St.
Dove St.
Eagle St.
Falcon St.
Goldfinch St.
Hawk St.
Ibis St.
Jackdaw St.
Ingalls St.
Lark St.
Randolph St.
Palmetto Way
Stephens St.
Barr Ave.
Hunter St.
Fort Stockton Dr.
Washington Pl.
Bush St.
Torrance St.
Reynard Way
Sutter St.
Kite St.
Walnut Ave.
Tupper St.
Puterbaugh St.
Guy St.
Linwood St.
Winder St.
India St.
Neale St.
Keating St.
Pringle St.
Mission Hills Blvd.
Clark St.
Henry St.
Titus St.
Hermosa Wy
Sierra Vista St.
St. James Pl.
Alameda Dr.
Sunset Blvd.
Orizaba St.
Pine St.
Ft. Stockton Dr.
Hickory St.
Witherby St.
Trias St.
Ampudia St.
Presidio Dr.
Whitman St.
Arista St.
California St.
San Diego Ave.
Noell St.
Hancock St.
Kurtz St.
Pacific Highway
Hortensia St.
Old Town Ave.
Juan St.
Conde St.
Congress St.
Harney St.
Twiggs St.
Jackson St.
Jefferson St.
5
Berta's Latin American Restaurant 1
Bino's Bistro 6
Bread & Cie 5
Bronx Pizza 4
El Agave Tequileria 2
Saffron Noodles and Saté 3
The Tractor Room 7
Urban Solace 6

Dining at the Beaches

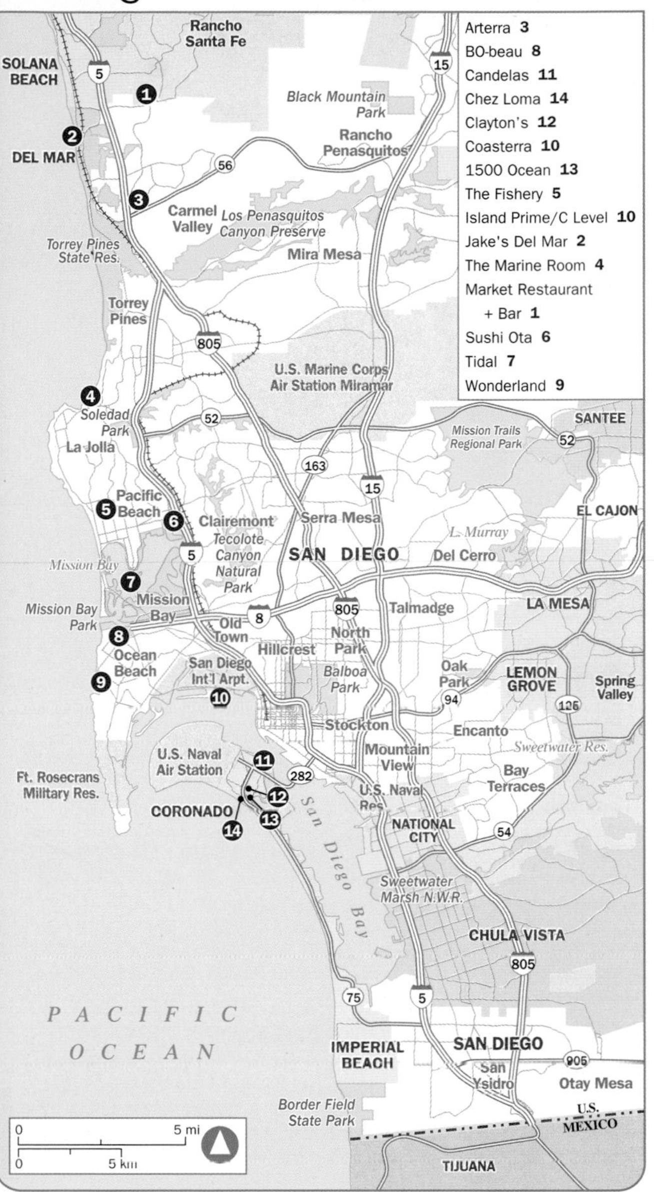

La Jolla Dining

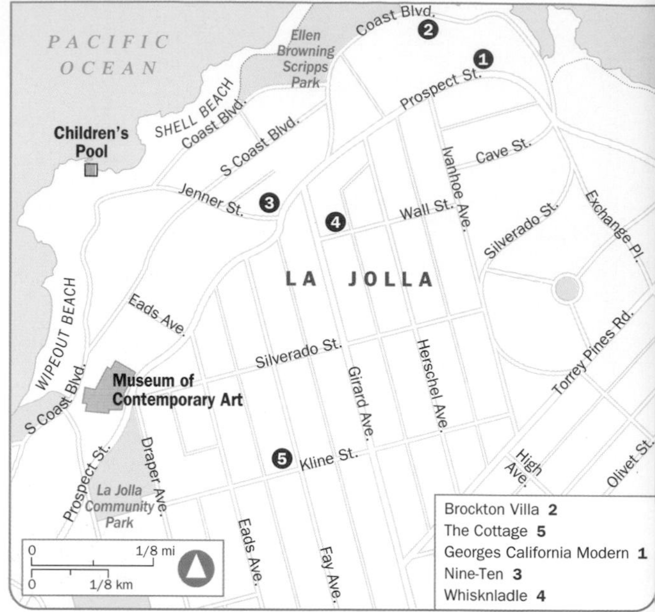

Dining A to Z

★★ 1500 Ocean CORONADO *CALIFORNIAN* The Hotel del Coronado's fine-dining option has a smart California Craftsman look and a Southland coastal cuisine menu that draws inspiration and top-quality products from throughout the region, from Baja to Santa Barbara. *1500 Orange Ave. (at the Hotel del Coronado). ☎ 619/522-8490. www.hoteldel.com/1500-ocean. Entrees $36–$75. AE, DC, DISC, MC, V. Tues–Sat 5:30–10pm. Bus: 901 or 904.*

★★ Arterra DEL MAR *CALIFORNIAN* There's a stylish outdoor lounge and a menu that's regularly adapted to meet the schedule of Mother Earth, featuring top products from local farms. *11966 El Camino Real (next to I-5 in the Marriott Del Mar). ☎ 858/369-6032. www.arterrarestaurant.com. Entrees $11–$19 breakfast, $12–$24 lunch, $17–$29 dinner. AE, DC, DISC, MC, V. Breakfast Mon–Fri 6:30–10:30am & Sat–Sun 7–11am; lunch Mon–Fri 11:30am–2pm; dinner Mon–Sat 5:30–10pm; lounge daily 11am–11:30pm.*

★ Berta's Latin American Restaurant OLD TOWN *LATIN AMERICAN* Faithfully re-creating the flavors of Central and South America, Berta's delves into favorites from Peru, Ecuador, and Brazil. *3928 Twiggs St. (at Congress St.). ☎ 619/295-2343. www.*

1500 Ocean.

bertasinoldtown.com. Entrees $7–$12 lunch, $14–$20 dinner. AE, DISC, MC, V. Tues–Sun 11am–10pm (lunch menu until 3pm). Bus: Numerous Old Town routes including 8, 9, 10, 28, or 30. Trolley: Old Town.

★★★ Bertrand at Mister A's BALBOA PARK *AMERICAN/MEDITERRANEAN* A bar/patio menu gives diners on a budget access to a seasonal menu and million-dollar vistas. *2550 Fifth Ave. (at Laurel St.). ☎ 619/239-1377. www.bertrandatmisteras.com. Entrees $19–$30 lunch, $29–$50 dinner. AE, DC, MC, V. Mon–Fri 11:30am–2:15pm; Mon–Thurs 5:30–9:30pm; Fri–Sun 5–9:30pm. Bus: 3 or 120.*

Bino's Bistro & Crêperie HILLCREST *EUROPEAN* After 14 years in Coronado, this casual, Euro-style spot is now in Hillcrest, still serving sweet and savory crepes, tapas, and entrees roaming the globe. *1260 University Ave. (btw. Richmond & Vermont sts.). ☎ 619/688-1674. www.binosbistro.com. Entrees $12–$26. AE, DISC, MC, V. Mon 11am–4pm; Tues–Thurs 11am–10pm; Fri–Sat 10am–midnight; Sun 8am–10pm. Bus: 1, 10, or 11.*

★★ BO-beau OCEAN BEACH *FRENCH* Sweet country cottage setting for French bistro favorites—the Brussels sprouts just might be the best in town. *4996 W. Point Loma Blvd. (at Bacon St.). ☎ 619/224-2884. www.cohnrestaurants.com. Entrees $16–$25. AE, DC, DISC, MC, V. Daily 4:30–closing (usually around 10pm). Bus: 35 or 923.*

★★★ Bracero LITTLE ITALY *MEXICAN* Celeb chef Javier Placencia's Baja-centric gourmet Mexican cuisine is all the rage on both sides of the border. Graze through the appetizer and taco menus for the finest flavors. *1490 Kettner St. (btw. Beech & Ash sts.). ☎ 619/756-7864. www.bracerococina.com. Entrees $12–$18 lunch, $26–$44 dinner. AE, MC, V. Sun–Mon 11:30am–9pm; Tues–Thurs 11:30am–10pm; Fri–Sat 11:30am–11pm. Bus: 83.*

★★ Bread & Cie HILLCREST *LIGHT FARE/MEDITERRANEAN* The traditions of European artisan bread-making are proudly carried on here. You can get a light breakfast or a great sandwich, as well as loaves of specialty breads. *350*

Bertrand at Mister A's.

BO-beau in Ocean Beach.

University Ave. (at Fourth St.). ☎ 619/683-9322. www.breadandcie.com. Sandwiches & light meals $6–$9. DISC, MC, V. Mon–Fri 7am–7pm; Sat 7am–6pm; Sun 7:30am–6pm. Bus: 1, 3, 10, 11, or 120.

Brian's 24 Restaurant Bar & Grill GASLAMP QUARTER *AMERICAN/ECLECTIC* If you have a hankering for chicken and waffles at 3am, this intimate 24-hour restaurant has you covered. *828 Sixth Ave. (at F St.). ☎ 619/702-8410. www.brians24.com. Entrees $11–$25. AE, DISC, MC, V. Open 24 hrs. Bus: 3, 120, or 992.*

★ **Brockton Villa** LA JOLLA *BREAKFAST/CALIFORNIAN* A restored 1894 beach bungalow, this charming cafe occupies a breathtaking perch overlooking La Jolla Cove. *1235 Coast Blvd. (across from La Jolla Cove). ☎ 858/454-7393. www.brocktonvilla.com. Entrees $8–$15 breakfast, $12–$22 lunch, $14–$30 dinner. AE, DISC, MC, V. Mon–Tues 8am–3pm; Wed–Sun 8am–9pm. Bus: 30.*

Bracero.

★★ **Bronx Pizza** HILLCREST *ITALIAN* This tiny pizzeria serves up arguably San Diego's best pies—other than calzones, that's all it makes. There's usually a line out the door. *111 Washington St. (at First Ave.). ☎ 619/291-3341. www.bronxpizza.com. Phone orders accepted for full pies. Pies $13–$19; $2.50 by the slice. Cash only. Sun–Thurs 11am–10pm; Fri–Sat 11am–11pm. Bus: 3, 10, or 83.*

★★ **Cafe Chloe** EAST VILLAGE *FRENCH* The conviviality of this bistro—combined with a short-but-sweet French-inspired menu covering breakfast, lunch, and dinner—makes for a winning dining experience. *721 Ninth Ave. (at G St.). ☎ 619/232-3242. www.cafechloe.com. Entrees $8–$13 breakfast & lunch, $24–$27 dinner. AE, MC, V. Mon–Fri 8am–10pm; Sat 8:30am–10pm; Sun 8:30am–9:30pm. Bus: 3, 5, 11, 901, or 929.*

★★ **Candelas** CORONADO *MEXICAN* Fill up with the buffet brunch before touring Coronado or stop by for a romantic bayview dinner. *1201 First St. (at the Ferry Landing), Coronado., ☎ 619/435-4900. www.candelas-coronado.com. Brunch $30 with bottomless mimosas, $25 without, $15 kids; entrees $13–$20 dinner. AE, DC, DISC, MC, V. Daily 8am–10pm. Bus: 901 or 904.*

★ **Chez Loma** CORONADO *FRENCH* Tables are scattered throughout this charming Victorian house; the enclosed garden terrace is especially lovely for brunch. *1132 Loma (off Orange Ave.). ☎ 619/435-0661. www.chezloma.com. Entrees $11–$16 brunch, $26–$37 dinner. AE, DC, DISC, MC, V. Sun–Wed 5–8:30pm, Thurs–Sat 5–9pm; brunch Sat–Sun 9:30am–2pm. Bus: 901 or 904.*

★ **Clayton's Coffee Shop** CORONADO *DINER* Jukeboxes, red vinyl booths, and chrome stools at the counter are sure-fire signs this classic coffee shop has been serving up eggs, bacon and hashbrowns for many a decade. The food's about as basic as it gets—burgers, dogs, and club sandwiches at lunch, and meatloaf and chicken fried steak at dinner. *979 Orange Ave. ☎ 619/435-5425. Entrees $7–$11. MC, V. Mon–Sat 6am–9pm; Sun 6am–8pm. Bus: 901 or 904.*

★★ **Coasterra** EMBARCADERO *MEXICAN* Downtown may lie just across the sparkling bay, but the waterside patio and elegant dining room feel miles away from reality. Chef Deborah Scott's trademark spicy flair elevates Mexican favorites toward gourmet status. *880 Harbor Island Dr. ☎ 619/814-1300. www.cohnrestaurants.com. Entrees $17–$36 lunch, $19–$48 dinner. AE, DISC, MC, V. Daily 11:30am–2:30pm, 5–10pm; patio dining daily 11:30am–10pm. Bus: 30.*

★ **The Cottage** LA JOLLA *BREAKFAST/LIGHT FARE* Maybe La Jolla's best breakfast, served at a turn-of-the-20th-century bungalow on a shady corner. The housemade granola is a favorite. *7702 Fay Ave. (at Kline St.). ☎ 858/454-8409. www.cottagelajolla.com. Entrees $12–$14 breakfast, $14–$20 lunch, $14–$26 dinner. AE, DISC, MC, V. Daily 7:30am–3pm; dinner Fri–Sat 4:30–9pm. Bus: 30.*

★★★ **Cowboy Star** EAST VILLAGE *AMERICAN* This restaurant and butcher shop is an unabashed homage to classic Hollywood westerns, specializing in dry-aged meats (including a $200 Japanese Wagyu filet chateaubriand) and game fowl. *640 10th Ave. (btw. G & Market sts.). ☎ 619/450-5880. www.cowboystarsd.com. Entrees $12–$26 lunch, $22–$100 dinner. AE, DISC, MC, V. Lunch Tues–Fri 11:30am–2:30pm; dinner Mon–Fri 5–10pm, Sat 4–10pm, Sun 5–9pm; Bus: 3, 5, 11, 901, or 929. Trolley: Park & Market.*

Seaside dining at Brockton Villa.

Cowboy Star.

★★★ Cucina Urbana BALBOA PARK *ITALIAN* One of the city's food-scene darlings, featuring rustic Italian fare that keeps one's pocketbook in mind while at no time sacrificing quality or creativity. *505 Laurel St. (at Fifth Ave.). ☎ 619/239-2222. www.urbankitchengroup.com. Entrees $15–$34. AE, DISC, MC, V. Sun 4:30–9pm; Mon 5–9pm; Tues–Thurs 5–10pm; Fri–Sat 5–10:30pm (limited menu until midnight); lunch Tues–Fri 11:30am–2pm. Bus: 3 or 120.*

★ Dobson's Bar & Restaurant GASLAMP QUARTER *CALIFORNIAN* By day it buzzes with the energy of movers and shakers; in the evening it segues from happy-hour watering hole to sophisticated pre-theater American bistro. *956 Broadway Circle (at Broadway). ☎ 619/231-6771. www.dobsonsrestaurant.com. Entrees $17–$22 lunch; $16–$42 dinner. AE, MC, V. Mon–Fri 11:30am–10pm; Sat 5–10pm. Bus: Numerous downtown routes including 7, 929, or 992. Trolley: Civic Center.*

Cucina Urbana.

★★★ El Agave Tequileria OLD TOWN *MEXICAN* The regional Mexican cuisine and rustic elegance here leave the touristy joints of Old Town far behind. Don't look for burritos and nachos here—the menu ranges through spicy moles, and savory truffle-like huitlacoche, to more than 850 tequilas and mezcals, and some of the best margaritas in town. *2304 San Diego Ave. (at Old Town Ave.). ☎ 619/220-0692. www.elagave.com. Entrees $13–$20 lunch, $22–$32 dinner. AE, MC, V. Daily 11am–10pm. Bus: Numerous routes including 8, 9, 10, 28, or 30. Trolley: Old Town.*

★ El Camino LITTLE ITALY *MEXICAN* This hipster cantina serves simple Mexican fare like open-face tacos created from organic products. It's also a casual nightspot with live music and DJs. *2400 India St. (at W. Kalmia St.). ☎ 619/685-3881. www.elcaminosd.com. Entrees $10–$15. AE, MC, V. Mon 5–10pm; Tues–Sat 5–11pm; Sun 11am–10pm; bar open nightly until 1 or 2am. Bus: 83.*

★★★ Extraordinary Desserts HILLCREST/LITTLE ITALY *DESSERTS/LIGHT FARE* Dozens of divine creations are available daily;

there's also an exclusive line of jams, syrups, spices, and confections for sale. The Little Italy location serves panini, salads, cheese, and alcohol; the Hillcrest outpost serves desserts only. *Hillcrest: 2929 Fifth Ave. (btw. Palm & Quince sts.). ☎ 619/294-7001. Bus: 3 or 120. Little Italy: 1430 Union St. (btw. Beech & Ash sts.). ☎ 619/294-7001. Bus: 30. www.extraordinarydesserts.com. Desserts $4–$12, salads & sandwiches $12–$15. AE, MC, V. Mon–Thurs 8:30am–11pm; Fri 8:30am–midnight; Sat 10am–midnight; Sun 10am–11pm.*

★ **Filippi's Pizza Grotto** LITTLE ITALY *ITALIAN* Walk through an Italian grocery and deli to get to the dining room, where the menu offers more than 15 pizzas, plus huge portions of pasta. *1747 India St. (btw. Date & Fir sts.). ☎ 619/232-5094. www.realcheesepizza.com. Entrees $6–$13. AE, DC, DISC, MC, V. Sun–Mon 11am–10pm; Tues–Thurs 11am–10:30pm; Fri–Sat 11am–11:30pm; deli opens daily at 8am. Bus: 83. Trolley: County Cntr/Little Italy. Other location: Pacific Beach, 962 Garnet Ave. (btw. Cass & Bayard sts.), ☎ 858/483-6222, Bus: 8/9.*

★ **The Fishery** PACIFIC BEACH *SEAFOOD* You're pretty well guaranteed fresh-off-the-boat seafood at this off-the-beaten-track establishment. It's really a wholesale warehouse and retail fish market with a casual restaurant attached. *5040 Cass St. (at Opal St.). ☎ 858/272-9985. www.pacshell.com. Entrees $12–$24 lunch, $16–$38 dinner. AE, DC, DISC, MC, V. Daily 11am–10pm. Bus: 30.*

★★ **The Fish Market/Top of the Market** EMBARCADERO *SEAFOOD/SUSHI* This view-enhanced, always-packed restaurant is a San Diego institution. Upstairs, fancy Top of the Market offers sea fare with souped-up

Extraordinary Desserts.

presentations. *750 N. Harbor Dr. ☎ 619/232-3474. www.thefishmarket.com. Entrees $15–$46 lunch & dinner (Top of the Market main courses $19–$30 lunch, $24–$55 dinner). AE, DC, DISC, MC, V. Daily 11am–10pm. Trolley: Seaport Village. Other location: Del Mar, 640 Via de la Valle (btw. S. Cedros Ave. & Solana Circle E), ☎ 858/755-2277.*

★★★ **Georges California Modern** LA JOLLA *CALIFORNIAN* This place has it all: stunning ocean views, style, impeccable service, and above all, a world-class chef. Those seeking fine food and incomparable views at more modest prices can head upstairs to Georges Ocean Terrace and George's Bar. *1250 Prospect St. (east of Ivanhoe Ave.). ☎ 858/454-4244. www.georgesatthecove.com. Entrees $28–$62. AE, DC, DISC, MC, V. Sun–Thurs 5:30–10pm; Fri–Sat 5–10pm. Ocean Terrace entrees $12–$18 lunch, $16–$27 dinner. Daily 11am–10pm (Fri–Sat till 10:30pm). Bus: 30.*

★★ **Island Prime/C Level** EMBARCADERO *STEAK/SEAFOOD* Spectacular bay and skyline vistas plus primo steaks are the main attraction at Island Prime, while the more casual C Level lounge claims the same vista with a more varied menu of sandwiches, salads, and seafood. *880 Harbor Island Dr. ☎ 619/298-6802. www.cohnrestaurants.com. Entrees Island Prime*

Appetizers at Jake's Del Mar.

$27–$50; C Level $15–$36 lunch & dinner. AE, DC, DISC, MC, V. Island Prime daily 5–10pm; C Level daily 11am–10pm. Bus: 923 or 992.

★ **Jake's Del Mar** DEL MAR *SEAFOOD/CALIFORNIAN* This seafood-and-view restaurant has a perfect seat next to the sand—the predictable menu can't live up to the panorama, but it's prepared competently. *1660 Coast Blvd. (at 15th St.). ☎ 858/755-2002. www.jakesdelmar.com. Entrees $14–$19 lunch, $15–$47 dinner, $10–$20 brunch. AE, DISC, MC, V. Tues–Sat 11:30am–2:30pm; Sun brunch 10am–2pm; daily 5–9pm (Fri–Sat till 9:30pm). Bus: 101.*

★★★ **The Marine Room** LA JOLLA *FRENCH/CALIFORNIAN* This shorefront institution has been San Diego's most celebrated dining room since 1941. Executive chef Bernard Guillas sees to it that the food lives up to its room with a view. *2000 Spindrift Dr. (at Torrey Pines Rd.). ☎ 866/644-2351. www.marineroom.com. Entrees $29–$48. AE, DC, DISC, MC, V. Sun–Thurs 5:30–9:30pm; Fri–Sat 5:30–10pm; lounge daily from 4pm. Bus: 30.*

★★★ **Market Restaurant + Bar** DEL MAR *CALIFORNIAN/SUSHI* This comfortably elegant restaurant specializes in Chef Carl Schroeder's acclaimed regional San Diego cuisine, showcasing the best ingredients from the area's top farms, ranches, and seafood providers. *3702 Via de la Valle (at El Camino Real). ☎ 858/523-0007. www.marketdelmar.com. Entrees $25–$35; sushi $12–$22. AE, MC, V. Sun–Thurs 5:30–9:30pm; Fri–Sat 5:30–10pm. Bus: 308.*

★★★ **Nine-Ten** LA JOLLA *CALIFORNIAN* The seasonal menu at this stylish spot is best enjoyed via small-plate grazing; better yet, turn yourself over to the "Mercy of the Chef" tasting menu. *910 Prospect St. (btw. Fay & Girard aves.). ☎ 858/964-5400. www.nine-ten.com. Entrees $13–$16 breakfast, $15–$20 lunch, $22–$40 dinner. AE, DC, DISC, MC, V. Breakfast Mon–Sat 6:30–11am, Sun 7:30–10:30am; lunch Mon–Sat 11:30am–2:30pm; dinner Sun–Mon 6–9:30pm, Tues–Sat 6–10pm; Sunday brunch 10:30am–2:30pm. Bus: 30.*

★★ **Nobu** GASLAMP QUARTER *SUSHI/ASIAN FUSION* Celebrity-approved fare from chef Nobu Matsuhisa. This place is pricey and has a full-volume ambience, but it's hard to argue with the textures, flavors, and beautiful presentations. *207 Fifth Ave. (at L St. in the Hard*

Saffron Noodles and Saté.

Nine-Ten.

Rock Hotel). ☎ *619/814-4124. www.noburestaurants.com. Entrees $29–$96, sushi $6–$14. AE, DC, DISC, MC, V. Sun–Thurs 5:30–10pm; Fri–Sat 5:30–10:45pm; lounge nightly 5–10:30pm (later on weekends if busy). Bus: 3, 11, or 120. Trolley: Gaslamp Quarter.*

★★ **The Oceanaire Seafood Room** GASLAMP QUARTER *SEAFOOD* Featuring top local products as well as fish brought in daily from around the globe, the menu incorporates elements of Pacific Rim, Italian, classic French, and Asian cuisine. *400 J St. (at Fourth Ave.).* ☎ *619/858-2277. www.theoceanaire.com. Entrees $19–$60. AE, DISC, MC, V. Sun–Thurs 5–10pm; Fri–Sat 5–11pm. Bus: 3, 11, or 120. Trolley: Convention Center.*

★★ **Puesto** EMBARCADERO *MEXICAN* The liveliest spot in the Headquarters at Seaport, with two indoor levels and a popular patio, serves killer street tacos costing far more than they would in Mexico, but the flavors, and the margaritas, are worth every penny. There's a second location in La Jolla (1026 Wall St.; ☎ 858/454-1260) open daily 11am–9pm (till 10pm Fri–Sat). *789 W. Harbor Dr.* ☎ *619/233-8880. www.eatpuesto.com. Entrees $11–$19. AE, DISC, MC, V. Daily 11am–10pm. Bus: 3 or 11. Trolley: Seaport Village.*

★★★ **Saffron Noodles and Saté** MISSION HILLS *THAI* Chef, author, and TV personality Su-Mei Yu earns endless kudos for creating healthy, easy meals and teaching children and adults to do the same. Her signature saffron-marinated chicken, along with two-dozen varieties of soups and noodles are take-out and dine-in comfort food. *3731-B India St.* ☎ *619/574-0177. www.saffronsandiego.com. Entrees $6–$10. AE, DISC, MC, V. Mon–Sat 10:30am–9pm, Sun 11am–8pm. Bus: 10, 83. Trolley: Washington St.*

★★★ **Sushi Ota** PACIFIC BEACH *SUSHI* Masterful chef-owner Yukito Ota creates San Diego's finest sushi in a nondescript location in a mini-mall. Discerning regulars look for the daily specials posted behind the counter. *4529 Mission Bay Dr. (at Bunker Hill).* ☎ *858/270-5670. www.sushiota.com. Entrees $10–$28 lunch, $16–$28 dinner, sushi $5.50–$17. AE, MC, V. Tues–Fri 11:30am–2pm & 5:30–10:30pm; Mon 5:30–10:30pm; Sat–Sun 5–10:30pm. Bus. 30.*

★★ **The Tractor Room** HILLCREST *AMERICAN* There's nothing staid about this menu. Game meats appear in buffalo corn dogs, venison meatloaf, and wild boar hash, though you can get a prime beef burger if you're feeling unadventurous. There's also a good

Whisknladle.

selection of scotch, whiskey, and bourbon. *3687 Fifth Ave. (at Pennsylvania Ave.). ☎ 619/543-1007. www.thetractorroom.com. Entrees $12–$25. AE, DISC, MC, V. Thurs 5–11pm; Fri 5pm–midnight; Sat 8:30am–2:30pm & 5:30pm–midnight; Sun 8:30am–2:30pm. Bus: 3 or 120.*

★★ kids **Tidal** MISSION BAY *SEAFOOD/CALIFORNIAN* The menu at this rambling waterfront resort restaurant is both sophisticated and kid-friendly—think foie gras or spaghetti. It's worth a visit to get a sense of the ultimate Mission Bay retreat. *1404 Vacation Rd. (Paradise Point Resort). ☎ 858/490-6363. www.paradisepoint.com. Entrees $26–$34. AE, DC, DISC, MC, V. Sun–Thurs 4–9pm; Fri–Sat 4–10pm. Bus: 8/9.*

★★ **Urban Solace** NORTH PARK *AMERICAN* This loud and cheerful eatery will speed you to a happy place with its creative, contemporary take on American comfort food. The bluegrass Sunday brunch keeps the good times rolling. *3823 30th St. (at University Ave.). ☎ 619/295-6464. www.urbansolace.net. Entrees $9–$16 lunch, $21–$28 dinner. Mon–Thurs 11am–10pm; Fri 11am–11pm; Sat 10:30am–11pm; Sun 9:30am–2:30pm & 4–9pm. Bus: 2, 6, 7, or 10.*

Urban Solace.

Wonderland.

★★ **Whisknladle** LA JOLLA *CALIFORNIAN* Gourmet comfort food—house-cured sausages, freshly churned ice cream, divine breads—created from top-quality local ingredients at modest sums, served in a sleek, glassed-in sidewalk cafe. The happy hour house-crafted sangria is the real deal. *1044 Wall St. (at Hershel Ave.). ☎ 858/551-7575. www.whisknladle.com. Entrees $13–$20 lunch, $21–$37 dinner. AE, DISC, MC, V. Mon–Thurs 11:30am–9pm; Fri–11:30am–6pm; Sat 10am–6pm, Sun 10am–9pm. Bus: 30.*

★★ **Wonderland** OCEAN BEACH *ECLECTIC* The music and exuberant patrons can be atrociously noisy, but you can't beat the view of surfers, pier, and waves; the craft beer selection; or the quirky Hawaiian, Mexican, Thai, Californian menu at this second-story hot spot with bar stools edging the open wall of windows. *5083 Santa Monica Ave., ☎ 619/255-3358. www.wonderlandob.com. Entrees $9–$18. AE, DC, DISC, MC, V. Mon–Tues 11am–midnight; Wed–Thurs 11am–1am; Fri 11am–2am; Sat 9am–2am; Sun 9am–midnight. Bus: 35.* ●

7 The Best Nightlife

Nightlife Best Bets

Best Bar with a View
★★★ Top of the Hyatt *1 Market Pl. (p 118)*

Best Concert Venue (Indoor)
★★★ Belly Up Tavern *143 S. Cedros Ave. (p 121)*

Best Concert Venue (Outdoor)
★★★ Humphreys *2241 Shelter Island Dr. (p 122)*

Best Rock 'n' Roll Club
★★ The Casbah *2501 Kettner Blvd. (p 121)*

Best Jazz Club
★ Dizzy's *4275 Mission Bay Dr. (p 121)*

Best Dive Bar
★ Nunu's Cocktail Lounge *3537 Fifth Ave. (p 118)*

Best Wine Bar
★★★ 3rd Corner *2265 Bacon St. (p 122)*

Best Megaclub
★★★ OMNIA *454 Sixth Ave. (p 119)*

Best Shoes-Optional Bar
★★ Wave House *3125 Ocean Front Walk (p 119)*

Best Brew Pub
★★ Ballast Point *2215 India St. (p 117)*

Best Open-Air Bar (High-Rise)
★★ Altitude Sky Lounge *660 K St. (p 117)*

Best Open-Air Bar (Low-Rise)
★★ LoungeSix *616 J St. (p 118)*

Best Place to Pick Up a Spare
★ East Village Tavern & Bowl *930 Market St. (p 117)*

Best 2-for-1 Experience
★★ The Onyx Room/Thin *852 Fifth Ave. (p 119)*

Best Art Collection
★★★ House of Blues *1055 Fifth Ave. (p 122)*

Best Spot for Latin Music
★★ Sevilla *555 Fourth Ave. (p 120)*

Best Drag Revue
★ Lips *3036 El Cajon Blvd. (p 122)*

Previous page: Humphreys Concerts by the Bay.

Downtown Nightlife

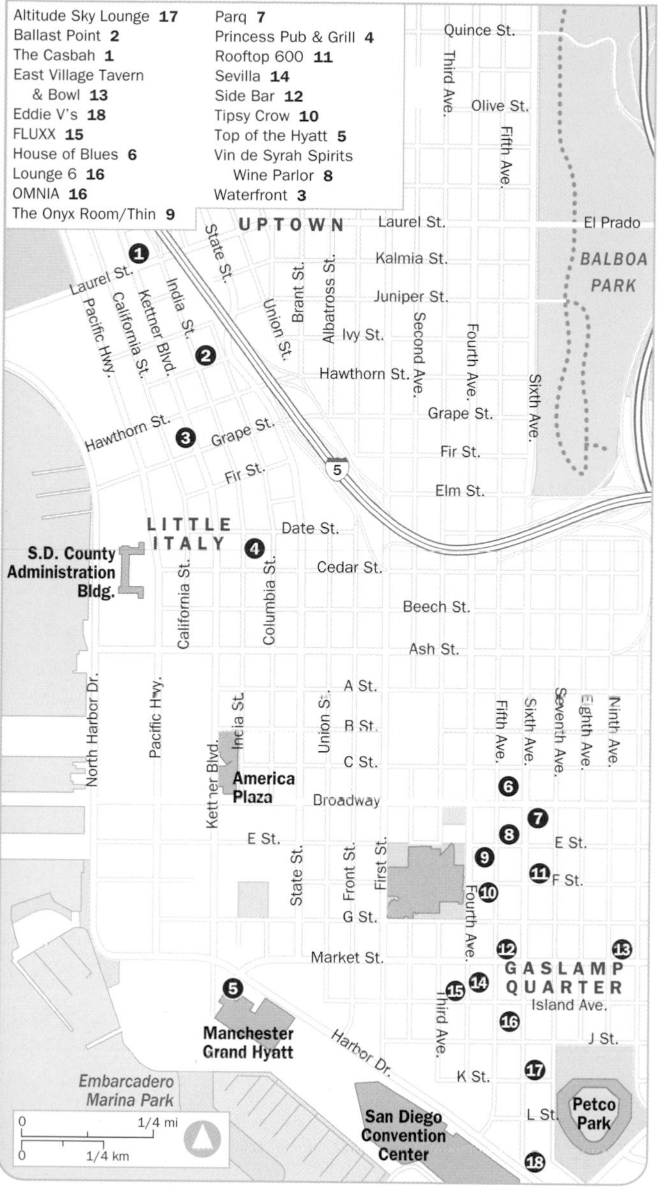
Altitude Sky Lounge 17
Ballast Point 2
The Casbah 1
East Village Tavern & Bowl 13
Eddie V's 18
FLUXX 15
House of Blues 6
Lounge 6 16
OMNIA 16
The Onyx Room/Thin 9
Parq 7
Princess Pub & Grill 4
Rooftop 600 11
Sevilla 14
Side Bar 12
Tipsy Crow 10
Top of the Hyatt 5
Vin de Syrah Spirits Wine Parlor 8
Waterfront 3
UPTOWN
LITTLE ITALY
GASLAMP QUARTER
BALBOA PARK
S.D. County Administration Bldg.
America Plaza
Manchester Grand Hyatt
Embarcadero Marina Park
San Diego Convention Center
Petco Park
Quince St.
Olive St.
Laurel St.
Kalmia St.
Juniper St.
Ivy St.
Hawthorn St.
Grape St.
Fir St.
Elm St.
Date St.
Cedar St.
Beech St.
Ash St.
A St.
B St.
C St.
Broadway
E St.
F St.
G St.
Market St.
Island Ave.
J St.
K St.
L St.
El Prado
Harbor Dr.
North Harbor Dr.
Pacific Hwy.
Kettner Blvd.
India St.
California St.
State St.
Union St.
Columbia St.
Brant St.
Albatross St.
Front St.
First St.
Second Ave.
Third Ave.
Fourth Ave.
Fifth Ave.
Sixth Ave.
Seventh Ave.
Eighth Ave.
Ninth Ave.
5
0
1/4 mi
1/4 km

Hillcrest Nightlife

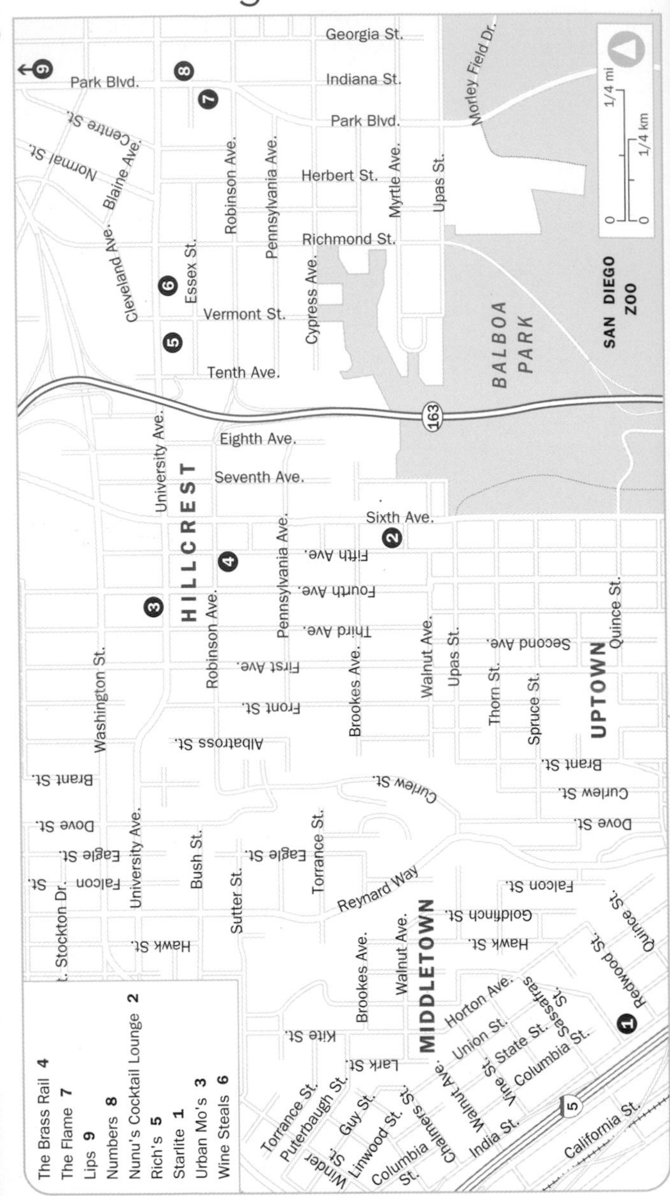
The Brass Rail 4
The Flame 7
Lips 9
Numbers 8
Nunu's Cocktail Lounge 2
Rich's 5
Starlite 1
Urban Mo's 3
Wine Steals 6
HILLCREST
MIDDLETOWN
UPTOWN
BALBOA PARK
SAN DIEGO ZOO
Georgia St.
Indiana St.
Park Blvd.
Morley Field Dr.
Centre St.
Normal St.
Blaine Ave.
Cleveland Ave.
Robinson Ave.
Pennsylvania Ave.
Herbert St.
Myrtle Ave.
Upas St.
Richmond St.
Essex St.
Cypress Ave.
Vermont St.
Tenth Ave.
University Ave.
Eighth Ave.
Seventh Ave.
Sixth Ave.
Fifth Ave.
Fourth Ave.
Third Ave.
Second Ave.
First Ave.
Front St.
Albatross St.
Washington St.
Walnut Ave.
Brookes Ave.
Thorn St.
Spruce St.
Quince St.
Brant St.
Curlew St.
Dove St.
Eagle St.
Falcon St.
Bush St.
Sutter St.
Torrance St.
Reynard Way
Goldfinch St.
Hawk St.
Stockton Dr.
Redwood St.
Horton Ave.
Sassafras St.
Union St.
State St.
Columbia St.
Kite St.
Lark St.
Puterbaugh St.
Guy St.
Winder St.
Linwood St.
Chalmers St.
Vine St.
India St.
California St.
163
5
0
1/4 mi
1/4 km

Nightlife on the Beaches

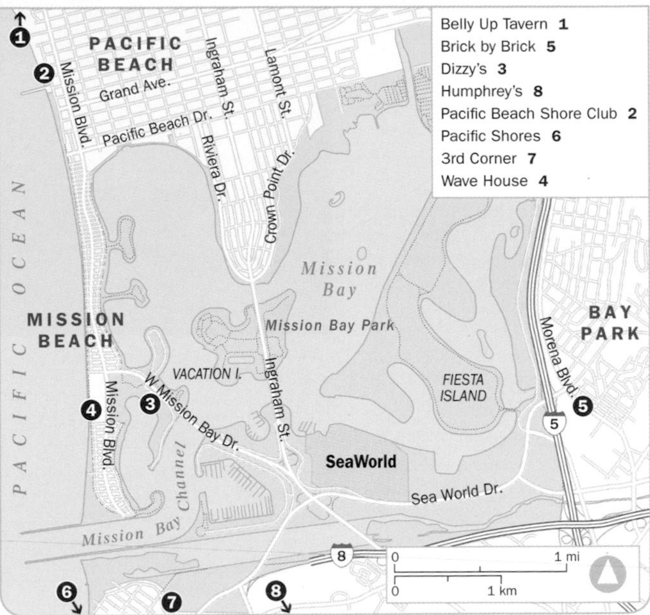

Nightlife A to Z

Bars

★★ Altitude Sky Lounge GASLAMP QUARTER Twenty-two stories up in a Marriott hotel, this long, narrow open-air space looks down on PETCO Park and the Convention Center. *660 K St. (btw. 6th & 7th aves.). ☎ 619/696-0234. www.altitudeskybar.com. No cover. Bus: 3, 11, 120, or 992. Trolley: Orange Line to Gaslamp Quarter. Map p 115.*

★★ Ballast Point LITTLE ITALY San Diego's many fine breweries tend to operate tasting rooms far outside central San Diego; this centrally located spot pours fine brews and serves hefty sandwiches and plates to share (try the pork belly mac 'n' cheese). *2215 India St. (btw. Ivy & Juniper sts.). ☎ 619/255-7213. www.ballastpoint.com. No cover. Bus: 83. Trolley: Blue Line to County Cntr/Little Italy. Map p 115.*

★ kids East Village Tavern & Bowl EAST VILLAGE Featuring 12 colorfully lit bowling lanes, as well as billiards and a separate bar area with outdoor seating, this raucous place has classic bar food and a good selection of brews on tap. Kids are allowed in until 9pm. *930 Market St. (btw. Ninth & 10th aves.). ☎ 619/677-2695. www.bowlevt.com. No cover. Bus: 3 or 11. Trolley: Gaslamp Quarter or Park & Market. Map p 115.*

★★ LoungeSix GASLAMP QUARTER On the 4th-floor pool deck of the Hotel Solamar, there are fire pits, cabanas, comfy lounges, and views of the Gaslamp Quarter action. *616 J St. (at Sixth Ave.). ☎ 619/531-8744. www.hotelsolamar.com. No cover. Bus: 3 or 120. Trolley: Orange Line to Gaslamp Quarter. Map p 115.*

★ Nunu's Cocktail Lounge HILLCREST Lots of 1960s Naugahyde style, plus cheap drinks and a kitchen that whips up specialties like the Jack Daniel's burger for an eclectic crowd. *3537 Fifth Ave. (at Ivy Lane). ☎ 619/295-2878. www.nunuscocktails.com. No cover. Bus: 3 or 120. Map p 116.*

★★ Pacific Shores OCEAN BEACH Old-timers coexist with hipsters floating through for inexpensive, generous cocktails. Take care with the booze, however, as the black lights and paintings of mermaids and bubbles could make you woozy. *4927 Newport Ave. (btw. Cable St. & Sunset Cliffs Blvd.). ☎ 619/223-7549. No cover. Bus: 35. Map p 117.*

★★ PB Shore Club PACIFIC BEACH It's packed, loud, and filled with hopeful singles plus a large contingent of active and retired Navy personnel (the bar supports all sorts of Vet programs) downing Vodka Red Bull slushies and lobster tacos. *4343 Ocean Blvd. (at Mission Beach Blvd). ☎ 858/272-7873. www.pbshoreclub.com. No cover. Bus: 8/9. Map p 117.*

★ Princess Pub & Grille LITTLE ITALY A local haunt for Anglophiles and others hankering for a pint o' Watney's and some bangers 'n' mash. *1665 India St. (at Date St.). ☎ 619/702-3021. www.princesspub.com. No cover. Bus: 83. Trolley: Blue Line to County Cntr/Little Italy. Map p 115.*

The Altitude Sky Lounge in Gaslamp Quarter.

★★ Side Bar GASLAMP QUARTER Ornate fixtures, dangling vintage bird cages, and erotic art add to the Victorian bordello feeling at this small, sexy lounge and nightclub. *536 Market St. (at Sixth Ave.). ☎ 619/696-0946. www.sidebarsd.com. Cover none–$15. Bus: 3 or 11. Trolley: Gaslamp Quarter. Map p 115.*

★★★ Tipsy Crow GASLAMP QUARTER This three-story nightlife compound hosts concerts, comedy, and DJs, and draws raves from fans who enjoy the lounge-style rooftop nest and the Underground space for dancing or comedy nights. *770 Fifth Ave. (at F St.). ☎ 619/338-9300. www.thetipsycrow.com. Cover varies. Bus: 3 or 11. Trolley: Gaslamp Quarter. Map p 115.*

★★★ Top of the Hyatt EMBARCADERO On the 40th floor of the West Coast's tallest waterfront building, this is San Diego's ultimate bar with a view. *1 Market Pl. (at Harbor Dr.). ☎ 619/232-1234. www.manchestergrand.hyatt.com. No cover. Trolley: Orange Line to Seaport Village. Map p 115.*

★★★ Waterfront LITTLE ITALY Long before Little Italy became a metrosexual hangout, this much-loved dive catered to 1930s workers at a nearby aerospace factory. These days it draws a more stylish crowd, with a few holdouts at the bar. Spicy bloody Marys and huevos rancheros draw Sunday brunchers; expect a line if you arrive after 9. *2044 Kettner Blvd (btw. W. Hawthorne & W. Grape sts.). ☎ 619/232-9656. www.waterfrontbarandgrill.com. No cover. Bus: 83. Map p 115.*

★★ Wave House MISSION BEACH A killer beachfront location, right alongside the Mission Beach amusement park. The 30,000 square-foot (2,800 sq. m) outdoor venue includes tiki bars, fire pits, beach cabanas, and a spot-on view of surfers tackling man-made curls in wave machines. *3125 Ocean Front Walk (at Mission Blvd. & W. Mission Bay Dr.). ☎ 858/228-9283. www.wavehousesd.com. No cover. Bus: 8/9. Map p 117.*

Dance Clubs

★ FLUXX GASLAMP QUARTER If you can make it past the doorman, you'll be wowed by the state-of-the-art sound and lighting and Vegas-style glitz (and prices) at this upscale club. Themes change monthly, hence the name. *500 Fourth Ave. (btw. Island Ave. & Market St.). ☎ 619/232-8100. www.fluxxsd.com. Cover $20. Bus: 3, 11, or 120. Trolley: Convention Center. Map p 115.*

★★★ OMNIA GASLAMP QUARTER The closest you'll come to a true Vegas-style club in San Diego is this offshoot of a Sin City hotspot. This three-level club has VIP boxes along the balcony above the main dance floor and a large rooftop deck. Vegas-level DJs mean big money; prepare to splurge. *454 Sixth Ave. (btw. Island Ave. & J St.). ☎ 619/544-9500. www.omnianightclub.com. Cover & tickets vary. Trolley: Orange Line to Gaslamp Quarter. Map p 115.*

★★ The Onyx Room/Thin GASLAMP QUARTER At street level is hyper-modern Thin, where cocktails mix with DJ grooves; subterranean Onyx is a classic lounge, featuring Latin, soul, jazz, and other live music. *852 Fifth Ave. (btw. E & F sts.). ☎ 619/235-6699. www.onyxroom.com. Cover Fri–Sat $10–$15 (covers both bars). Bus: 3, 120, 992, or any Broadway route. Trolley: Fifth Ave. Map p 115.*

★★ Parq Nightclub GASLAMP QUARTER This dress-to-impress dance club has flashy decor, dizzying light shows, and top-notch DJs.

Cocktails at the Top of the Hyatt.

The Onyx Room.

Enter through the fancy, and quite good, restaurant. *615 Broadway (at Sixth Ave.). ☎ 619/727-6789. www.parqsd.com. Cover $15–$25. Bus: All Broadway routes. Trolley: Blue or Orange Line to Fifth Ave. Map p 115.*

★★ **RoofTop 600** GASLAMP QUARTER A dance floor and overall sexy vibe draws the beautiful people to this open-air bar with equally beautiful views. *600 F St. (btw. Sixth & Seventh aves. at the Andaz Hotel). ☎ 619/814-2055. www.rooftop600.com. Bus: 3 or 120. Trolley: Gaslamp Quarter. Map p 115.*

★★ **Sevilla** GASLAMP QUARTER This Spanish-themed club is the place for salsa and merengue lessons and Latin music nights; there's also a tapas bar and dining room in Cafe Sevilla upstairs. *555 Fourth Ave. (at Market St.). ☎ 619/233-5979. www.sevillanightclub.com. Cover $5–$15. Bus: 3, 11, or 120. Trolley: Convention Center. Map p 115.*

Gay & Lesbian Bars & Clubs

★ **The Brass Rail** HILLCREST San Diego's oldest gay bar features VIP rooms and bottle service. Theme nights vary, but there's usually one for karaoke, hip-hop, and Latin music. *3796 Fifth Ave. (at Robinson St.). ☎ 619/298-2233. www.thebrassrailsd.com. Cover $5. Bus: 1, 3, or 120. Map p 116.*

★ **Numbers** HILLCREST It's a predominantly male crowd at this busy dance emporium. Every second and fourth Saturday is Sabbat Goth night. *3811 Park Blvd. (at University Ave.). ☎ 619/294-7583. www.numberssd.com. Cover $3–$10. Bus: 1, 7, 10, or 11. Map p 116.*

★★ **Rich's** HILLCREST Dance your heart and feet out in two cavernous rooms with separate DJs

Concert at Belly Up.

Concert at House of Blues.

and swift bartenders. Thursday Lez Night is jammed. *1051 University Ave. (btw. 10th Ave. & Vermont St.). ☎ 619/295-2195. www.richssandiego.com. Cover varies. Bus: 3. Map p 116.*

★★ Urban Mo's HILLCREST Always packed with festive revelers, this restaurant and bar segues into a club at night, with country line dancing, diva performances, and DJ nights. *308 University Ave. (at Third Ave.). ☎ 619/491-0400. www.urbanmos.com. No cover. Bus: 3. Map p 116.*

Live Music Venues

★★★ Belly Up Tavern SOLANA BEACH A 30-minute drive from downtown, this venerable concert bar hosts international artists of all genres and is arguably San Diego's best spot for live music. *143 S. Cedros Ave. (south of Lomas Santa Fe Dr.). ☎ 858/481-9022 (recorded info) or 858/481-8140 (box office). www.bellyup.com. $15–$50. Bus: 101. Map p 117.*

★★ Brick by Brick MISSION VALLEY There's nothing fussy or fancy here—just a bare-bones bar with pool table, pinball machine, and reasonably priced drinks. But it's a favorite with bands of all genres seeking an up-close gathering of avid fans. *1130 Buenos Ave. (btw. W. Morena Blvd. & Naples Place). ☎ 619/276-3990. www.brickbybrick.com. Cover charge $8–$25. Bus: 44. Map p 117.*

★★ The Casbah LITTLE ITALY This rockin' club has a well-earned rep for showcasing rock, alternative and punk bands that either are, were, or will be famous; live music can be counted on at least 6 nights a week. *2501 Kettner Blvd. (at Laurel St.). ☎ 619/232-4355. www.casbahmusic.com. Cover charge $8–$25. Bus: 83. Map p 115.*

★ Dizzy's PACIFIC BEACH You'll find uncompromising, straight-ahead jazz at this oddly situated venue in the showroom at San Diego Jet Ski Rentals. All ages welcome. *4275 Mission Bay Dr. (at Rosewood St.). No phone. www.dizzyssandiego.com. $10–$15 (tickets available at the door; cash only). Bus: 8. Map p 117.*

★★ Eddie V's DOWNTOWN This stylish restaurant's V Lounge is the best spot downtown for martinis and live jazz. *789 W. Harbor Dr. (at Seventh Ave.). ☎ 619/615-0281. www.eddiev.com. No cover. Trolley: Orange Line to Seaport Village. Map p 115.*

★★★ **Humphreys** SHELTER ISLAND This locally beloved 1,300-seat outdoor venue is alongside the water next to bobbing sailboats. An indoor lounge, Humphreys Backstage, also has music nightly. *2241 Shelter Island Dr. ☎ 619/523-1010 (general info) or 619-224-3577 (reservations). www.humphreysconcerts.com. Ticket prices vary. Bus: 28. Map p 117.*

Supper Clubs

★★★ **House of Blues** DOWNTOWN Filled with cool art, there are two stages and a restaurant serving Southern-inspired cuisine (also open for lunch and Sunday Gospel brunch). *1055 Fifth Ave. (btw. Broadway & C St.). ☎ 619/299-2583. www.hob.com/sandiego. Ticket prices vary. Bus: 3, 120, or numerous Broadway routes. Trolley: Fifth Ave. Map p 115.*

★ **Lips** NORTH PARK This drag revue has a different show nightly, such as Bitchy Bingo on Wednesday and celebrity impersonations on Thursday; Sunday there's a Gospel brunch. Weekend late shows are 21 and over only. *3036 El Cajon Blvd. (at 30th St.). ☎ 619/295-7900. www.lipssd.com. Cover $3–$5, food minimum $10–$15. Bus: 1 or 15. Map p 116.*

The bar at Starlite.

★★ **Starlite** MIDDLETOWN This hip restaurant and bar eschews the large-scale dine-and-dance scene that's popular in the Gaslamp Quarter for an intimate, mondo-exotica lounge feel. *3175 India St. (at Spruce St.). ☎ 619/358-9766. www.starlitesandiego.com. No cover. Bus: 83. Trolley: Blue Line to Middletown. Map p 116.*

Wine Bars

★★★ **3rd Corner** OCEAN BEACH This convivial wine bar multitasks as a restaurant and as a wine shop where you can meander through racks of wines looking for the right one to uncork. *2265 Bacon St. (btw. Voltaire St. & W. Point Loma Blvd.). ☎ 619/223-2700. www.the3rdcorner.com. Bus: 35 or 923. Map p 117.*

★★ **Vin de Syrah Spirits & Wine Parlor** GASLAMP QUARTER This hot spot has a hidden, speakeasy entrance and an oddball *Alice in Wonderland* decor. It morphs into a jamming club Friday and Saturday nights. *901 Fifth Ave. (at E St.). ☎ 619/234-4166. www.syrahwineparlor.com. Bus: 3, 120, or numerous Broadway routes. Trolley: Fifth Ave. Map p 115.*

★ **Wine Steals** HILLCREST Specialty nights include wine tastings, reduced-price flights, and mimosa pints, and there's no corkage fee for bottles sold at the shop. Pizzas, sandwiches and cheeseboards are available. *1243 University Ave. (btw. Richmond & Vermont sts.). ☎ 619/295-1188. www.winestealssd.com. Bus: 1, 10, or 11 (Hillcrest). Map p 116.*

8 The Best Arts & Entertainment

A&E Best Bets

Best **Classical Music Festival**
★★★ La Jolla Music Society SummerFest *various locations (p 126)*

Best **Sports Venue**
★★★ San Diego Padres' PETCO Park *100 Park Blvd. (p 129)*

Best **Goal-Oriented Kicks**
★★ San Diego Sockers *2260 Jimmy Durante Blvd. (p 129)*

Best **Place for Culture in a Mall**
★★ San Diego Repertory Theatre *Horton Plaza (p 130)*

Best **Place for Foreign & Indie Film**
★★★ Hillcrest Cinema *3965 Fifth Ave. (p 127)*

Most **Extreme Screen**
★★★ Fleet Science Center IMAX Dome Theater *Balboa Park (p 127)*

Best **Restored Venues**
★ North Park Theatre *2891 University Ave. (p 126)* and ★★★ Balboa Theatre *868 Fourth Ave. (p 126)*

Best **Use of Strings & Pyrotechnics**
★★ San Diego Symphony Summer Pops *Embarcadero Marina Park South (p 126)*

Best **Broadway-Bound Fare**
★★★ La Jolla Playhouse *2910 La Jolla Village Dr. (p 130)*

Best **Place to Be a Groundling**
★★★ Old Globe Theatre *Balboa Park (p 130)*

Best **Place to Get Your Dance On**
★★ Dance Place at NTC Promenade *2650 Truxton Rd. (p 126)*

Best **Place for Tragic Heroines**
★★ San Diego Opera *1200 Third Ave. (p 128)*

Best **Place for Horsing Around**
★★★ Del Mar Races *2260 Jimmy Durante Blvd. (p 129)*

An evening of music on the beach with the La Jolla Music Society. Previous page: San Diego Symphony.

Downtown/Balboa Park A&E

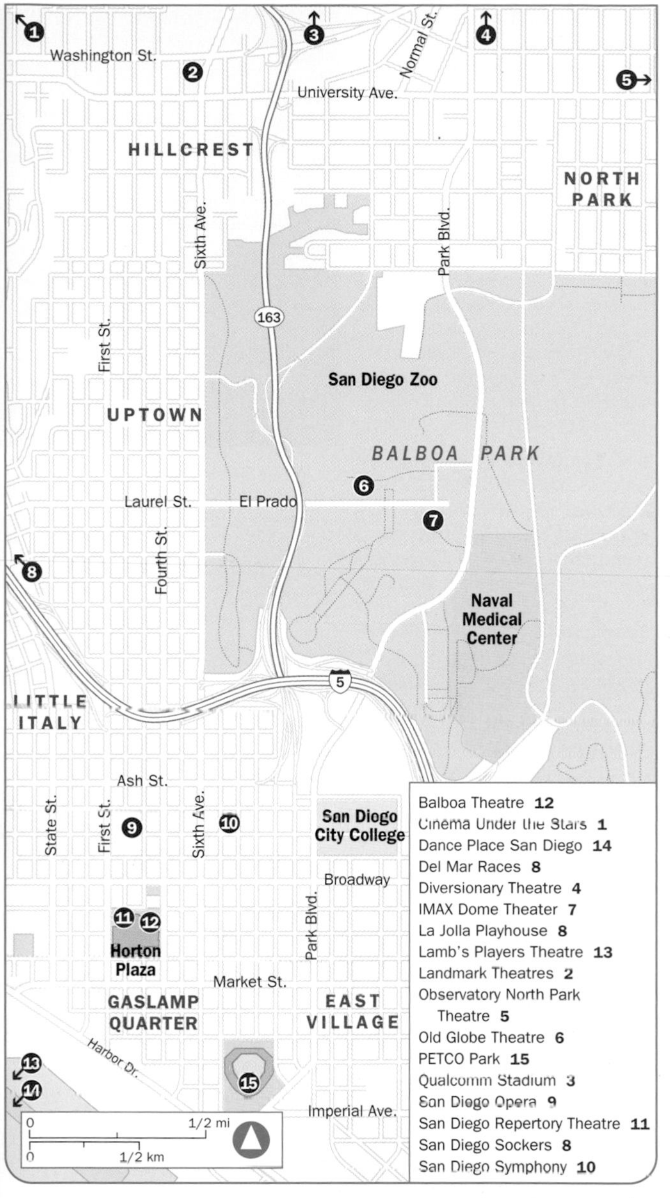

Balboa Theatre 12
Cinema Under the Stars 1
Dance Place San Diego 14
Del Mar Races 8
Diversionary Theatre 4
IMAX Dome Theater 7
La Jolla Playhouse 8
Lamb's Players Theatre 13
Landmark Theatres 2
Observatory North Park Theatre 5
Old Globe Theatre 6
PETCO Park 15
Qualcomm Stadium 3
San Diego Opera 9
San Diego Repertory Theatre 11
San Diego Sockers 8
San Diego Symphony 10

A&E A to Z

Classical Music

★★★ La Jolla Music Society VARIOUS LOCATIONS This well-respected organization has been bringing marquee names to San Diego since 1968; the annual SummerFest in August is always highly anticipated, featuring concerts, lectures, and workshops. *Performances at Athenaeum Music & Arts Library, Sherwood Auditorium at the Museum of Contemporary Art in La Jolla, Neurosciences Institute, Copley Symphony Hall, Balboa Theatre, & San Diego Civic Theatre. ☎ 858/459-3728. www.ljms.org. Tickets $25–$110.*

★★ San Diego Symphony DOWNTOWN/EMBARCADERO Top talent performs at Copley Symphony Hall, then transfers to the waterfront for an open-air Bayside Summer Nights summer pops season. *Symphony Hall, 750 B St. (at Seventh Ave.). ☎ 619/235-0804. www.sandiegosymphony.com. Bus: Numerous Broadway routes Trolley: Blue or Orange Line to 5th Ave. Embarcadero Marina Park South (behind the Convention Center), Trolley: Orange Line to Gaslamp Quarter. Tickets $20–$100.* *See p 125.*

Heikoff Giant Dome Theater featuring the IMAX® film, Coral Reef Adventure.

A show at Balboa Theatre.

Concert & Performance Venues

★★★ Balboa Theatre GASLAMP QUARTER A gilded 1924 beauty spared from the wrecking ball and reopened in 2008, this downtown icon presents music, dance, theater, and film. *868 Fourth Ave. (southwest corner of Fourth Ave. & E St.). ☎ 619/570-1100 or 619/615-4000. www.sdbalboa.org. Bus: 3, 120, or all Broadway routes. Trolley: Fifth Ave.* *See p 125.*

★ Observatory North Park – North Park Theatre NORTH PARK This gloriously restored vaudeville house has been through various incarnations and is now an SRO concert venue with an adjacent tavern. *2891 University Ave. (at Kansas St.). ☎ 619/239-8836. www.observatorysd.com. Ticket prices vary. Bus: 2, 6, 7, or 10.* *See p 125.*

Dance

★★ Dance Place San Diego POINT LOMA This former San Diego Naval Training Center is now

What a Deal

Half-price tickets to theater, music, and dance events are available at the ARTS TIX booth in Horton Plaza Park, at Broadway and Third Avenue. The kiosk is open Tuesday through Thursday 10am to 4pm, Friday and Saturday 10am to 6pm, and Sunday 10am to 2pm. Half-price tickets are available only for same-day shows, except for Monday performances, which are sold on Sunday. For a daily listing of offerings, call ☎ 858/381-5595 or check out www.sdartstix.com; the website also sells half-price tickets for some shows. Full-price advance tickets are also available—the booth doubles as a Ticketmaster outlet.

the heart of the city's dance scene, providing studio, performance, and educational space for the **San Diego Ballet** (☎ 619/294-7378; www.sandiegoballet.org), **Malashock Dance** (☎ 619/260-1622; www.malashockdance.org), and **Jean Isaacs San Diego Dance Theater** (☎ 619/225-1803; www.sandiegodancetheater.org). *2650 Truxton Rd. (at Dewey Rd.). ☎ 619/573-9260. www.ntclibertystation.com. Bus: 28. Map p 125.*

Film

★★ Cinema Under the Stars MISSION HILLS An intimate, outdoor movie-going experience that runs from spring through fall, featuring both classics and new releases. You can lounge in zero-gravity chairs or sit at cafe tables. *4040 Goldfinch St. (at Fort Stockton Dr.). ☎ 619/295-4221. www.topspresents.com. Tickets $16. Bus: 10 or 83. Map p 125.*

★★★ kids IMAX Dome Theater BALBOA PARK The Reuben H. Fleet Science Center features a variety of nature- and science-themed movies projected onto the 76-foot (23m) tilted-dome screen (shows are daily, with evening screenings on Friday). *Balboa Park (adjacent to Park Blvd.). ☎ 619/238-1233. www.rhfleet.org. Tickets $17–$20. Bus: 7. Map p 125.*

★★★ Landmark Theatres HILLCREST/LA JOLLA Indie and foreign films play the Hillcrest theater's five screens and the single screen at the venerable Ken Cinema in Kensington. *www.landmarktheatres.com. Hillcrest Cinema: 3965 Fifth Ave. (btw. University Ave. & Washington St.). ☎ 619/298-2904. Bus: 1, 3, 10, 11, 83, or 120. Ken Cinema: 4061 Adams Ave. (at Park Place.). ☎ 619/283-3227. Bus: 11. Tickets $8–$11. Map p 125.*

San Diego Opera.

Sure Bets

San Diego County has 18 Native American reservations, many of which operate casinos. The most accessible from downtown is **Viejas Casino** (5000 Willows Rd., Alpine; ☎ 800/847-6537 or 619/445-5400; www.viejas.com)—it's a straight shot out I-8 (exit Willows Rd.), less than a half-hour's drive away. Viejas also has an outlet center with more than 40 brand-name retailers. **Barona Resort & Casino** (1932 Wildcat Canyon Rd., Lakeside; ☎ 888/722-7662 or 619/443-2300; www.barona.com) has 2,000 Vegas-style slots, 70 table games, and an off-track betting area. The resort includes 400 guest rooms, a spa, and an 18-hole championship golf course. Take I-8 east to Highway 67 north; at Willows Road, turn right and continue to Wildcat Canyon Road; turn left, and continue 6 miles (10km) to the reservation (allow 40 min. from downtown). **Sycuan Resort & Casino** is outside El Cajon, at 5469 Casino Way (☎ 800/279-2826 or 619/445-6002; www.sycuan.com). Follow I-8 east for 10 miles (16km) to the El Cajon Boulevard exit. Take El Cajon 3 blocks to Washington Avenue, turning right and continuing on Washington as it turns into Dehesa Road. Stay on Dehesa for 5 miles (8km), and follow the signs (allow 30 min. from downtown). Sycuan features 2,000 slots, 60 game tables, a 1,200-seat bingo palace, and a 450-seat theater that features name touring acts; Sycuan's 54 holes of golf are also some of San Diego's best.

Opera

★★ **San Diego Opera** DOWNTOWN A season of both well-trod warhorses and edgier works runs from late January to mid-May, performed at the Civic Theatre by name talent from around the world, as well as local singers. *1200 Third Ave. (at B St.). ☎ 619/533-7000 (box office). www.sdopera.com. Tickets $30–$210. Bus: Numerous Broadway routes. Trolley: Blue or Orange Line to Civic Center.* *Map p 125.*

Del Mar Races.

PETCO Park, home of the Padres.

Spectator Sports

★★★ Del Mar Races DEL MAR Thoroughbred racing takes place at the Del Mar Race Track from mid-July to early September and in a second season in November. Party crowds come for post-race concerts and other special events; there's year-round satellite wagering at the fairgrounds' Surfside Race Place (☎ 858/755-1167; www.surfsideraceplace.com). *2260 Jimmy Durante Blvd. (at Via de la Valle). ☎ 858/755-1141. www.dmtc.com. Tickets $6–$15. Bus: 101. Map p 125.*

★ San Diego Chargers MISSION VALLEY The city's NFL team plays at Qualcomm Stadium; the season runs from August to December. Heated discussions about a new stadium or the team's desertion from San Diego have been underway for years. *9449 Friars Rd. (btw. I-805 & I-15). ☎ 800/745-3000. www.chargers.com. Tickets $54–$98. Trolley: Green Line or special event Blue Line to Qualcomm Stadium. Map p 125.*

★★★ San Diego Padres EAST VILLAGE Major League Baseball action at PETCO Park, an architecturally striking downtown facility; season runs April to September. *100 Park Blvd. (bordered by Seventh & 10th aves. at J St.). ☎ 877/374-2784 or 619/795-5000. www.padres.com. Tickets $5–$63. Trolley: Orange or special event line to Gaslamp Quarter; Blue or Orange Line to 12th & Imperial Transit Center or Park & Market. Map p 125.*

★★ San Diego Sockers DEL MAR San Diego's most successful sports franchise (11 championships) is part of the Professional Arena Soccer League; the season is November to February. The team plays at the Valley View Casino Center. *3500 Sports Arena Blvd. (at Midway Dr.). ☎ 866/799-4625. www.sdsockers.com. Tickets $11–$20. Bus: 9, 10. Map p 125.*

San Diego Chargers.

Montego Glover (center) and the cast of La Jolla Playhouse's Tony Award–winning production of Memphis.

Theater

★★ Diversionary Theatre UNIVERSITY HEIGHTS This 104-seat theater focuses on plays with gay and lesbian themes. *4545 Park Blvd. (btw. Madison & Monroe aves.). ☎ 619/220-0097. www.diversionary.org. Tickets $10–$35, $10 student rush 1 hour prior to curtain. Bus: 11. Map p 125.*

★★★ La Jolla Playhouse LA JOLLA The Tony Award–winning Playhouse is known for its contemporary takes on classics and its commitment to *commedia dell'arte* style, as well as producing Broadway-bound blockbusters. *2910 La Jolla Village Dr. (at Torrey Pines Rd.). ☎ 858/550-1010. www.lajollaplayhouse.org. Tickets $35–$90. Bus: 30, 41, 101, 150, or 921. Map p 125.*

★★ Lamb's Players Theatre CORONADO Featuring a true resident ensemble, Lamb's presents both premieres and classics, keeping things on the safe, noncontroversial side. *1142 Orange Ave. (at C Ave.). ☎ 619/437-0600. www.lambsplayers.org. Tickets $40–$60. Bus: 901 or 904. Map p 125.*

★★★ Old Globe Theatre BALBOA PARK This Tony Award–winning, three-theater complex attracts big-name playwrights and performers and has spawned a number of Broadway hits. The summer Shakespeare Festival features three works by the Bard. *Balboa Park (behind the Museum of Man). ☎ 619/234-5623. www.theoldglobe.org. Tickets $39–$85. Bus: 3, 7, or 120. Map p 125.*

★★ San Diego Repertory Theatre GASLAMP QUARTER The Rep mounts plays and musicals with a strong multicultural bent, performing in the two-stage Lyceum Theatre at Horton Plaza. *79 Broadway Circle, in Horton Plaza. ☎ 619/544-1000. www.sdrep.org. Tickets $25–$53. Bus: All Broadway routes. Trolley: Civic Center. Map p 125.* ●

The Old Globe Theatre at Balboa Park.

9 The Best **Lodging**

Lodging Best Bets

Best **Historic Hotel**
★★★ Hotel Del Coronado $$$$ *1500 Orange Ave. (p 139)*

Best **for a Romantic Getaway**
★★★ The Lodge at Torrey Pines $$$$ *11480 N. Torrey Pines Rd. (p 141)*

Best **for Families**
★★★ Paradise Point Resort & Spa $$$ *1404 Vacation Rd. (p 143)*

Best **Moderately Priced Hotel**
★ Horton Grand $$ *311 Island Ave. (p 139)*

Best **Budget Hotel**
★★ La Pensione Hotel $ *606 W. Date St. (p 141)*

Best **Bed & Breakfast**
★★ Britt Scripps Inn $$$ *406 Maple St. (p 136)*

Best **Boutique Inn**
★★ Hotel Palomar $$$$ *1047 5th Ave. (p 139)*

Spa at L'Auberge Del Mar. Previous page: The Catamaran on Mission Bay and Pacific Beach.

Best **Place to Stay on the Beach**
★★★ Tower 23 $$$$ *723 Felspar St. (p 143)*

Best **Place to Stay over the Beach**
★★★ Crystal Pier Hotel $$$ *4500 Ocean Blvd. (p 136)*

Best **Green Hotel**
★★ Hotel Indigo $$$ *509 Ninth Ave. (p 139)*

Best **Place to Watch a Concert from Your Room**
★★ Hard Rock Hotel $$$ *207 Fifth Ave. (p 138)*

Best **Rooftop Pool**
★★ Andaz Hotel $$$ *650 F St. (p 136)*

Best **Golf Resort**
★★★ Park Hyatt Aviara Resort $$$$ *7100 Four Seasons Point (p 143)*

Best **Place to Adjust Your Chakras**
★★ Omni La Costa Resort and Spa $$$$ *2100 Costa del Mar Rd. (p 142)*

Best **for Baseball Fans**
★★★ Omni San Diego Hotel $$$$ *675 L St. (p 142)*

Best **for Modernists**
★★ Keating Hotel $$$$ *432 F St. (p 140)*

Best **for Traditionalists**
★★ The Westgate Hotel $$$$ *1055 Second Ave. (p 144)*

Best **Place to Get Away from It All**
★★ Loews Coronado Bay Resort $$$$ *4000 Coronado Bay Rd. (p 142)*

Downtown Hotels

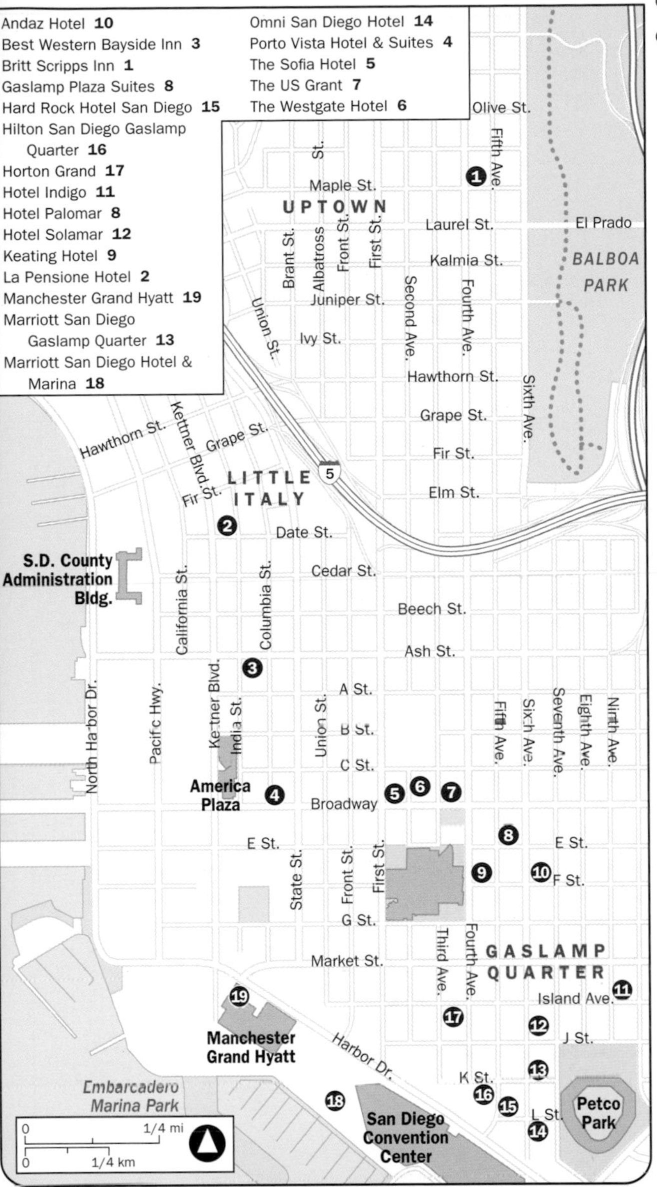
Andaz Hotel 10
Best Western Bayside Inn 3
Britt Scripps Inn 1
Gaslamp Plaza Suites 8
Hard Rock Hotel San Diego 15
Hilton San Diego Gaslamp Quarter 16
Horton Grand 17
Hotel Indigo 11
Hotel Palomar 8
Hotel Solamar 12
Keating Hotel 9
La Pensione Hotel 2
Manchester Grand Hyatt 19
Marriott San Diego Gaslamp Quarter 13
Marriott San Diego Hotel & Marina 18
Omni San Diego Hotel 14
Porto Vista Hotel & Suites 4
The Sofia Hotel 5
The US Grant 7
The Westgate Hotel 6
UPTOWN
LITTLE ITALY
GASLAMP QUARTER
BALBOA PARK
El Prado
Olive St.
Maple St.
Laurel St.
Kalmia St.
Juniper St.
Ivy St.
Hawthorn St.
Grape St.
Fir St.
Elm St.
Date St.
Cedar St.
Beech St.
Ash St.
A St.
B St.
C St.
Broadway
E St.
F St.
G St.
Market St.
Island Ave.
J St.
K St.
L St.
Harbor Dr.
Brant St.
Albatross St.
Front St.
First St.
Second Ave.
Third Ave.
Fourth Ave.
Fifth Ave.
Sixth Ave.
Seventh Ave.
Eighth Ave.
Ninth Ave.
Union St.
Kettner Blvd.
India St.
Columbia St.
California St.
Pacific Hwy.
North Harbor Dr.
State St.
5
S.D. County Administration Bldg.
America Plaza
Manchester Grand Hyatt
San Diego Convention Center
Petco Park
Embarcadero Marina Park
0 1/4 mi
0 1/4 km

Mission Bay Hotels

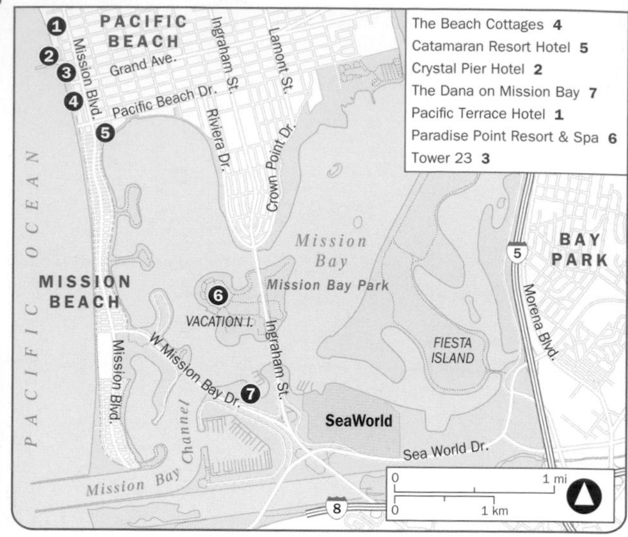
PACIFIC BEACH
Grand Ave.
Mission Blvd.
Pacific Beach Dr.
Ingraham St.
Lamont St.
Riviera Dr.
Crown Point Dr.
PACIFIC OCEAN
MISSION BEACH
Mission Bay
Mission Bay Park
VACATION I.
W. Mission Bay Dr.
Mission Bay Channel
SeaWorld
Sea World Dr.
FIESTA ISLAND
Morena Blvd.
BAY PARK
5
8
0
1 mi
1 km
The Beach Cottages 4
Catamaran Resort Hotel 5
Crystal Pier Hotel 2
The Dana on Mission Bay 7
Pacific Terrace Hotel 1
Paradise Point Resort & Spa 6
Tower 23 3

La Jolla Hotels

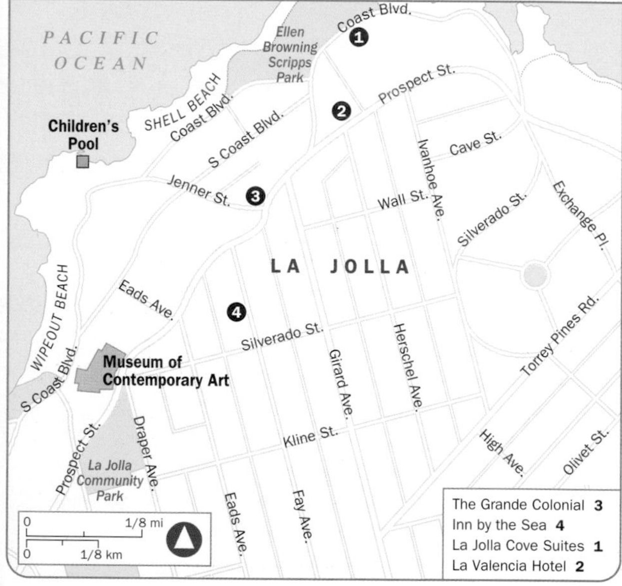
PACIFIC OCEAN
Ellen Browning Scripps Park
Coast Blvd.
Prospect St.
SHELL BEACH
Coast Blvd.
S Coast Blvd.
Children's Pool
Jenner St.
Cave St.
Ivanhoe Ave.
Wall St.
Silverado St.
Exchange Pl.
LA JOLLA
WIPEOUT BEACH
Eads Ave.
Silverado St.
Museum of Contemporary Art
S Coast Blvd.
Girard Ave.
Herschel Ave.
Torrey Pines Rd.
Prospect St.
Draper Ave.
La Jolla Community Park
Kline St.
High Ave.
Olivet St.
Eads Ave.
Fay Ave.
0
1/8 mi
1/8 km
The Grande Colonial 3
Inn by the Sea 4
La Jolla Cove Suites 1
La Valencia Hotel 2

Hotels at the Beaches

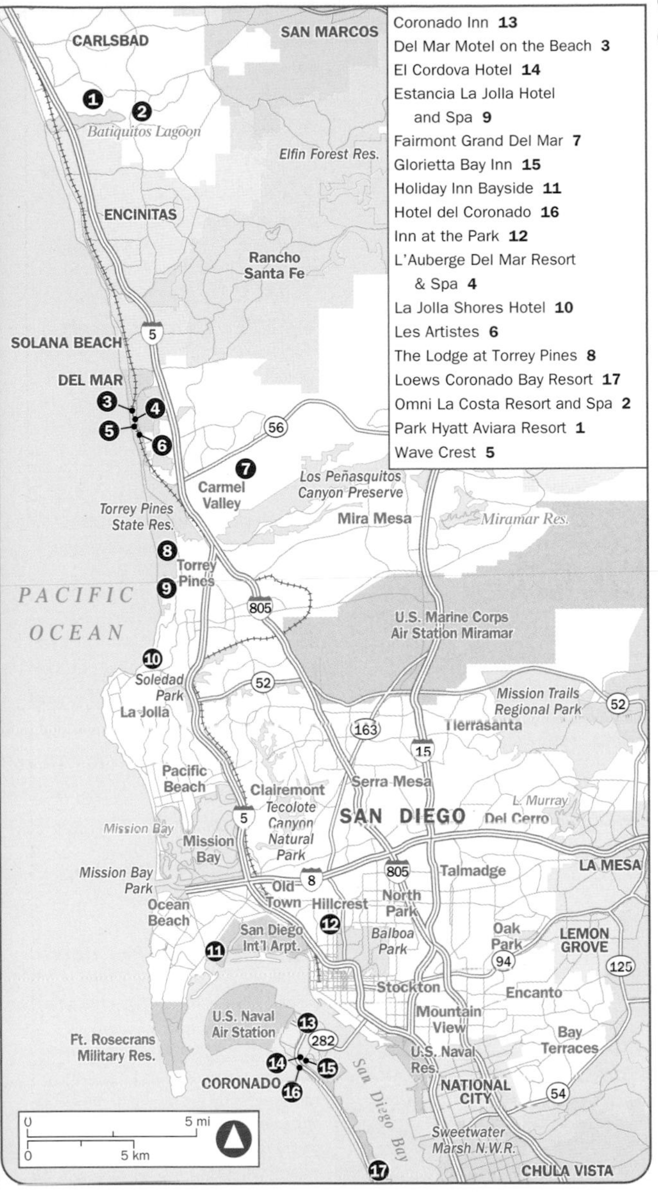
Coronado Inn 13
Del Mar Motel on the Beach 3
El Cordova Hotel 14
Estancia La Jolla Hotel and Spa 9
Fairmont Grand Del Mar 7
Glorietta Bay Inn 15
Holiday Inn Bayside 11
Hotel del Coronado 16
Inn at the Park 12
L'Auberge Del Mar Resort & Spa 4
La Jolla Shores Hotel 10
Les Artistes 6
The Lodge at Torrey Pines 8
Loews Coronado Bay Resort 17
Omni La Costa Resort and Spa 2
Park Hyatt Aviara Resort 1
Wave Crest 5
CARLSBAD
SAN MARCOS
Batiquitos Lagoon
Elfin Forest Res.
ENCINITAS
Rancho Santa Fe
SOLANA BEACH
DEL MAR
Carmel Valley
Los Peñasquitos Canyon Preserve
Mira Mesa
Miramar Res.
Torrey Pines State Res.
Torrey Pines
PACIFIC OCEAN
U.S. Marine Corps Air Station Miramar
Soledad Park
La Jolla
Mission Trails Regional Park
Tierrasanta
Pacific Beach
Clairemont
Tecolote Canyon Natural Park
Serra Mesa
L. Murray
SAN DIEGO
Del Cerro
Mission Bay
Mission Bay
Mission Bay Park
Old Town
Hillcrest
Talmadge
LA MESA
North Park
Ocean Beach
San Diego Int'l Arpt.
Balboa Park
Oak Park
LEMON GROVE
Stockton
Encanto
U.S. Naval Air Station
Mountain View
Ft. Rosecrans Military Res.
U.S. Naval Res.
Bay Terraces
CORONADO
San Diego Bay
NATIONAL CITY
Sweetwater Marsh N.W.R.
CHULA VISTA
5
56
805
52
163
15
8
94
125
282
54
0
5 mi
0
5 km

Lodging A to Z

★★ **Andaz Hotel** GASLAMP QUARTER A sexy vibe prevails, yet this chic hotel works for business travelers as well. It features a nightclub and rooftop pool/entertainment area. *600 F St. (btw. Sixth & Seventh aves.). ☎ 877/489-4489. www.andazsandiego.com. 159 units. Doubles from $229. AE, DC, DISC, MC, V. Bus: 3 or 120. Map p 133.*

★ **The Beach Cottages** PACIFIC BEACH This family-owned operation has been around since 1948 and offers a variety of guest quarters, including cottages just steps from the sand. *4255 Ocean Blvd. (1 block south of Grand Ave.). ☎ 858/483-7440. www.beachcottages.com. 61 units. Doubles from $185. AE, DISC, MC, V. Bus: 8/9 or 30. Map p 134.*

★ **Best Western Bayside Inn** DOWNTOWN Accommodations here are basic chain-hotel issue, but they are well maintained and have balconies overlooking the bay or downtown. *555 W. Ash St. (at Columbia St.). ☎ 800/341-1818. www.baysideinn.com. 122 units. Doubles from $170 w/breakfast. AE, DISC, MC, V. Bus: 83. Trolley: Blue or Orange Line to America Plaza. Map p 133.*

Governors room at Britt Scripps.

★★ **Britt Scripps Inn** BANKERS HILL A glorious Victorian house lovingly converted into an intimate hotel close to Balboa Park and Hillcrest. *406 Maple St. (at 4th Ave.). ☎ 888/881-1991. www.brittscrippsinn.com. 9 units. Doubles from $133. DC, MC, V. Bus: 3 or 120. Map p 133.*

★★ kids **Catamaran Resort Hotel** PACIFIC BEACH Right on Mission Bay, this Polynesian-themed resort has its own beach, complete with watersports facilities. Family cruises in the *Bahia Belle* sternwheeler, outdoor movies, play areas, and suites with kitchenettes all help keep kids busy and happy. *3999 Mission Blvd. (4 blocks south of Grand Ave.). ☎ 800/422-8386. www.catamaranresort.com. 313 units. Doubles from $249. AE, DISC, MC, V. Bus: 8/9. Map p 134.*

★ **Coronado Inn** CORONADO This tropically flavored 1940s motel is centrally located and terrifically priced, and it maintains a friendly ambience. Some units have kitchenettes or full kitchens. *266 Orange Ave. (corner of 3rd St.). ☎ 619/435-4121. www.coronadoinn.com. 30 units. Doubles from $129 w/breakfast. AE, DISC, MC, V. Bus: 901 or 904. Map p 135.*

★★★ kids **Crystal Pier Hotel** PACIFIC BEACH This utterly unique cluster of cottages literally sits over the surf on the vintage Crystal Pier. There's a 2-night minimum stay in winter and 3 nights in summer. *4500 Ocean Blvd. (at Garnet Ave.). ☎ 800/748-5894. www.crystalpier.com. 29 units. Doubles from $300. DISC, MC, V. Bus: 8/9, 27, or 30. Map p 134.*

The gardens at Estancia La Jolla Hotel and Spa.

★★ kids The Dana on Mission Bay MISSION BAY Some rooms here overlook bobbing sailboats in the recreational marina; beaches are a 15-minute walk away and an aerial tram reaches Sea World. *1710 W. Mission Bay Dr. (off Ingraham St.). ☎ 800/445-3339. www.thedana.com. 271 units. Doubles from $130. AE, DISC, MC, V. Bus: 8/9. Map p 134.*

★ Del Mar Motel on the Beach DEL MAR The only property in Del Mar right on the beach, this simply furnished little white-stucco motel has been here since 1946. *1702 Coast Blvd. (at 17th St.). ☎ 800/223-8449. www.delmarmotelonthebeach.com. 44 units. Doubles from $169. AE, DISC, MC, V. Bus: 101. Map p 135.*

★★ El Cordova Hotel CORONADO With its courtyard, meandering pathways, and prime location across from the Hotel del Coronado, this Spanish hacienda is a popular option. *1351 Orange Ave. (at Adella Ave.). ☎ 844/591-8930. www.elcordovahotel.com. 40 units. Doubles from $169. AE, DISC, MC, V. Bus: 901 or 904. Map p 135.*

★★★ Estancia La Jolla Hotel and Spa LA JOLLA This romantic, California rancho-style property features meticulously maintained gardens, an award-winning restaurant, and an indulgent spa. *9700 N. Torrey Pines Rd. (north of Almahurst Row). ☎ 877/437-8262. www.estancialajolla.com. 210 units. Doubles from $219. AE, DISC, MC, V. Bus: 101. Map p 135.*

★★★ Fairmont Grand Del Mar DEL MAR The name is no idle boast. Resembling a Tuscan villa, this luxury resort has a Vegas-like opulence and incorporates a Tom Fazio–designed golf course and one of San Diego's finest restaurants. *5300 Grand Del Mar Court (off Carmel Country Rd.). ☎ 855/314-2030. www.thegranddelmar.com. 249 units. Doubles from $395. AE, DC, DISC, MC, V. No public transportation. Map p 135.*

★★ Gaslamp Plaza Suites GASLAMP QUARTER At 11 stories, this was San Diego's first skyscraper, built in 1913. Most rooms are spacious and offer luxuries rare in this price range. *520 E St. (corner of Fifth Ave.). ☎ 800/874-8770. www.gaslampplaza.com. 64 units. Doubles from $119 w/breakfast. AE, DISC, MC, V. Bus: 3, 120, or any Broadway route. Trolley: Blue or Orange Line to Fifth Ave. Map p 133.*

Pool at the Fairmont Grand Del Mar.

★★★ **Glorietta Bay Inn** CORONADO Across the street from the Hotel del Coronado, this pretty hotel consists of the charmingly historic John D. Spreckels mansion (1908) and several less attractive motel-style buildings. *1630 Glorietta Blvd. (near Orange Ave.). ☎ 800/283-9383. www.gloriettabayinn.com. 100 units. Doubles from $149 w/breakfast. AE, DISC, MC, V. Bus: 901 or 904. Map p 135.*

★★★ **The Grande Colonial** LA JOLLA This refined, elegant hotel possesses an old-world European flair that's more London or Georgetown than seaside La Jolla. *910 Prospect St. (btw. Fay & Girard aves.). ☎ 888/828-5498. www.thegrandecolonial.com. 93 units. Doubles from $219. AE, MC, V. Bus: 30. Map p 134.*

★★ **Hard Rock Hotel San Diego** GASLAMP QUARTER This 12-story condo-hotel has a sweet location, a celebrity-chef restaurant, and an outdoor concert space. The Black Eyed Peas designed one of the "Rock Star" suites. *207 Fifth Ave. (btw. K & L sts.). ☎ 866/751-7625. www.hardrockhotelsd.com. 420 units. Doubles from $249. AE, DISC, MC, V. Trolley: Orange Line to Gaslamp Quarter. Map p 133.*

★★ **Hilton San Diego Gaslamp Quarter** GASLAMP QUARTER This handsome hotel incorporates elements of a historic building. It's also a great place for guests who want to be in the heart of the Gaslamp action. *401 K St. (at Fourth Ave.). ☎ 800/445-8667. www3.hilton.com. 283 units. Doubles from $170. AE, DC, DISC, MC, V. Trolley: Orange Line to Gaslamp Quarter or Convention Center. Map p 133.*

★ kids **Holiday Inn Bayside** POINT LOMA With one new tower in 2016, this sprawling property is close to the airport, the Embarcadero, and downtown and has plenty of family-friendly amenities. *4875 N. Harbor Dr. (at Ash St.). ☎ 800/662-8899. www.holinnbayside.com. 291 units. Doubles from $160. AE, DC, MC, V. Bus: 28. Map p 135.*

Hotel Del Coronado.

Guest room at Hotel Indigo overlooking PETCO Park.

★ **Horton Grand** GASLAMP QUARTER The charming Horton Grand combines two hotels built in 1886. Both were saved from demolition and moved to this spot. *311 Island Ave. (at 4th Ave.). ☎ 800/542-1886. www.hortongrand.com. 132 units. Doubles from $179. AE, MC, V. Bus: 3, 11, or 120. Trolley: Orange Line to Convention Center. Map p 133.*

★★★ **Hotel del Coronado** CORONADO Opened in 1888 and designated a National Historic Landmark in 1977, the Hotel Del is the last of California's stately old seaside hotels and a monument to Victorian grandeur. *1500 Orange Ave. (at Dana Pl.). ☎ 800/468-3533. www.hoteldel.com. 757 rooms. Doubles from $350. AE, DC, DISC, MC, V. Bus: 901 or 904. Map p 135.*

★★ **Hotel Indigo** EAST VILLAGE Green is the primary color at this boutique property—it's San Diego's first LEED-certified hotel. The state-of-the-art rooms have a livable, residential feel and don't scrimp on comfort. Pets are welcome and pampered. *509 Ninth Ave. (at Island Ave.). ☎ 877/834-3613. www.hotelindigo.com/sandiego. 210 units. Doubles from $259. AE, DC, DISC, MC, V. Bus: 3, 11, 901, or 929. Map p 133.*

★★ **Hotel Palomar** DOWNTOWN This high-style, design-centric hotel features an Asian-chic vibe and a happening pool lounge where the beautiful people come to party. *1047 Fifth Ave. (at Broadway). ☎ 888/288-6601. www.hotelpalomar-sandiego.com. 184 units. Doubles from $239. AE, DISC, MC, V. Bus: 3, 120, or numerous Broadway routes. Trolley: Fifth Ave. Map p 133.*

★★ **Hotel Solamar** GASLAMP QUARTER This stylishly urban and sophisticated property provides excellent Gaslamp digs. The 4th-floor pool bar is a hot spot.

Hotel Solomar.

The Fresca Spa Suite at Hotel Keating.

435 Sixth Ave. (btw. J St. & Island Ave.). ☎ 877/230-0300. www.hotelsolamar.com. 235 units. Doubles from $229. AE, DISC, MC, V. Bus: 3 or 120. Trolley: Orange Line to Gaslamp Quarter. Map p 133.

★ Inn at the Park HILLCREST This eight-story property, built in 1926, occupies a prime corner overlooking Balboa Park. Rooms have fully stocked kitchens and there's a guest laundry, making it a good choice for extended stays. *525 Spruce St. (btw. Fifth & Sixth aves.). ☎ 877/499-7163. www.shellhospitality.com. 82 units. Doubles from $149. AE, DISC, MC, V. Bus: 3 or 120. Map p 135.*

★ Inn by the Sea LA JOLLA Occupying an enviable location in the heart of La Jolla's charming village, this property is just a short walk from the cliffs and beach. *7830 Fay Ave. (btw. Prospect & Silverado sts.). ☎ 800/526-4545. www.innbytheseaatlajolla.com. 129 units. Doubles from $135 w/breakfast. AE, DISC, MC, V. Bus: 30. Map p 134.*

★★ Keating Hotel GASLAMP QUARTER The Italian design group behind Ferrari and Maserati made its first foray into hotel design with this ultra-contemporary project, set in a gorgeous structure built in 1890. *432 F St. (btw. Fourth & Fifth aves.). ☎ 619/814-5700. www.thekeating.com. 35 units. Doubles from $189. AE, DISC, MC, V. Bus: 3, 120, or 992. Map p 133.*

★★★ L'Auberge Del Mar Resort & Spa DEL MAR An excellent spa and one of the area's finest restaurants highlight this elegant hotel, across from Del Mar's shopping and dining scene, and a short walk (down a private path) from the beach. *1540 Camino del Mar (at 15th St.). ☎ 800/245-9757. www.laubergedelmar.com. 120 units. Doubles from $380. AE, DC, MC, V. Bus: 101. Map p 135.*

★ La Jolla Cove Suites LA JOLLA Across from Ellen Browning Scripps Park, this family-run, updated 1950s-era hotel has to-die-for ocean views and is steps away from the Cove. *1155 Coast Blvd. (across from La Jolla Cove). ☎ 858/459-2621. www.lajollacove.com. 113 units. Doubles from $140. AE, DISC, MC, V. Bus: 30. Map p 134.*

★ kids La Jolla Shores Hotel LA JOLLA Spend time on the beach right by your room or the courts at the adjacent La Jolla

Suite at La Valencia Hotel.

The Lodge at Torrey Pines.

Beach and Tennis Club at this three-story 1960s hotel in a mainly residential enclave. *8110 Camino del Oro (at Avenida de la Playa). ☎ 855/923-8058. www.ljshoreshotel.com. 128 units. Doubles from $229. AE, DISC, MC, V. Bus: 30. Map p 135.*

★★ La Pensione Hotel LITTLE ITALY This place has a lot going for it: modern amenities, remarkable value, a convenient location, a friendly staff, and free parking. *606 W. Date St. (at India St.). ☎ 800/232-4683. www.lapensionehotel.com. 75 units. Doubles from $130. MC, V. Bus: 83. Trolley: Blue Line to County Cntr/Little Italy. Map p 133.*

★★★ La Valencia Hotel LA JOLLA This bluff-top hotel, which looks like a Mediterranean villa, has been the centerpiece of La Jolla since opening in 1926; a recent remodel replaced the venerable Whaling Bar with a French cafe. *1132 Prospect St. (at Herschel Ave.). ☎ 858/454-0771. www.lavalencia.com. 113 units. Doubles from $265. AE, DC, DISC, MC, V. Bus: 30. Map p 134.*

★ Les Artistes DEL MAR A funky, informal hotel, just a few blocks from downtown Del Mar, where the rooms have been redone as tributes to favored artists like Diego Rivera. *944 Camino del Mar (btw. Ninth & 10th sts.). ☎ 858/755-4646. www.lesartistesinn.com. 12 units. Doubles from $179 w/breakfast. MC, V. Bus: 101. Map p 135.*

★★★ The Lodge at Torrey Pines LA JOLLA This resort is a Craftsman-style fantasy brimming with clinker-brick masonry, Stickley furniture, and exquisite pottery. Some rooms overlook the golf course and the ocean. *11480 N. Torrey Pines Rd. (at Callan Rd.). ☎ 858/453-4420. www.lodgetorreypines.com. 171 units. Doubles from $305. AE, DC, DISC, MC, V. Bus: 101. Map p 135.*

Sea Spa at Lowes Coronado.

The Splash Landing pool area at Omni La Costa.

★★ kids **Loews Coronado Bay Resort** CORONADO Located on its own private peninsula 4 miles (6.5km) south of downtown Coronado, this isolated resort destination has a plethora of water-related activities. *4000 Coronado Bay Rd. (off Silver Strand Blvd.). ☎ 800/235-6397. www.loewshotels.com. 439 units. Doubles from $219. AE, DC, DISC, MC, V. Bus: 901. Map p 135.*

★ **Manchester Grand Hyatt San Diego** EMBARCADERO This twin-towered behemoth is adjacent to the Convention Center and Seaport Village shopping center, creating a neatly insular, if touristy, little world. *1 Market Place (Market St. at Harbor Dr.). ☎ 619/232-1234. www.manchestergrand.hyatt.com. 1,628 units. Doubles from $269. AE, DC, DISC, MC, V. Trolley: Orange Line to Seaport Village. Map p 133.*

★★ **Marriott San Diego Gaslamp Quarter** GASLAMP QUARTER This formerly mainstream hotel now has a stylish boutique feel. Check out the open-air bar on the 22nd floor. *660 K St. (btw. Sixth & Seventh aves.). ☎ 888/800-8118. www.sandiegogaslamphotel.com. 306 units. Doubles from $209. AE, DC, DISC, MC, V. Trolley: Orange Line to Gaslamp Quarter. Map p 133.*

★ **Marriott San Diego Hotel & Marina** EMBARCADERO Convention goers are drawn to the scenic 446-slip marina, lush grounds, waterfall pool, and breathtaking bay-and-beyond views. *333 W. Harbor Dr. (at Front St.). ☎ 800/228-9290. www.marriott.com. 1,360 units. Doubles from $289. AE, DC, DISC, MC, V. Trolley: Orange Line to Convention Center. Map p 133.*

★★ kids **Omni La Costa Resort and Spa** CARLSBAD This campus-like golf and tennis resort has a California mission style. There's also a 42-room spa and the new-age Chopra Center for adults, and waterslides and entertainment for the kids. *2100 Costa del Mar Rd. (at El Camino Real). ☎ 888/444-6664. www.omnihotels.com. 610 units. Doubles from $299. AE, DC, DISC, MC, V. Bus: 309. Map p 133.*

★★★ **Omni San Diego Hotel** GASLAMP QUARTER This swank 32-story high-rise has lots of

A room at the Manchester Grand Hyatt.

An aerial view of Paradise Point.

baseball memorabilia and a 4th-floor "skybridge" that connects it with PETCO Park—it's baseball fan heaven and a great downtown option whatever your interests. *675 L St. (at Sixth Ave.). ☎ 888/444-6664. www.omnihotels.com. 511 units. Doubles from $229. AE, DC, DISC, MC, V. Trolley: Orange Line to Gaslamp Quarter. Map p 133.*

★ Pacific Terrace Hotel PACIFIC BEACH More upscale than most of the casual places nearby, this boardwalk hotel features a South Seas–meets–Spanish Colonial ambience. *610 Diamond St. (west of Mission Blvd.). ☎ 800/344-3370. www.pacificterrace.com. 73 units. Doubles from $264. AE, DISC, MC, V. Bus: 30. Map p 134.*

★★★ kids Paradise Point Resort & Spa MISSION BAY Smack dab in the middle of Mission Bay, this hotel complex rambles over 44 acres beside Mission Bay. Low-rise cottages with parking spots are clustered by the beach and several pools. *1404 Vacation Rd. (off Ingraham St.). ☎ 800/344-2626. www.paradisepoint.com. 462 units. Doubles from $242. AE, DC, DISC, MC, V. Bus: 8/9. Map p 134.*

★★★ Park Hyatt Aviara Resort CARLSBAD This ocean-view property is no longer a Four Seasons, but it's still a sumptuous resort with an outstanding spa, restaurant, and golf course. *7100 Four Seasons Point (at Aviara Pkwy.). ☎ 760/448-1234. www.parkaviara.hyatt.com. 329 units. Doubles from $280. AE, DC, DISC, MC, V. No public transportation. Map p 135.*

★ Porto Vista Hotel & Suites DOWNTOWN The least-expensive rooms are simple, but as the price climbs, amenities include bathtubs, balconies with bay views, and expanded wet bars including coffeemaker (in all rooms), microwave, and fridge. *1835 Columbia St. (at Broadway). ☎ 619/544-0164. www.portovistasd.com. 189 units. Doubles from $115. MC, V. Bus: 3, 120, or numerous Broadway routes. Trolley: America Plaza. Map p 133.*

★ The Sofia Hotel DOWNTOWN This remake of one of San Diego's oldest hotels has a European feel with tiny rooms and a fun brasserie. *150 W. Broadway (at First Ave.) ☎ 619/234-9200. www.thesofiahotel.com. 211 units. Doubles from $199. MC, V. Bus: 2, 7, 923, 929 & all Broadway routes. Trolley: Blue or Orange Line to Civic Center. Map p 133.*

★★★ Tower 23 PACIFIC BEACH This sophisticated modernist beach hotel with a great

Patio of Tower 23.

restaurant and popular bar sits right alongside the boardwalk in Pacific Beach. *723 Felspar St. (west of Mission Blvd.). ☎ 866/869-3723. www.t23hotel.com. 44 units. Doubles from $359. AE, MC, V. Bus: 8/9, 27, or 30. Map p 134.*

★★★ **The US Grant** DOWNTOWN Built in 1910, this grandiose 11-story property is a Beaux Arts beauty and one of San Diego's most historic hotels. The clubby Grant Grill has long been a spot for power lunches and dinners. *326 Broadway (btw. Third & Fourth aves., main entrance on Fourth Ave.). ☎ 866/716-8136. www.usgrant.net. 270 units. Doubles from $279. AE, DC, DISC, MC, V. Bus: 2, 3, 120, 992 & all Broadway routes. Trolley: Orange or Blue Line to Civic Center. Map p 133.*

★★ **Wave Crest** DEL MAR On a bluff overlooking the Pacific, these gray-shingled bungalow condominiums are beautifully maintained and wonderfully private. *1400 Ocean Ave. (south of 15th St.). ☎ 858/755-0100. www.wavecrestresort.com. 31 units. Studios from $220. MC, V. Bus: 101. Map p 135.*

★★ **The Westgate Hotel** DOWNTOWN With its regal and lavish decor, this is about as "old world" as San Diego gets. It's a hub of cultural and culinary activities, as well. *1055 Second Ave. (btw. Broadway & C St.). ☎ 800/522-1564. www.westgatehotel.com. 223 units. Doubles from $155. AE, DC, DISC, MC, V. Bus: 2, 7, 923, 929 & all Broadway routes. Trolley: Blue or Orange Line to Civic Center. Map p 133.* ●

The US Grant.

10 The Best Day Trips

North County

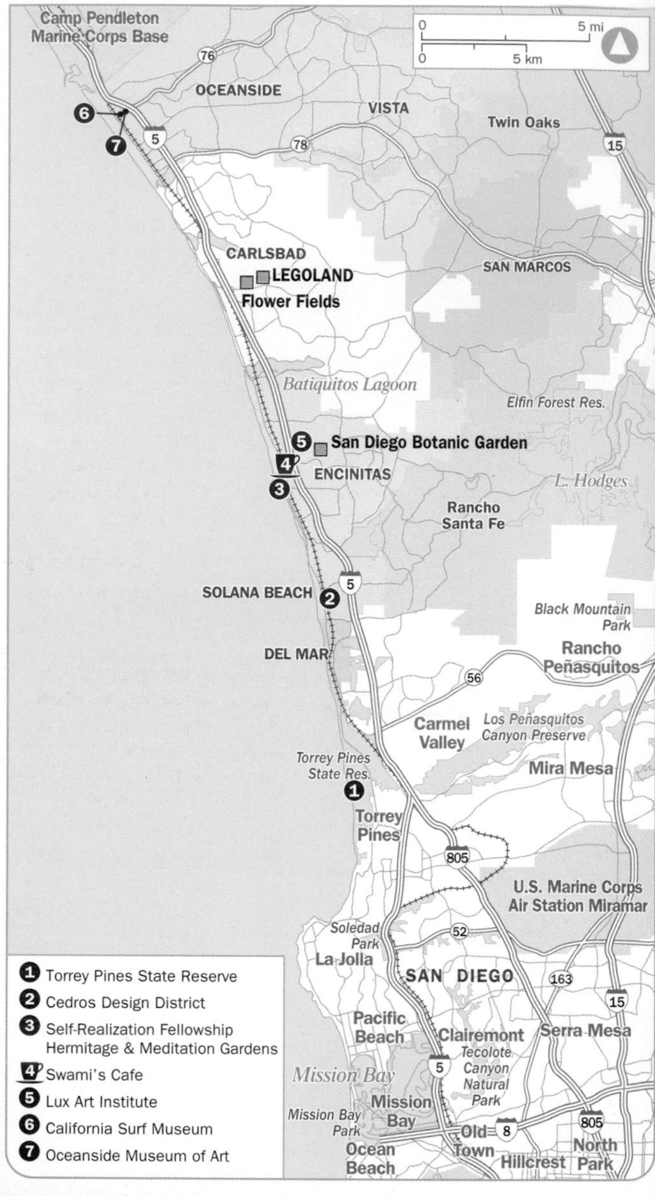
Camp Pendleton Marine Corps Base
OCEANSIDE
VISTA
Twin Oaks
CARLSBAD
LEGOLAND
Flower Fields
SAN MARCOS
Batiquitos Lagoon
Elfin Forest Res.
San Diego Botanic Garden
ENCINITAS
L. Hodges
Rancho Santa Fe
SOLANA BEACH
Black Mountain Park
DEL MAR
Rancho Peñasquitos
Carmel Valley
Los Peñasquitos Canyon Preserve
Mira Mesa
Torrey Pines State Res.
Torrey Pines
U.S. Marine Corps Air Station Miramar
Soledad Park
La Jolla
SAN DIEGO
Pacific Beach
Clairemont
Serra Mesa
Tecolote Canyon Natural Park
Mission Bay
Mission Bay Park
Mission Bay
Ocean Beach
Old Town
Hillcrest
North Park
0 5 mi
0 5 km
1 Torrey Pines State Reserve
2 Cedros Design District
3 Self-Realization Fellowship Hermitage & Meditation Gardens
4 Swami's Cafe
5 Lux Art Institute
6 California Surf Museum
7 Oceanside Museum of Art

Previous page: Balloon ride in Temecula.

Don't be fooled by the laidback, surf-dude ethic that prevails among the string of picturesque coastal communities north of La Jolla. For decades, the area's slower pace and stunning physical beauty have attracted artists, writers, celebrities, spiritualists, and others who could afford a piece of coastal solitude. The result is a casual sophistication and territorial pride that distinguishes this region from the county's lower reaches. **START: Del Mar is 18 miles (29km) north of downtown San Diego, Carlsbad about 33 miles (53km), and Oceanside approximately 36 miles (58km). If you're driving, follow I-5 north; Del Mar, Solana Beach, Encinitas, Carlsbad, and Oceanside all have freeway exits. The northernmost point, Oceanside, will take about 45 minutes. The other choice by car is to wander up the old coast road, known as Camino del Mar, "PCH" (Pacific Coast Highway), Old Highway 101, and County Highway S21. The Breeze 101 bus route traverses 101 from La Jolla to Oceanside. From San Diego, the Coaster commuter train provides service to Solana Beach, Encinitas, Carlsbad, and Oceanside, and Amtrak stops in Solana Beach and Oceanside. The Coaster makes the trip a number of times (6:30am–7pm) on weekdays, four times on Saturday; Amtrak passes through about 11 times daily each way. For the Coaster, call ☎ 800/262-7837 or 511, or visit www.transit.511sd.com; check with Amtrak at ☎ 800/872-7245 or www.amtrak.com. If you are driving, be aware of rush-hour traffic.**

❶ ★★★ Torrey Pines State Natural Reserve. Simply one of the most breathtaking locations in San Diego County, this park is home to the gnarled little tree that's the rarest native pine in North America. ⏲ *At least 1 hr.* *See p 93.*

❷ ★★★ Cedros Design District. This vivacious neighborhood is loaded with home decor and clothing boutiques, art galleries, and cafes. ⏲ *At least 1 hr.* *See p 78.*

❸ ★★ Self-Realization Fellowship Hermitage and Meditation Gardens. Paramahansa Yogananda, a guru born and educated in India, opened this retreat with the exotic lotus domes in 1937. He lived for many years in the

Torrey Pines Natural State Reserve.

Hermitage, and today the site serves as a spiritual sanctuary for his followers. The serene meditation gardens offer spectacular ocean views and are a terrific place to cool off on a hot day (and no disciples will give you a sales pitch). *⏲ 30 min. 215 W. K St. (off S. Coast Hwy. 101). ☎ 760/753-2888. www.yogananda-srf.org. Free admission. Tues–Sat 9am–5pm, Sun 11am–5pm (Hermitage open Sun 2–5pm).*

Meditation Gardens, Self-Realization Fellowship.

Locals crowd into casual 4 ★ **Swami's Cafe** for tasty, health-conscious breakfasts and lunch. It gets its name from the legendary surf spot across the highway, which in turn was named for the yogi's retreat on the clifftop. *1163 S. Coast Hwy. 101 (at W. K St.). ☎ 760/944-0612. www.swamiscafesd.com. Mon–Sat 7am–9pm, Sun 7am–3pm. $7–$12.*

5 ★★ Lux Art Institute. This unique facility allows visitors to watch as an artist in residence paints, sculpts, or draws in a studio environment. The building itself is a work of art. *⏲ 45 min. 1550 S. El Camino Real (north of Manchester Ave.). ☎ 760/436-6611. www.luxartinstitute.com. Admission $5 adults (good for 2 visits), free for ages 20 & under. Thurs–Fri 1–5pm; Sat 11am–5pm.*

6 ★ California Surf Museum. This slick, oceanfront facility opened in 2009 and features an extensive collection documenting the early days of surfing. The gift shop sells surf-themed goods. *⏲ 45 min. 312 Pier View Way (at N. Cleveland St.). ☎ 760/721-6876. www.surfmuseum.org. Admission $5 adults, $3 seniors & students, free for*

Grape Escape

Over the line in Riverside County, 60 miles (97km) north of San Diego via I-15, is the wine country of Temecula (pronounced "ta-*meck*-you-la"). Some believe Franciscan friars planted the first grapevines here in the early 1800s. There are now 25-plus wineries in the region (most are along Rancho California Road). Harvest time is generally from mid-August to September, but visitors are invited year-round to tour, taste, and stock up. For more information, contact the **Temecula Valley Winegrowers Association** (☎ 800/801-9463; www.temeculawines.org) or the **Temecula Valley Convention and Visitors Bureau** (☎ 888/363-2852; www.temeculacvb.com), which can provide information on accommodations, golf, fishing, and the Temecula Valley Balloon & Wine Festival, held in June. **Grapeline** (☎ 888/894-6379; www.gogrape.com) can pick you up from your hotel and shuttle you on a wine country tour.

Flower Power

San Diego's North County is a noted flower-growing region, and there are two places that will be of special interest to the horticulturally minded: the ★ **San Diego Botanic Garden** in Encinitas and the ★ **Flower Fields** at Carlsbad. The serene Botanic Garden, 230 Quail Gardens Dr. (☎ 760/436-3036; www.sdbgarden.org), boasts the country's largest bamboo collection, plus some 35 acres (14 hectares) of native and exotic flora. The Flower Fields, 5704 Paseo del Norte (☎ 760/431-0352; www.theflowerfields.com), is a working nursery where a spectacular sea of ranunculus blossom every March to mid-May. Visitors can tour the grounds and enjoy a number of special floral installations.

Flower Fields at Carlsbad.

kids 11 & under. Daily 10am–4pm (Thurs till 8pm).

7 ★★ Oceanside Museum of Art. Cutting-edge and classic California Deco architecture cozy up together at this beautiful museum presenting contemporary artwork by both regional and international artists. 🕓 *45 min. 704 Pier View Way (at N. Ditmar St.) ☎ 760/435-3720. www.oma-online.org. Admission $8 adults, $5 seniors, free for students & military. Tues–Sat 10am–4pm, Sun 1–4pm.*

Julian

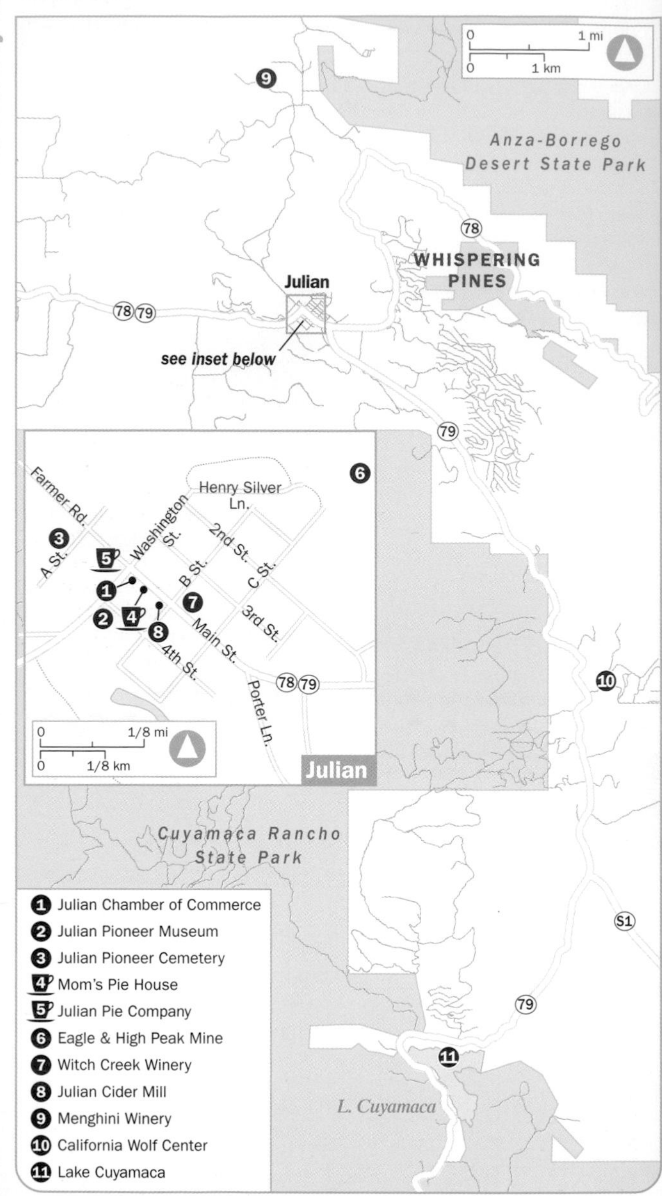

0 1 mi
0 1 km
Anza-Borrego
Desert State Park
78
WHISPERING
PINES
Julian
78 79
see inset below
79
Farmer Rd.
Henry Silver
Ln.
Washington
St.
2nd St.
A St.
B St.
C St.
3rd St.
Main St.
4th St.
78 79
Porter Ln.
0 1/8 mi
0 1/8 km
Julian
Cuyamaca Rancho
State Park
S1
79
L. Cuyamaca
1 Julian Chamber of Commerce
2 Julian Pioneer Museum
3 Julian Pioneer Cemetery
4 Mom's Pie House
5 Julian Pie Company
6 Eagle & High Peak Mine
7 Witch Creek Winery
8 Julian Cider Mill
9 Menghini Winery
10 California Wolf Center
11 Lake Cuyamaca

A trip to Julian offers a taste of the Old West, and its successor in these parts: the apple. Prospectors first ventured into these fertile hills (elevation 4,225 feet/1,288m) in search of gold in the late 1860s, and within 10 years, 18 mines were operating, producing up to an estimated $13 million worth of gold. After the rush played out, this quaint Victorian town (pop. 3,000) found fame thanks to another mother lode: apples. **START: Julian is not accessible via public transportation. You can make the 90-minute drive on Highway 78 or I-8 to Highway 79; try taking one route going and the other on the way back (Highway 79 winds through Rancho Cuyamaca State Park, while Highway 78 traverses open country and farmland). Weekend crowds can be heavy, especially during the fall apple-harvest season. Fall temperatures are brisk; snow is possible in winter.**

❶ Julian Chamber of Commerce. Located in the foyer of the creaky old Town Hall (built in 1913), the visitors center is where you can find enthusiastic staffers who always have suggestions for local activities and events. Before you leave the visitors center, be sure to duck into the auditorium itself to check out the photos of Julian's bygone days. Main Street is only 6 blocks long, and shops, cafes, and some lodgings are on it or a block away—town maps and accommodations fliers are available on the Town Hall porch. Public restrooms are behind the building. *2129 Main St. (at Washington St.). ☎ 760/765-1857. www.julianca.com. Daily 10am–4pm.*

A horse-drawn carriage ride in Julian.

❷ Julian Pioneer Museum. This small museum is dedicated to illuminating the life and times of Julian's townspeople from 1869 to 1913. It displays clothing, tools, gold-mining equipment, household and military items, and a fine collection of lace doilies, quilts, and scarves. Look out back for the Julian Transportation Garage museum, with its vintage machinery and vehicles. The museum is staffed by volunteers and hours vary. ⏱ *30 min. 2811 Washington St. (south of Fourth St.). ☎ 760/765-0227. www.julianpioneermuseum.org. $3 donation requested. Thurs–Sat 10am–4pm.*

❸ ★ Julian Pioneer Cemetery. This small, hillside graveyard is straight out of *Our Town.* Julian's citizenry have been laid to rest here since 1870, when the only way to deliver caskets to the gravesite was to carry them up the long, stone staircase in front. If you don't want to huff and puff up the stairs (just imagine carrying a casket), there's a parking lot behind the cemetery that provides easy access. ⏱ *20 min. A St. (at Farmer Rd).*

You've waited long enough—it's time for some pie. You can observe the mom-on-duty rolling crust and crimping edges at 4 ★★ **Mom's Pie House.** The shop routinely bakes several varieties of apple pie as well as seasonal specialties. A limited selection of sandwiches and soups is available at lunchtime. *2119 Main St. ☎ 760/765-2472. www.momspiesjulian.com. Mon–Thurs 7am–5pm; Fri & Sun 7am–5:30pm; Sat 7am–6pm. $5–$18.*

Or enjoy the outdoor seating at 5 ★★ **Julian Pie Company,** where overhanging apples are literally up for grabs. Among its specialties is a no-sugar-added pie; light lunches of soup and sandwiches are offered weekdays (11am–2pm). *2225 Main St. ☎ 760/765-2449. www.julianpie.com. Daily 9am–5pm. $5–$16.*

Fresh picked fruit in Julian.

6 ★ kids **Eagle and High Peak Mine.** Although seemingly a tourist trap, this mine, which dates from around 1870, offers an interesting and educational look at the town's one-time economic mainstay. Tours take you underground to the 1,000-foot (305m) hard-rock tunnel to see the mining and milling process; antique engines and authentic tools are on display. ◷ *1 hr. End of C St. (at Old Miner's Trail). ☎ 442/777-8646. www.theeaglemining.com. $10 adults, $5 children 6–11, $1 for children under 6 (cash only). Hour-long tours are usually given beginning at 10am, but hours vary so it's best to call ahead.*

Freshly baked pies in Julian.

7 **Witch Creek Winery.** There are a handful of wineries in the Julian area, but this is the only wine-tasting operation right in town. What it lacks in ambience, it makes up for in convenience and friendliness. ◷ *30 min. 2000 Main St. (btw. B & C sts.). ☎ 760/765-2023. www.witchcreekwinery.com. Daily 11am–5pm.*

8 ★★ **Julian Cider Mill.** You can see cider presses at work here October through March. It offers free tastes of the fresh nectar, and jugs to take home. Throughout the year, the mill also carries the area's widest selection of food products, from apple butters and jams to berry preserves, several varieties of local honey, candies, and other goodies. ◷ *20 min. 2103 Main St.*

(at B St.). ☎ 760/765-1430. www.juliancidermillinc.com. Mon–Thurs 9:30am–5pm, Fri–Sun 9:30am–5:30pm.

❾ ★★ **Menghini Winery.** The rustic facilities and rolling picnic grounds of this winery make it a popular spot not only for wine tasting, but also for special events like the annual Grape Stomp Festa and Julian Music Festival in September, and the Apple Days Festival in October. It's located about 3 miles (5km) out of town. ◷ *1 hr. 1150 Julian Orchards Dr. (at Wynola Rd.). ☎ 760/765-2072. www.menghiniwinery.com. Mon–Fri 10am–4pm, Sat–Sun 10am–5pm.*

❿ ★★ kids **California Wolf Center.** Animal lovers should look into this education and conservation center, located about 4 miles (6.5km) from town, where you can learn about wolves and visit with the resident wolf pack. Reservations required. ◷ *1 hr. 18457 Hwy. 79 (at KQ Ranch Campground, look for Wolf Center sign). ☎ 760/765-0030. www.californiawolfcenter.org. Admission $20 for adults, $15 for seniors, military, students and children 12 and under. Sat & Sun at 10am & 2pm; private tours can be arranged.*

⓫ ★ kids **Lake Cuyamaca.** Eight miles (13km) south of Julian, this 110-acre (45-hectare) lake offers boating, fishing, and camping. Anglers try for trout (stocked year-round), bass, catfish, crappie, and bluegill. There's also a general store and restaurant at the lake's edge. ◷ *At least 1 hr. 15027 Hwy. 79 (btw. Milk Ranch & Wolahi roads.). ☎ 877/581-9904. www.lakecuyamaca.org. Fishing fee $8 per day, $4 per day for ages 8–15, free for children under 8. A California fishing license is required & sold here: $14.86 for the day. Rowboats $25 per day, motorboat $50 per day ($35 after 1pm), canoes & paddleboats (summer only) $15 per hour. Daily 6am–sunset (weather permitting).*

Tijuana

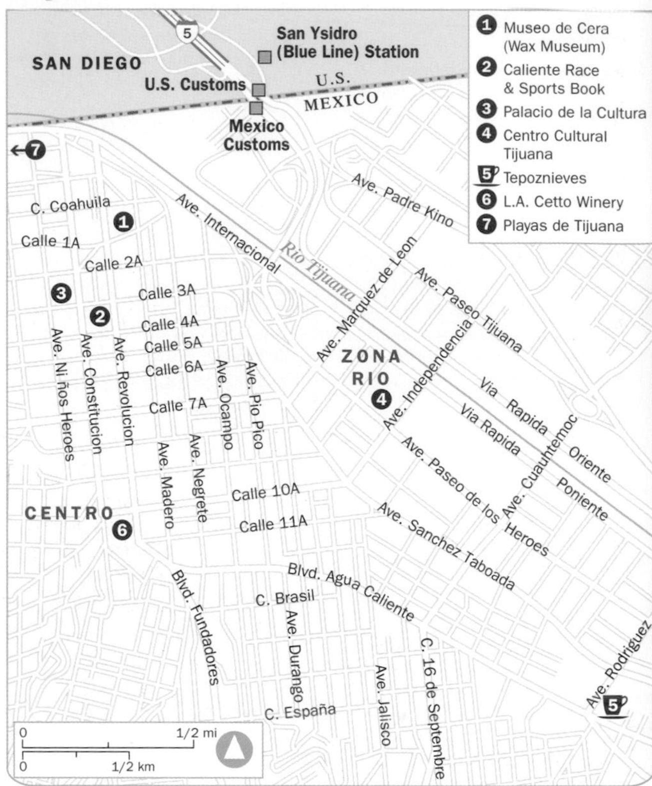

Vibrant, chaotic, colorful, and confounding, Tijuana is Mexico's fourth-largest city and just a 20-minute drive from downtown San Diego. T.J., as San Diegans call it, was little more than a village at the turn of the 20th century, but it grew explosively in response to the needs of San Diego and the rest of California, providing a workforce for factories and fields, especially during World War II. It also offered succor, becoming a decadent playground for Americans deprived of booze and gambling by Prohibition and moral reformers. Today's Tijuana, unfortunately, does not possess an attractive urban landscape—its beauty lies within its fabulous restaurants, burgeoning art and music scene, plentiful shopping opportunities, and legendary nightlife. **START: Take the Blue Line trolley to San Ysidro (it's the last stop). From the trolley, cross the street**

and head up the ramp that accesses the border-crossing bridge. Tijuana's shopping and nightlife district, Avenida Revolución, is a $5 taxi ride from the border, or you can walk the mile (.6km) into the tourist area. The trolley takes about 40 minutes from downtown San Diego; the one-way fare is $2.50. The last trolley to San Ysidro departs downtown around midnight (3am on Sat); the last returning trolley from San Ysidro is at 1am (2am on Sat). Unless you plan on driving farther into Mexico, it's best to park your car on the U.S. side and walk across. Taxis are cheap, plentiful, and safe in Tijuana (you will need to negotiate a price with cab drivers; the white taxis with red stripes are metered and a better deal). If you drive, take I-5 south; purchasing Mexican auto insurance north of the border is also highly recommended.

❶ Museo de Cera (Wax Museum). This creepy sideshow is filled with characters from Mexican history and lore, and includes a few incongruous figures like Bill Clinton and Whoopi Goldberg. And despite her presence here, there was no kindly rancho matriarch named Tía (aunt) Juana for whom the city was named. Tijuana derives its name from "tycuan," an indigenous word meaning "near the water," a reference to a broad, shallow river that is now little more than a trickle (except during storms) running down a concrete wash. 🕔 *30 min. 8281 Calle 1 (btw. avs. Revolución & Maderas).* ☎ *664/688-2478. Admission $2. Daily 10am–6pm.*

The Millennial Arch at Avenida Revolución.

❷ Caliente Race & Sports Book. This attractive, flagstone-fronted space has all the bells and whistles of a Vegas sports book. You can bet on international sporting events including NFL, NBA, and soccer games; there's also electronic gaming. About a 10-minute cab ride away is Hipódromo Caliente (Caliente Racetrack), at Blv. Agua Caliente and Tapachula (☎ 664/633-7300), where there's daily greyhound racing. It's also home to the Estadio Caliente stadium and Los Xolos, Tijuana's hugely popular and successful soccer team. 🕔 *At least 15 min. Av. Revolución at Calle 4.* ☎ *664/688-3425. www.caliente.com.mx. Hours vary but usually daily 11am–midnight.*

❸ ★ Palacio de la Cultura. Showcasing the work of local artists, this large complex is set in the Antigua Palacio Municipal, which served as a seat of government from 1930 to 1986, and is one of the area's few remaining historical buildings. This is a great side trip off touristy Revolución—adjacent are the Cathedral and Mercado el Popo, a quintessentially Mexican marketplace selling nuts, candy, and produce. 🕔 *1 hr. Calle 2 at Av.*

Crossing the World's Busiest International Border

U.S. citizens need a passport, passport card, or similarly secure document such as a SENTRI card (used by frequent border crossers) to cross the border; those 15 and under must have a birth certificate or naturalization certificate. Non-U.S. citizens will need a passport, an I-94, a multiple-entry visa, or a Resident Alien Card. For more information, check with the U.S. Department of State (☎ 202/647-5225; www.travel.state.gov) before your visit. Waits of up to 2 hours are not uncommon when crossing back to the U.S.

If you walk across to Mexico, the first structure you'll see on your left is a **Visitor Information Center** (☎ 664/607-3097), open daily 9am to 6pm. Here you'll find maps, safety tips, and brochures that cover the city's highlights. There's also an information booth on the east side of Avenida Revolución at Third. The **Tijuana Convention & Visitors Bureau** (☎ 664/684-0537; www.descubretijuana.com) is across the street from the Centro Cultural at Paseo de los Héroes 9365, Suite 201. It's open Monday to Friday 9am to 6pm. For English-speaking tourist assistance, dial ☎ 078 (it operates 24/7); for emergencies, dial ☎ 066. When calling numbers from the U.S., dial 011-52 then the 10-digit number.

English is widely spoken and dollars are accepted just about everywhere; Visa and MasterCard are accepted in many places, but never assume they will be—ask before dining or purchasing. You're permitted to bring $800 worth of purchases back across the border duty-free, including 1 liter of alcohol per person (for adults 21 and older). You can also bring back about a month's supply (50 dosages) of some medicines that require a prescription in the U.S. In 2009, the Mexican government decriminalized possession of small amounts of drugs, including marijuana, cocaine, heroin, and LSD. This does not mean that you can't end up in a world of trouble if you're caught holding these substances. Do yourself a favor and stay away from narcotics and those who deal them while in Mexico.

The following countries have consulate offices in Tijuana: the United States (☎ 664/977-2000), Canada (☎ 664/684-0461), and the United Kingdom (☎ 664/681-7323).

The easiest way to visit TJ is with a guided tour. **Turista Libre** (www.turistalibre.com) offers fun, insightful tours focusing on street eats, sports, cultural, and other interests. The tours are led by an American journalist and start on the U.S. side of the border, alleviating all border-crossing dilemmas.

Centro Cultural Tijuana.

Constitución. ☎ 664/688-1721. www.imac.tijuana.gob.mx. Free admission. Hours vary but usually daily 10am–6pm.

❹ ★★ Centro Cultural Tijuana. A short cab ride away in the Zona Río is Tijuana's cultural icon, which opened in 1982. This ultramodern complex features a gigantic, sand-colored sphere, "La Bola," that houses an IMAX Dome Theater (some English-language films on weekends), and "El Cubo," a state-of-the-art gallery that hosts traveling exhibitions. CECUT (pronounced see-*coot*) also has a museum that covers the history of Tijuana and Baja, from pre-Hispanic times through the modern era (descriptions are in both Spanish and English). Music, theater, and dance performances are held in the center's acoustically excellent concert hall; there's also a cafe and a great museum bookshop. ⏱ *At least 1 hr. Paseo de los Héroes, at Av. Independencia. ☎ 664/687-9600. www.cecut.gob.mx. Museum admission $2; film & exhibition tickets vary. Tues–Sun 9am–9pm; extended hours for films & special events.*

In the heart of Tijuana's Zona Río fine-dining district, you'll find 5 **★ Tepoznieves.** This unique ice-cream parlor serves up treats that are sure to intrigue and delight, like wine- or spirit-infused sorbets, and traditional ice creams made with everything from rose petals to prunes (and yes, chocolate, too). *Blvd. Sánchez Taboada 10737 (at Francisco Sarabia). ☎ 664/634-6532. $1–$3.*

❻ ★★ L.A. Cetto Winery (Cava de Vinos). This impressive barrel-shaped winery and visitor center provides an introduction to Mexican viniculture. The Valle de Guadalupe, a fertile region southeast of Tijuana, produces most of Mexico's wine, and many high-quality vintages are exported to Europe; most are unavailable in the United States. L.A. Cetto also sells fine tequila, brandy, olive oil, and more. ⏱ *1 hr. Av. Cañón Johnson 2108 (at Av. Constitución Sur). ☎ 664/685-3031. www.cettowines.com. Admission $2 for tour & tasting (18 & over; under 18 are admitted free with an adult but cannot taste*

Tijuana Safety Alert

Violence rises and falls unpredictably in Tijuana, mostly due to the presence of organized drug-related crime—but tourists are not the targets. There is petty crime, too, so observe the same precautions as in any large city: Don't flash a lot of cash or expensive jewelry, and stick to populated areas. *Mordida,* "the bite," is also still known to occur. That's when uniformed police officers extort money in exchange for letting you off for some infraction, like a traffic ticket. If you find yourself dealing with an official, never offer a bribe—you may find yourself in much more trouble than you bargained for. And if you meet up with corruption, you have little recourse but to comply, and then report the incident to your consulate (be sure to note the officer's name, as well as badge and patrol car numbers, but be discreet as you do so). Another option is the city of Tijuana Internal Affairs 24-hour hotline at ☎ 664/688-2810; the San Diego Police Department will take crime reports and forward them to the proper agency as well. For the latest security advisories, go to http://travel.state.gov; you can also call toll-free ☎ 888/407-4747 Monday through Friday 5am to 5pm. From Mexico, dial 001-202-501-4444 (tolls apply).

the wines), $5 with souvenir wine glass. Mon–Sat 10am–5pm.

7 ★★ kids Playas de Tijuana. This large, sandy beach is popular among families. It features a line of ramshackle restaurants and cafes arranged on a bluff overlooking the surf, offering great spots for lunch and a cold beer. A stone's throw away is the bullring-by-the-sea known as Plaza Monumental; bullfighting season runs March to November (☎ 664/680-1808; www.plazamonumental.com). Perhaps the most notable thing here, though, is the imposing fence that disappears into the ocean, dividing the U.S. and Mexico. It provides a stark contrast to the laughing children splashing in the water next to it. ***At least 1 hr. About 6 miles (9.5km) west of the Zona Centro, off the scenic toll road that heads toward Rosarito & Ensenada (but before you reach the first toll booth).***

The Savvy Traveler

Before You Go

Tourist Offices

Contact the **San Diego Tourism Authority** (750 B St., Suite 1500, San Diego, CA 92101; ☎ 619/232-3101; www.sandiego.org). The *Official Visitors Planning Guide* features excellent maps and information on accommodations, activities, and attractions. The organization's **International Visitor Information Center** (☎ 619/236-1242; www.sandiego.org) is on the Embarcadero at 996B N. Harbor Dr. at Broadway (open daily 9am–4pm). The **La Jolla Village Information Center** is at 1162 Prospect St. (☎ 858-454-5718; www.lajollabythesea.com).This office is open daily in summer, from 10am until 6pm; from September to May the center is open daily from 10am until 5pm. The **Coronado Visitors Center** (1100 Orange Ave.; ☎ 619/437-8788; www.coronadovisitorcenter.com) dispenses maps, newsletters, and information-packed brochures. Inside the Coronado Museum, it's open Monday through Friday 9am to 5pm, Saturday and Sunday 10am to 5pm. For information about Del Mar, contact the **Del Mar Community & Visitor Center,** 1104 Camino del Mar, Del Mar (☎ 858/755-4844; www.delmarmainstreet.com). It's open Monday through Friday 9am to 4pm. The **Solana Beach Visitor Center** is near the train station at 103 N. Cedros (☎ 858/350-6006; www.visitsolanabeach.com). The **Carlsbad Visitor Information Center,** 400 Carlsbad Village Dr. (in the old Santa Fe Depot; ☎ 760/434-6093; www.visitcarlsbad.com), has information about LEGOLAND and flower fields and nursery touring. Oceanside's **California Welcome Center,** 928 N. Coast Hwy. (☎ 800/350-7873; www.visitoceanside.org), provides information on local attractions, dining, and accommodations; it also has a gift shop.

Previous page: Paddleboarding in Mission Bay.

The Best Times to Go

With its coastal setting, the city of San Diego maintains a moderate climate year-round. Although the temperature can change 20 to 30 degrees (F) between day and evening, it rarely reaches a point of extreme heat or cold; daytime highs above 100°F (38°C) are unusual, and the mercury dropping below freezing can be counted in mere hours once or twice each year. San Diego receives very little precipitation (just 10 in./103cm of rainfall in an average year); what rain does fall comes primarily between November and April. Fall and spring are great times to be here; beachgoers should note that late spring and early summer tanning sessions are often compromised by a local phenomenon called **May Gray** and **June Gloom**—a layer of low-lying clouds or fog along the coast that doesn't burn off until noon (if at all) and returns before sunset. San Diego is busiest between Memorial Day and Labor Day; if you visit in summer, expect fully booked beachfront hotels and crowded parking lots. The beach is at its best in September, when the crowds are gone, the water is still relatively warm, and the sun shines daily.

Festivals & Special Events

SPRING. Wildflowers bloom in the desert between late February and the end of March at **Anza-Borrego Desert State Park**

AVERAGE MONTHLY TEMPERATURES (°F & °C) & RAINFALL (IN.)

	JAN	FEB	MAR	APR	MAY	JUNE
High (°F/°C)	66/18	66/18	68/18	69/20	72/20	76/22
Low (°F/°C)	48/8	50/10	52/11	55/12	58/14	61/16
Days of Precip.	2.2	1.6	1.9	0.8	0.2	0.1

	JULY	AUG	SEPT	OCT	NOV	DEC
High (°F/°C)	77/24	77/25	74/25	71/23	66/21	42/18
Low (°F/°C)	65/18	66/18	65/18	60/15	53/11	49/9
Days of Precip.	0	0.1	0.2	0.4	1.1	1.4

(☎ 760/767-5311; www.parks.ca.gov). The peak of blooming lasts for a few weeks and timing varies from year to year, depending on the winter rainfall. **Mardi Gras in the Gaslamp Quarter** (☎ 619/233-5227; www.gaslamp.org) is the largest Mardi Gras party on the West Coast. The celebration of "Fat Tuesday" features a Mardi Gras parade and an outdoor celebration in downtown's historic Gaslamp Quarter. The **San Diego Latino Film Festival** (☎ 619/230-1938; www.sdlatinofilm.com), held in mid-March, has grown to become one of the largest and most successful Latino film events in the country. More than 100 movies from throughout Latin America and the United States are shown, complemented by gala parties, seminars, a music series, and art exhibits. The **St. Patrick's Day Parade** (☎ 858/268-9111; www.stpatsparade.org) takes place the Saturday prior to March 17; it's followed by a festival in Balboa Park. **The San Diego Crew Classic** (☎ 619/225-0300; www.crewclassic.org) brings thousands of rowers from around the country to Mission Bay. Some university alumni groups plan huge gatherings and cheer on their teams from the shore. The **Flower Fields at Carlsbad Ranch** (☎ 760/431-0352; www.theflowerfields.com) provides one of the most spectacular sights in North County: the yearly blossoming of a gigantic sea of bright ranunculuses during March and April. Visitors are welcome to view and tour the fields. **ArtWalk** (☎ 619/615-1090; www.missionfederalartwalk.org) is the largest art event in the San Diego/Tijuana region, showcasing hundreds of visual and performing artists. It takes place along the streets of Little Italy in late April. Held the weekend closest to May 5, **Fiesta Cinco de Mayo** (☎ 619/291-4903; www.cincodemayooldtown.com) commemorates the 1862 triumph of Mexican soldiers over the French. The festivities include a battle re-enactment, mariachi music, and margaritas galore.

SUMMER. The **Rock 'n' Roll Marathon** (☎ 800/311-1255; www.runrocknroll.com) in early June not only offers runners a unique course through Balboa Park, downtown, and around Mission Bay, it pumps them (and spectators) up with live bands on 26 stages along the course. There is a pre-race fitness expo and post-race concert, featuring big-name talent. Annually, the biggest local event is the **San Diego County Fair** (☎ 858/793-5555; www.sdfair.com), mid-June to early July. Livestock competitions, thrill rides, flower-and-garden shows, gem and mineral exhibits, food and crafts booths, carnival games, and home arts exhibits dominate the event. There are also grandstand concerts by name performers. The **World Championship Over the Line Tournament** (☎ 619/688-0817; www.ombac.org) in mid-July is a San Diego original. It's a beach softball event renowned for boisterous, beer-soaked, anything-goes behavior. The **San Diego LGBT Pride Parade, Rally, and Festival** (☎ 619/297-7683; www.sdpride.org), held the third or fourth weekend in July, is one of San Diego's biggest draws. It begins Friday night with a rally in Balboa Park, reconvenes at 11am on Saturday for a parade through Hillcrest, followed by a massive 2-day festival in the park. The "turf meets the surf" in Del Mar during the **thoroughbred racing season** at the Del Mar Race Track (☎ 858/755-1167; www.dmtc.com). The ponies run mid-July to early September and again in November. Upward of 60,000 people attend America's largest comic-book convention, **Comic-Con International** (☎ 619/491-2475; www.comic-con.org), each late July. It's a long weekend of auctions, dealers, celebrities, and seminars focusing on graphic novels, fantasy, and sci-fi. (***Note:*** Single-day tickets sell out; preregistration is encouraged.) **La Jolla SummerFest** (☎ 858/459-3728; www.ljms.org) is perhaps San Diego's most prestigious annual music event. It features a wide spectrum of classical and contemporary music, with guest composers and musicians ranging from the likes of Chick Corea to Yo-Yo Ma. SummerFest also offers master classes, open rehearsals, and workshops.

FALL. The country's largest rough-water swimming competition, the **La Jolla Rough Water Swim** (www.ljrws.com) began in 1916. It takes place the Sunday after Labor Day at La Jolla Cove. Up in the mountain town of Julian (☎ 760/765-1857; www.julianca.com), the **fall apple harvest** from mid-September to mid-November draws big crowds. Every weekend local artisans display their wares, and there's plenty of cider and apple pie, plus entertainment and brilliant fall foliage. San Diego's acclaimed local breweries, along with guest brewers from around California and beyond, strut their stuff at the **Festival of Beer** (www.sdbeerfest.org) in mid-September. Some 150 different beers are on tap, along with food and live music. **Fleet Week** (www.fleetweeksandiego.org) is a bit of a misnomer. It's the nation's largest military appreciation event and it lasts the entire month of October. It includes Navy ship tours, a college football game, an auto race of classic speedsters, and the renowned Miramar Air Show. One of the West's most impressive celebrations of Italian culture takes place at the **Little Italy Festa** (☎ 619/233-3898; www.littleitalysd.com) in mid-October. The streets come alive with traditional food, music, and entertainment, including stickball and chalk-art street painting competitions. The **San Diego Bay Wine & Food Festival** (☎ 619/312-1212; www.worldofwineevents.com), held in mid-November, is Southern California's biggest wine and culinary event. More than 200 wineries and restaurants participate. Some two-dozen bands perform at the **San Diego Thanksgiving Dixieland Jazz Festival** (☎ 619/297-5277; www.dixielandjazzfestival.org). This annual festival is held over the long Thanksgiving weekend and features vintage jazz sounds like ragtime, swing, and, of course, pure New Orleans Dixieland.

WINTER. During the first Friday and Saturday nights of December, San Diego's fine urban park is decked out in holiday splendor for **Balboa Park December Nights** (☎ 619/239-0512; www.balboapark.org). There's a candlelight procession, caroling, entertainment, and ethnic food; park museums are all free, too. **Whale-watching season** begins in mid-December and continues until about mid-March, as more than 20,000 Pacific gray whales make the trek from chilly Alaskan seas to the warm-water breeding lagoons of Baja California, and then back again. There are a variety of ways to witness the procession, from both land and sea (www.sandiego.org). San Diego is home to two college football bowl games: the **Holiday Bowl** (☎ 619/283-5808; www.holidaybowl.com) and the **Poinsettia Bowl** (☎ 619/285-5061; www.poinsettiabowl.net), both held in late December. The Holiday Bowl pits top teams from the Pac 10 and Big 12 Conferences; the Poinsettia Bowl pits a team from the Mountain West Conference against an at-large opponent. The Holiday Bowl features several special events, including the nation's biggest balloon parade of giant inflatable characters. The PGA Tour stop at Torrey Pines Golf Course has been an annual event since 1952, featuring the finest professional golfers in the world. Now known as the **Farmers Insurance Open** (☎ 858/886-4653; www.farmersinsuranceopen.com), it takes place in late January, attracting more than 100,000 spectators. Local restaurants of all levels offer special set-price dinners during **San Diego Restaurant Week** (www.sandiegorestaurantweek.com), which runs for 2 weeks in late January and again in mid-September. Reservations are a must.

Useful Websites

- **www.sandiego.org** is maintained by the San Diego Tourism Authority and includes up-to-date weather data, a calendar of events, and a hotel booking engine.
- **www.sandiegomagazine.com**, the *San Diego Magazine* website, offers feature stories and dining and events listings.
- **www.sandiegoreader.com**, the site of the free weekly *San Diego Reader,* is a great resource for club and show listings. It has printable coupons for discount dining and other services, plus arts, eats, and entertainment critiques.
- **www.sdcitybeat.com**, the site of the free weekly *San Diego City Beat* offers news from hip neighborhoods, with a special focus on downtown's many sectors, and lots of info on clubs, music, bars, and events.
- **www.sandiegouniontribune.com** is the *San Diego Union-Tribune* site, offering headline news, plus reviews and information on restaurants, music, movies, performing arts, museums, outdoor recreation, beaches, and sports.
- **socalpulse.com** provides information on arts, culture, special events, shopping, and dining for San Diego, Orange County, and Los Angeles. You can also make hotel reservations through the site.
- **www.voiceofsandiego.org** is an excellent online news source that offers information on what's happening in the city politically and culturally.
- **www.sezio.org** is a hip spot where you can check in with the local art and music scene and learn about the latest openings and shows.

Getting **There**

By Plane

San Diego International Airport (☎ 619/400-2404; www.san.org), also known as Lindbergh Field (airport code: SAN), is just 3 miles (4.8km) northwest of downtown San Diego. It isn't a connecting hub for domestic airlines, and most international travel arrives via Los Angeles or points east. San Diego is seeing an increase in international flights, however, with service to the U.K. and Japan along with several airlines serving Mexico. Planes land at Terminal 1 or 2, though most flights to and from Southern California airports use the Commuter Terminal, a half-mile (.8km) away; the Airport Flyer ("red bus") provides free service from the main airport to the Commuter Terminal, or there's a footpath. The main airport underwent a major expansion recently, with a totally remodeled Terminal 2 opening in 2015. Several local restaurants and shops have opened outlets in the terminal, and it's actually worth arriving early for your flight to check them out. General **information desks** with visitor materials, maps, and other services are near the baggage claim areas of both Terminal 1 and 2. You can exchange foreign currency at **Travelex America** (☎ 619/681-1941; www.travelex.com) in Terminal 2 on the second level (*inside* the security area, near the gates). **Hotel reservation** and **car-rental courtesy phones** are in the baggage-claim areas of Terminal 1 and 2. Major airlines flying into San Diego include **Air Canada** (☎ 888/247-2262; www.aircanada.com), **Alaska Airlines/Horizon Air** (☎ 800/252-7522; www.alaskaair.com), **Allegiant Air** (☎ 702/505-8888; www.allegiantair.com), **American Airlines** (☎ 800/433-7300; www.aa.com), **British Airways** (☎ 800/247-9297; www.britishairways.com, **Delta Airlines** (☎ 800/221-1212; www.delta.com), **Frontier Airlines** (☎ 800/432-1359; www.frontierairlines.com), **Hawaiian Airlines** (☎ 800/367-5320; www.hawaiianair.com), **Japan Airlines** (☎ 800/525-3663; www.jal.com), **JetBlue Airways** (☎ 800/538-2583; www.jetblue.com), **Southwest Airlines** (☎ 800/435-9792; www.southwest.com), **Spirit Airlines** (☎ 800/401-2222; www.spirit.com), **Sun Country Airlines** (☎ 800/359-6786; www.suncountry.com), **United Airlines** (☎ 800/864-8331; www.united.com), **Virgin America** (☎ 877/359-8474; www.virginamerica.com), **Volaris** (☎ 866/988-3257; www.volaris.com), and **WestJet** (☎ 888/937-8538; www.westjet.com). The Commuter Terminal is used by regional carriers **American Eagle** and **United Express** and for connecting flights to Los Angeles (for flight info, contact the parent carriers).

The **Metropolitan Transit System** (☎ 619/233-3004; www.transit.511sd.com) operates the San Diego Transit Flyer—bus route no. 992—providing service between the airport and downtown San Diego, running along Broadway. Bus stops are at each of Lindbergh Field's three terminals. The one-way fare is $2.25, and exact change is required. If you're connecting to another bus or the San Diego Trolley, you'll need to purchase a Day Pass; a 1-day pass starts at $5 and is available from the driver or online. The ride takes about 15 minutes, and buses come at 10- to 15-minute intervals.

Taxis line up outside both terminals, and the trip to a downtown location, usually a 10-minute ride, is about $10 (plus tip); budget $25 to $40 for Coronado or Mission Beach, and $35 to $50 for La Jolla. **Uber** (www.uber.com) is especially valuable in San Diego, where distances between popular sights can be significant and taxi fares are high.

Several airport **shuttles** run regularly from the airport to points around the city; you'll see designated pick-up areas outside each terminal. The fare is about $8 per person to downtown hotels; Mission Valley and Mission Beach hotels are $20; and Coronado and La Jolla hotels are $23 and $29, respectively. Rates to a residence are about $5 to $10 more than the above rates for the first person. **SuperShuttle** (☎ 800/974-8885; www.supershuttle.com) serves all of San Diego County.

If you're **driving** to downtown from the airport, take Harbor Drive south to Broadway, the main east–west thoroughfare, and turn left. To reach Hillcrest or Balboa Park, exit the airport toward I-5, and follow the signs for Laurel Street. To reach Mission Bay, take I-5 north to I-8 west. To reach La Jolla, take I-5 north to the La Jolla Parkway exit, bearing left onto Torrey Pines Road.

By Bus & Train

Greyhound buses (☎ 800/231-2222, www.greyhound.com) from Los Angeles, Phoenix, Las Vegas, and other points in the Southwest arrive at the station in downtown San Diego at 120 W. Broadway (☎ 619/515-1100). Local buses stop in front and the San Diego Trolley line is nearby.

Trains from all points in the United States and Canada will take you to Los Angeles, where you'll need to change trains for the journey to San Diego. The city's Santa Fe Station (☎ 619/239-9021) is at the west end of Broadway, on Kettner Boulevard between Pacific Highway and India Street, within walking distance of many downtown hotels and the Embarcadero. Taxis line up outside the main door, the trolley station is across the street, and a dozen local bus routes stop on Broadway or Pacific Highway. **Amtrak** (☎ 800/872-7245; www.amtrak.com) trains run between downtown Los Angeles and San Diego about 11 times daily each way. They stop in Anaheim (Disneyland), Santa Ana, San Juan Capistrano, Oceanside, and Solana Beach. Two trains per day also stop in San Clemente. The travel time from Los Angeles to San Diego is about 2 hours and 45 minutes (for comparison, driving time can be as little as 2 hr., or as much as 4 hr. during rush hour). A one-way ticket to San Diego is $37, or $51 for a reserved seat in business class. International visitors can buy a **USA Rail Pass,** good for 15, 30, or 45 days of unlimited travel on Amtrak.

By Boat

San Diego's **B Street Cruise Ship Terminal** is at 1140 N. Harbor Dr., right at the edge of downtown (☎ 800/854-2757; www.portofsandiego.org). Carnival Cruise Lines (☎ 888/227-6482; www.carnival.com) counts San Diego as a year-round homeport, while several others, including Holland America Line (☎ 800/426-0327; www.hollandamerica.com), Royal Caribbean (☎ 800/327-6700; www.royalcaribbean.com), and Celebrity (☎ 800/437-3111; www.celebritycruises.com) make seasonal stops here.

By Car

Three main interstates lead into San Diego. **I-5** is the primary route from San Francisco, central California, and Los Angeles; it runs straight through downtown to the

Tijuana border crossing. **I-8** cuts across California from points east like Phoenix, terminating just west of I-5 at Mission Bay. **I-15** leads from the deserts to the north through inland San Diego; as you enter Miramar, take **Highway 163** south to reach the central parts of the city.

Getting **Around**

By Car

If you plan to drive in San Diego, study your maps in advance of your travels, paying close attention to freeway entrances and exits. Though typically reasonably courteous, some San Diego drivers are loath to yield to the uninitiated on freeways. Most downtown streets run one-way, in a grid pattern. However, outside downtown, canyons and bays often make streets indirect. Finding a parking space can be tricky in the Gaslamp Quarter, Old Town, Mission Beach, and La Jolla, but parking lots are often centrally located. Rush hour on the freeways is generally concentrated from 7 to 9am and 4 to 6pm (for up-to-the-minute traffic info, dial ☎ 511). A few things to note: San Diego's gas prices are often among the highest in the country; California has a seat-belt law for both drivers and passengers; drivers are required to use hands-free cellphone technology; text messaging while driving is illegal; and smoking in a car with a child age 17 or under is punishable by a $100 fine. You may turn right at a red light after stopping unless a sign says otherwise; likewise, you can turn left on a red light from a one-way street onto another one-way street after coming to a full stop. Penalties in California for drunk driving are among the toughest in the country; the main beach arteries (Grand, Garnet, and Mission) sometimes have random checkpoints set up to catch impaired drivers. If you plan to drive to Mexico, be sure to check with your insurance company at home to verify exactly the limits of your policy. Mexican car insurance is available—and highly recommended—from various agencies (visible to drivers heading into Mexico) on the U.S. side of the border.

All the major car-rental firms have an office at the airport and several have them in larger hotels. Some of the national companies include **Alamo** (☎ 800/462-5266; www.alamo.com), **Avis** (☎ 800/633-3469; www.avis.com), **Budget** (☎ 800/527-0700; www.budget.com), **Dollar** (☎ 800/800-4000; www.dollar.com), **Enterprise** (☎ 855/266-9289; www.enterprise.com), **Hertz** (☎ 800/654-3131; www.hertz.com), **National** (☎ 800/227-7368; www.nationalcar.com), and **Thrifty** (☎ 800/847-4389; www.thrifty.com).

By Bus

The **MTS Transit Store** at the 12th & Imperial Transit Center (☎ 619/234-1060; www.sdmts.com) dispenses passes, tokens, timetables, maps, brochures, and lost-and-found information. It issues ID cards for seniors 60 and older, and for travelers with disabilities, all of whom pay $1.10 per ride. The office is open Monday through Friday 9am to 5pm. Most bus fares are $2.25. Buses accept dollar bills and coins, but drivers can't give change. If you need to make a connection with another bus or trolley, purchase a $5 day pass from the driver, at the Transit Store, at a trolley station ticket vending machine, or online. It gives you unlimited use of most bus and trolley routes for the rest of the service day. For assistance with route information from a living, breathing entity, call ☎ 619/233-3004. You can also view timetables, maps, and fares online at www.transit.511sd.com. If you know your route and just need schedule information—or automated answers to FAQs—call **Info Express** (☎ 619/685-4900) from any touch-tone phone, 24 hours a day.

By Trolley

The San Diego Trolley is great for visitors, particularly if you're staying downtown or plan to visit Tijuana. There are three routes. The **Blue Line** travels from the Mexican border (San Ysidro) north through downtown and Old Town, with some trolleys continuing into Mission Valley. The **Orange Line** runs from downtown east through Lemon Grove and El Cajon. The **Green Line** runs from Old Town through Mission Valley to Qualcomm Stadium, San Diego State University, and on to Santee. The trip to the border takes 40 minutes from downtown; from downtown to Old Town takes 10 to 15 minutes. Trolleys operate on a self-service fare-collection system; riders buy tickets from machines in stations before boarding (some machines require exact change). It's a flat fare of $2.50 for travel between any two stations; a $5 day pass is also available, good for all trolley trips and most bus routes. Fare inspectors board trains at random to check tickets. The lines run every 15 minutes during the day and every 30 minutes at night; during peak weekday rush hours, the Blue Line runs every 10 minutes. There is also expanded service to accommodate events at PETCO Park and Qualcomm Stadium. Trolleys stop at each station for only 30 seconds. To open the door for boarding, push the lighted green button; to open the door to exit the trolley, push the lighted white button. For recorded transit information, call ☎ 619/685-4900. To speak with a customer service representative, call ☎ 619/233-3004 (TTY/TDD 619/234-5005), daily from 5:30am to 8:30pm. For wheelchair lift info, call ☎ 619/595-4960. The trolley generally operates daily from 5am to about midnight; the Blue Line provides limited but additional service between Old Town and San Ysidro throughout the night from Saturday evening to Sunday morning; check the website at www.transit.511sd.com for additional details.

By Train

San Diego's express rail commuter service, the **Coaster,** travels between the downtown Santa Fe Depot station and the Oceanside Transit Center, with stops at Old Town, Sorrento Valley, Solana Beach, Encinitas, and Carlsbad. Fares range from $4 to $6.50 each way, depending on how far you go, and can be paid by credit card at vending machines at each station. Eligible seniors and riders with disabilities pay $2 to $2.75. The scenic trip between downtown San Diego and Oceanside takes 1 hour. Trains run Monday through Friday, from about 6:30am to 7pm, with four trains in each direction on Saturday; call ☎ 800/262-7837 or log on to www.transit.511sd.com for info. The **Sprinter** rail service runs west to east alongside Highway 78, from Oceanside to Escondido. The Sprinter operates Monday through Friday from about 4am to 9pm daily, with service every 30 minutes in both directions. On weekends, trains run every half-hour from 9:30am to 5:30pm (westbound) and

10:30am to 6:30pm (eastbound). There is hourly service before and after those times. Basic one-way fare is $2, $1 for seniors and travelers with disabilities.

By Taxi

Rates are based on mileage and can add up quickly in sprawling San Diego—a trip from downtown to La Jolla will cost $35 to $50. Other than in the Gaslamp Quarter after dark, taxis don't cruise the streets as they do in other cities, so you have to call ahead for quick pickup. Among the local companies are **Orange Cab** (☎ 619/291-3333), **San Diego Cab** (☎ 619/226-8294), and **Yellow Cab** (☎ 619/444-4444). The **Coronado Cab Company** (☎ 619/435-6211) serves Coronado.

By Ferry & Water Taxi

There's regularly scheduled ferry service between San Diego and Coronado (☎ 800/442-7847 or 619/234-4111; www.flagshipsd.com for information). Ferries leave from the Broadway Pier (1050 N. Harbor Dr., at the intersection with Broadway) and the Convention Center Marina (600 Convention Way, behind the Convention Center). Broadway Pier departures are scheduled Sunday through Thursday on the hour from 9am to 9pm, and Friday and Saturday until 10pm. They return from the Ferry Landing in Coronado to the Broadway Pier Sunday through Thursday every hour on the half-hour from 9:30am to 9:30pm and Friday and Saturday until 10:30pm. Trips from the Convention Center depart about every 2 hours beginning at 9:25am, with the final departure at 8:25pm (10:25pm Fri and Sat); return trips begin at 9:17am, then run about every 2 hours thereafter until 8:17pm (10:17pm Fri and Sat). The ride takes 15 minutes. The fare is $4.75 each way; buy tickets at the San Diego Harbor Excursion kiosk on Broadway Pier, the Convention Center Marina, or the Ferry Landing in Coronado. ***Note:*** The ferries do not accommodate cars.

Private water taxis (☎ 619/235-8294; www.flagshipsd.com) are available for groups up to 33 persons.

By Bicycle

San Diego is ideal for exploration by bicycle, and many roads have designated bike lanes. Bikes are available for rent in most areas. San Diego Ridelink publishes a comprehensive map of the county detailing bike *paths* (for exclusive use by bicyclists), bike *lanes* (alongside motor vehicle ways), and bike *routes* (shared ways designated only by bike-symbol signs). The free San Diego Region Bike Map is available online at www.511sd.com, or by calling ☎ 619/699-1900; it can also be found at visitor centers. **The San Diego County Bicycle Coalition** (☎ 858/487-6063; www.sdcbc.org) is also a great resource.

Fast **Facts**

AREA CODES San Diego's main area code is **619,** used primarily for downtown, uptown, Mission Valley, Point Loma, Coronado, La Mesa, El Cajon, and Chula Vista. The area code **858** is used for northern and coastal areas, including Mission Beach, Pacific Beach, La Jolla, Del Mar, Rancho Santa Fe, and Rancho Bernardo. Use **760** to reach the remainder of San Diego County, including Encinitas, Carlsbad, Oceanside, Escondido, Ramona, Julian, and Anza-Borrego.

ATMs & BANKS One of California's most popular banks is Wells Fargo, a member of the Star, PLUS, and Interlink systems. It has hundreds of ATMs at branches and stores (including most Vons supermarkets) throughout San Diego County. Another statewide bank is Bank of America, which accepts PLUS, Star, Cirrus, and Interlink cards. Banks are open weekdays, 9am to 4pm or later, and sometimes Saturday morning.

BABYSITTERS **Marion's Childcare** (☎ 888/891-5029; www.hotelchildcare.com) has bonded babysitters available to come to your hotel room; rates start at $20 per hour with a 4-hour minimum, cash only. **Panda's Domestic Service Agency** (☎ 619/295-3800; www.sandiegobabysitters.com) is also available.

B&Bs Check with the **San Diego Bed & Breakfast Guild** (www.bandbguildsandiego.org).

BEACH & WEATHER REPORT Call ☎ 619/221-8824. You can also check www.sandiego.gov/lifeguards/beaches for descriptions and water quality info.

CONSULATES & EMBASSIES All embassies are in the nation's capital, Washington, D.C. Some consulates are in major U.S. cities, and most nations have a mission to the United Nations in New York City. For addresses and phone numbers of embassies in Washington, D.C., call ☎ 202/555-1212 or log on to www.embassy.org/embassies. The **Mexican Consulate** is at 1549 India St., San Diego, CA 92101 (☎ 619/231-8414).

DENTISTS For dental referrals, contact the San Diego County Dental Society at ☎ 800/201-0244 (www.sdcds.org), or call ☎ **800/DENTIST** (www.1800dentist.com).

DISABLED TRAVELERS **Accessible San Diego** (☎ 619/325-7550; www.access-sandiego.org) has an info line that helps travelers find accessible hotels, tours, attractions, and transportation. The annual *Access in San Diego* pamphlet, a citywide guide with specifics on which establishments are accessible for those with visual, mobility, or hearing disabilities can be downloaded for $4. Manual wheelchairs with balloon tires are available free of charge daily at the main lifeguard stations in Ocean Beach, Mission Beach, Pacific Beach, La Jolla, and Del Mar, among others. Beach conditions permitting, the Mission Beach, Coronado, and Oceanside lifeguard stations also have electric wheelchairs available. For Mission Beach information call (☎ 619/525-8247); for Coronado information call ☎ 619/522-7346, Del Mar ☎ 858/755-1556, Oceanside ☎ 760/435-4018. Airport transportation for travelers with disabilities is available in vans holding one or two wheelchairs from **SuperShuttle** (☎ 800/974-8885, TDD 866/472-4497; www.supershuttle.com).

DOCTORS For a doctor referral, contact the **San Diego County Medical Society** (☎ 858/565-8888; www.sdcms.org) or **Scripps Health** (☎ 800/727-4777; www.scripps.org.

ELECTRICITY Like Canada, the United States uses 110–120 volts AC (60 cycles), compared to 220–240 volts AC (50 cycles) in most of Europe, Australia, and New Zealand. Downward converters that change 220–240 volts to 110–120 volts can be difficult to find in the United States, so bring one with you.

EMERGENCIES Call ☎ 911 for fire, police, or ambulance. The main police station is at 1401 Broadway, at 14th Street (☎ 619/531-2000, or TTY/TDD 619/233-3323). If you encounter serious problems, contact the San Diego chapter of **Traveler's Aid International** at ☎ 619/295-8393, or log on to www.travelersaid.org to help direct you to a local branch. This nationwide, nonprofit, social-service organization is geared to helping travelers in difficult straits, including reuniting families separated while traveling, providing food and/or shelter to people stranded without cash, or emotional counseling.

HOSPITALS Near downtown San Diego, **UCSD Medical Center–Hillcrest** (200 W. Arbor Dr.; ☎ 619/543-6222; health.ucsd.edu) has the most convenient emergency room. In La Jolla, **UCSD Thornton Hospital** (9300 Campus Point Dr.; ☎ 858/657-7000; health.ucsd.edu) has a good emergency room, and you'll find another in Coronado, at **Sharp Coronado Hospital** (250 Prospect Pl., opposite the Marriott Resort; ☎ 619/522-3600; www.sharp.com).

HOTLINES AIDS/STD/Hepatitis Hotline (☎ 800/367-2437); Alcoholics Anonymous (☎ 619/265-8762); Debtors Anonymous (☎ 619/525-3065); Mental Health referral and Suicide Crisis Line (☎ 800/273-8255).

INSURANCE/LOST LUGGAGE On flights within the U.S., checked baggage is covered up to $3,300 per ticketed passenger. Liability limits vary for international travel; check with your carrier for specifics. If you plan to check items more valuable than what's covered by the standard liability, see if your homeowner's policy covers your valuables or get baggage insurance as part of a comprehensive travel-insurance package. If your luggage is lost, immediately file a lost-luggage claim at the airport, detailing the luggage contents. Most airlines require that you report delayed, damaged, or lost baggage within 24 hours of arrival. The airlines are required to deliver luggage, once they have found it, directly to your house or destination free of charge.

INSURANCE/MEDICAL Unlike many European countries, the United States does not usually offer free or low-cost medical care to its citizens or visitors. Doctors and hospitals are expensive, and in most cases will require advance payment or proof of coverage before they render their services. Good policies will cover the cost of an accident, repatriation, or death. Packages, such as **Europ Assistance's Worldwide Healthcare Plan,** are sold by European automobile clubs and travel agencies at attractive rates; you can contact **Europ Assistance USA** at ☎ 240/330-1000 (www.worldwideassistance.com). Though lack of health insurance may prevent you from being admitted to a hospital in non-emergencies, don't worry about being left on a street corner to die: The American way is to fix you now and bill the living daylights out of you later.

INSURANCE FOR BRITISH TRAVELERS Most big travel agents offer their own insurance and will probably try to sell you their package when you book a holiday. Think before you sign. **Britain's Consumers' Association** recommends that you insist on seeing the policy and reading the fine print before buying travel insurance. **The Association of British Insurers** (☎ 020/7600-3333; www.abi.org.uk) can provide advice; you might also shop around for better deals: Try **Columbus Direct** (☎ **0800/0680-060**; www.columbusdirect.net).

INSURANCE FOR CANADIAN TRAVELERS Canadians should check with their provincial health plan offices or call **Health Canada** (☎ 866/225-0709; www.hc-sc.gc.ca) to find out the extent of their coverage and what documentation and receipts they must take home in case they are treated in the United States.

INSURANCE/TRIP CANCELLATION This will help retrieve your money if you have to back out of a trip or depart early, or if your travel supplier goes bankrupt. Permissible reasons for trip cancellation can range from sickness to natural disasters to the State Department declaring a destination unsafe for travel. For more information, contact one of the following recommended insurers: **Allianz** (☎ 866/884-3556; www.allianztravelinsurance.com), **MH Ross Travel Insurance Services** (☎ 800/423-3632; www.mhross.com), **Travel Guard International** (☎ 800/826-4919; www.travelguard.com), **Travel Insured International** (☎ 800/243-3174; www.travelinsured.com), and **Travelex Insurance Services** (☎ 800/228-9792; www.travelex-insurance.com).

INTERNET If you have your laptop, cafes, coffeehouses, and hotels provide a multitude of wireless options. For those without a computer, you can find terminals at all **public libraries,** including the downtown central library (330 Park Blvd. ☎ 619/236-5800; www.sandiego.gov); the Pacific Beach branch (4275 Cass St., ☎ 858/581-9934); the Ocean Beach branch (4801 Santa Monica Ave., ☎ 619/531-1532); and La Jolla (7555 Draper Ave., ☎ 858/552 1657). Another option is **Lestat's Coffee House,** 3343 Adams Ave., Normal Heights (☎ 619/291-4043; www.lestats.com) and 4496 Park Blvd., Hillcrest (☎ 619/501-6638); both locations are open 24 hours.

LIQUOR LAWS The legal age for purchase and consumption of alcoholic beverages in California is 21. Proof of age is a necessity—it's often requested at bars, nightclubs, and restaurants, even from those well into their 30s and 40s, so always bring ID when you go out. Beer, wine, and hard liquor are sold daily from 6am to 2am and are available in grocery stores. Do not carry open containers of alcohol in your car or any public area that isn't zoned for alcohol consumption—the police can fine you on the spot. **Alcohol is forbidden at all city beaches, boardwalks, and coastal parks.** Pay heed or pay the price: First-time violators face a $250 fine.

MAIL At press time, domestic postage rates are 35¢ for a postcard and 49¢ for a letter. For international mail, a first-class letter of up to 1 ounce costs $1.20; a first-class postcard costs the same as a letter. For more information, go to www.usps.com.

San Diego's main post office is in the boondocks, but the former main office, just west of Old Town at 2535 Midway Dr., is a good alternative; it's open Monday through Friday 8am to 5pm, and Saturday 8am to 4pm. Downtown post offices are at 815 E St. (Mon–Fri 9am–5pm) and at 51 Horton Plaza, next to the Westin Hotel (Mon–Fri 9:30am–5pm, Sat 10am–4pm). Additionally, a post office is in Ocean Beach, 4833 Santa Monica Ave. (Mon–Fri 8:30am–5pm, Sat 8:30am–noon), and at the Mission Valley Shopping Center, next to Macy's (Mon–Fri 9:30am–5pm, Sat 9:30am–3pm).

PASSPORTS Always keep a photocopy of your passport with you when traveling. If it's lost or stolen, having a copy facilitates the reissuing process at a local consulate or embassy. Keep your passport and other valuables in either the hotel's or the room's safe.

RESTROOMS Toilets can be found in hotel lobbies, bars, restaurants, museums, department stores, railway and bus stations, and service stations. Large hotels and fast-food restaurants are often the best bet for clean facilities. Restaurants and bars in resorts or heavily visited areas may reserve their restrooms for patrons. Horton Plaza, the Headquarters, and Seaport Village downtown, Balboa Park, Old Town State Historic Park in Old Town, and the Ferry Landing Marketplace in Coronado all have well-marked public restrooms. In general, you won't have a problem finding one.

SAFETY San Diego is a relatively safe destination, by big-city standards. Of the 10 largest cities in the United States, it historically has had the lowest incidence of violent crime, per capita. Virtually all areas of the city are safe during the day. In Balboa Park, caution is advised in areas not frequented by regular foot traffic (particularly off the walkways on the Sixth Avenue side of the park). Transients are common in San Diego—especially downtown, in Hillcrest, and in the beach area. They are rarely a problem, but can sometimes be unpredictable. Downtown areas to the east of PETCO Park are sparsely populated after dusk, and poorly lit. Parts of the city that are usually safe on foot at night include the Gaslamp Quarter, Hillcrest, Old Town, Mission Valley, La Jolla, Coronado, and Mission, Pacific, and Ocean beaches.

SMOKING Smoking is prohibited in nearly all indoor public places, including theaters, hotel lobbies, and enclosed shopping malls. State law prohibits smoking in all restaurants and bars, except those with outdoor seating. San Diego has also banned smoking from all city beaches and parks, which includes Mission Bay Park and Balboa Park, as well as piers and boardwalks. It is also illegal to smoke in a vehicle with a child 17 or younger present; you can't be pulled over for this but an officer can tack it on to another infraction.

TAXES Sales tax in restaurants and shops is 8%. Hotel tax is 10.5%, or 12.5% for properties with more than 70 rooms.

TELEPHONES **Local calls** made from public pay phones cost either 35¢ or 50¢. Pay phones do not accept pennies, and few will take anything larger than a quarter. Most long-distance and international calls can be dialed directly from any phone. **For calls within the United States and to Canada,** dial 1 followed by the area code and the seven-digit number. **For other international calls,** dial 011 followed by the country code, city code, and the number you are calling. For **reversed-charge or collect calls,** and for person-to-person calls, dial the number 0 then the area code and number; an operator will come on the line, and you should specify whether you are calling collect, person-to-person, or both. If your operator-assisted call is international, ask for the overseas operator. For **local directory assistance** ("information"), dial 411; for long-distance information, dial 1 and then the appropriate area code and 555-1212.

TIME ZONE San Diego, like the rest of the West Coast, is in the Pacific Standard Time zone, which is 8 hours behind Greenwich Mean Time. Daylight saving time is observed.

TIPPING In hotels, tip **bellhops** at least $1 per bag ($2–$3 if you have a lot of luggage) and tip the **chamber staff** $1 to $2 per day (more if you've left a disaster area to clean up). Tip the **doorman** or **concierge** only if he or she has provided you with some specific service (for example, calling a cab for you or obtaining difficult-to-get theater tickets). Tip the **valet-parking attendant** $1 to $2 every time you get your car. In restaurants, bars, and nightclubs, tip **service staff** 15% to 20% of the check, tip **bartenders** 10% to 15%, and tip **checkroom attendants** $1 per garment. Tip **cab drivers** 15% of the fare; tip **skycaps** at airports at least $1 per bag ($2–$3 if you have a lot of luggage); and tip **hairdressers** and **barbers** 15% to 20%.

TRANSIT INFORMATION Call ☎ 619/233-3004 (TTY/TDD 619/234-5005), or log onto www.transit.511sd.com. If you know your bus route and just need schedule information, call ☎ 619/685-4900.

A Brief **History**

It's believed humans first arrived in San Diego's coastal areas some 20,000 years ago, while others settled in the desert about 8,000 years later. The first cultural group, which is now referred to as the San Dieguito people, date back to 7,500 B.C. They were followed by the La Jollan culture, which populated the coastal mesas until about 1,000 to 3,000 years ago. The Diegueños followed about 1,500 years ago, and existed in two groups: the Ipai, who lived along the San Diego River and northeast toward what is now Escondido, and the Tipai, or Kumeyaay, who lived south of the river into Baja California and east toward Imperial Valley.

In 1542, a Portuguese explorer in the employ of Spain, **Juan Rodríguez Cabrillo,** set out from the west coast of Mexico, principally in search of a northwest passage that might provide an easier crossing between the Pacific Ocean and Europe. En route he landed at a place he charted as San Miguel, spending 6 days to wait out a storm and venture ashore—doing a meet-and-greet with a group of fearful Kumeyaay (who had heard tales of white men killing natives to the east and south)—before heading north along the coast. Although Cabrillo wrote favorably about what he saw, it would be 60 years before Europeans visited San Miguel again. When Spanish explorer Sebastián Vizcaíno sailed into the bay on the feast day of San Diego de Alcalá in 1602, he renamed it in honor of the saint. But despite Vizcaíno calling it "a port which must be the best to be found in all the South Sea," San Diego Bay was all but ignored by invaders for the next century and a half.

In 1768, Spain, fearing that Russian enclaves in Northern California might soon threaten Spanish settlements to the south, decreed the founding of colonies in Southern California. The following year, after an arduous 110-day voyage from the tip of Baja California, the *San Carlos* arrived into San Diego Bay on April 29, 1769, carrying the scouting team for "the sacred expedition" of **Father Junípero Serra,** a priest who had been charged with the task of spreading Christianity to the indigenous people. Serra would arrive about 2 months later via an overland route.

The site for a mission was selected just above the San Diego River, on a prominent hill that offered views onto plains, mesas, marshes, and the sea. A rudimentary fort, the **Presidio de San Diego,** was established to protect the mission, the first of 21 to be built in Alta California (the first mission in Baja California was established in 1697). The local populace was initially hostile to the Spanish incursion, but the tribes were eventually subdued by the settlers' firepower. After 4 years, Father Serra requested permission to relocate the mission to Nipaguay, a site 6 miles (10km) up the valley, next to an existing village. Irrigation projects were begun, crops planted, and herds of cattle and sheep introduced, but the cost for the Kumeyaay was high. Their culture was mostly lost; communities were shattered by foreign diseases from which they had no natural immunities; and those who defied the Spaniards or deserted the new settlements were dealt with cruelly.

In 1821, as what is now known as **Old Town** started to take shape, Mexico declared independence from Spain. California's missions were secularized; the Mexican government lost all interest in the native people and instead focused on creating sprawling rancheros. The Mexican flag flew over the Presidio, and in 1825, San Diego became the informal capital of the California territory.

The **Mexican-American War** took root in 1846, spreading west from Texas, leading to brutal battles between the Californios and invading American troops. By 1847, the Californios had surrendered, the treaty of Guadalupe-Hidalgo was signed a year later, and Mexico was paid $15 million for what became the southwestern United States. In 1848, gold was discovered near Sacramento and the **gold rush** began. In 1850, California was made the 31st state, and San Diego was established as both a city and county.

In 1850, William Heath Davis, a San Francisco financier, purchased 160 acres (65 hectares) along the bay and made plans to develop a "new town." Residents of Old Town scoffed, and despite Davis' construction of a wharf and installation of several prefabricated houses, the citizens stayed rooted at the base of the Presidio and labeled the project "Davis' Folly." But in 1867, another developer, Alonzo Horton, also saw the potential of the area and bought 960 acres (389 hectares) of bayfront land for $265. This time, people started moving into New Town, and by 1869 San Diego had a population of 3,000; a devastating fire in Old Town in 1872 proved to be the final blow for the original settlement.

In 1915, despite a competing event in San Francisco, San Diego's **Panama-California Exposition** was a fabulous success, and it spurred the development of 1,400-acre (567-hectare) **Balboa Park** into fairgrounds of lasting beauty. The barrage of publicity from the 2-year fair touted San Diego's climate and location, and helped put the city on the map.

Toward the end of the 19th century, the **U.S. Navy** began using San Diego as a home port; in 1908 the Navy sailed into the harbor with its battleship fleet and 16,000 sailors, and the War Department laid plans to dredge the bay to accommodate even larger ships. Aircraft innovator Glenn Curtiss convinced the Navy to designate $25,000 to the development of aviation, and soon after he opened a flying school at North Island, the northwestern lobe of the Coronado peninsula. World War I meant construction projects, and North Island was established as a Marine base. The Navy built a shipyard at 22nd Street in downtown, and constructed a naval training station and hospital in 1921. America's first aircraft carrier docked in San Diego in 1924.

Aviator T. Claude Ryan started Ryan Aviation to build military and civilian aircraft and equipment, and in 1927 he built ***The Spirit of St. Louis*** for Charles A. Lindbergh, a young airmail pilot. Only a few weeks after taking off from North Island, Lindbergh landed in Paris and was toasted as the first to fly solo across the Atlantic. In 1928, San Diego's airport was dedicated as **Lindbergh Field.**

A second world's fair, the 1935–36 **California-Pacific International Exposition,** allowed the Spanish colonial architecture in Balboa Park to be expanded, and many tourists were so enamored with what they saw, they became residents. In the decades to come, though, downtown stumbled the way many urban centers did in the 1960s and 1970s, filled after dark with the homeless and inebriated. In 1974, the **Gaslamp Quarter**—the new name for Alonzo Horton's New Town—was designated as a historic district. Little occurred to revitalize downtown at first, but a redevelopment plan was established and the first step was taken when **Seaport Village,** a waterside shopping complex at the south end of the Embarcadero, opened in the early '80s. In 1985, a $140-million shopping center next to Horton Plaza opened to raves, and San Diegans responded immediately, coming downtown to shop and dine as they hadn't in a generation. Another wave of downtown development saw the opening of the $474-million ballpark **PETCO Park** in 2004, along with the beginnings of a new downtown neighborhood, called East Village. Today, both the village and Little Italy are dense residential and commercial zones with high-rise condo towers, trendy restaurants and bars, and little to no parking.

Today's San Diego owes much to **medical and high-tech industries**—biotechnology, pharmaceutical, and telecommunications in particular. One economic think tank declared the city to be the nation's number one "biotech cluster," supported by a steady flow of research from academic institutions like the University of California, San Diego; the Scripps Research Institute; and the Salk Institute. The biotech industry here also provides a home base for a gaggle of science-based Nobel Prize winners and is directly responsible for tens of thousands of jobs and billions of dollars in local economic impact.

Index

See also Accommodations and Restaurant indexes, below.

A

Accommodations, 132–144. *See also* Accommodations Index
    best, 132
Africa and Beyond, 74
Airport shuttles, 165
Air travel, 164–165
Albright, Harrison, 67, 68
Alcazar Garden, 22
Altitude Sky Lounge, 11, 117
Antiques and collectibles, 74
Antique Warehouse, 78
Anza-Borrego Desert State Park, 5–6, 95, 160
Apple Box, 76
Area codes, 168–169
Art galleries, 74–75
Arts and entertainment, 124–130
    best, 124
ARTS TIX, 127
ArtWalk, 161
Athenaeum Music & Arts Library, 61
ATMs/banks, 169

B

Baby Del (Livingston House), 67
Babysitters, 169
Backesto Building, 47
Balboa Park, 3, 9–10, 20, 21, 23–27
Balboa Park December Nights, 163
Balboa Park Miniature Railroad and Carousel, 27
Balboa Park Municipal Golf Course, 41
Balboa Theatre, 45, 126
Ballast Point, 117
Barona Resort & Casino (Lakeside), 128
Bars, 117–119
    wine, 122
Baum, L. Frank, 67
Bay Books, 75
Bayside Trail, 91
Bazaar del Mundo, 77
Beach and weather report, 169
Beaches, 83–87. *See also specific beaches*
    Tijuana, 158
Bed & breakfasts (B&Bs), 169
Belly Up Tavern, 121
Belmont Park, 33
Berkeley (ferry), 55–56
Biking, 168
Birch Aquarium at Scripps, 32
Bird-watching, 97, 98
Black's Beach, 83
Blondstone Jewelry Studio, 79
Boat tours and cruises, 4, 56
Bookstores, 75–76
Botanical Building and Lily Pond, 25
Brass Rail, 65
The Brass Rail, 120
Brick by Brick, 121
British travelers, insurance for, 170
Brokers Building, 49
Brown, Michael, 38
B Street Cruise Ship Terminal, 165
Bullfighting, Tijuana, 158
Bus travel, 165, 166–167

C

Cabrillo, Juan, 35
Cabrillo Bridge, 21
Cabrillo National Monument, 3, 13, 35, 89–91
Cabrillo Statue, 89–90
Caliente Race & Sports Book (Tijuana), 155
Caliente Racetrack (Tijuana), 155
California Surf Museum (North County), 148
California Welcome Center (Oceanside), 160
California Wolf Center (Julian), 153
Canadian travelers, insurance for, 170–171
Carlsbad, 147
Carlsbad Premium Outlets, 80
Carlsbad Visitor Information Center, 160
Carnival Cruise Lines, 165
Car travel, 165–166
The Casbah, 121
Casinos, 128
Cedros Design District, 78, 147
Cedros Soles, 76
Celebrity cruises, 165
Centro Cultural Tijuana, 157
Children's Pool, 4, 60, 83
Chinese Mission, 49
Chuck Jones Gallery, 74
Chula Vista Nature Center, 32
Cinema Under the Stars, 127
CityPass, Southern California, 30
Classical music, 126
Climate, 160
The Coaster, 167
Coast Walk, 61
Colorado House, 51
Comic-Con International, 162
Consulates, 169
Coronado, neighborhood walk, 66–68
Coronado Beach, 84
Coronado Ferry, 56
Coronado Library, 68
Coronado Municipal Golf Course, 41
Coronado Visitors Center, 160
County Administration Center, 55
Cowles Mountain, 93
Crown Manor, 67
Crown Point, 97
Cruise ships, 165
Cuyamaca Peak, 95
Cuyamaca Rancho State Park, 95

D

Dance clubs, 119–120
Dance performances, 126–127
David Alan Collection, 78
Davis-Horton House, 48–49
Davis-Horton House Museum, 38–39
Del Mar, 147
Del Mar Beach, 84–85
Del Mar Community & Visitor Center, 160
Del Mar Plaza, 80
Del Mar Races, 129
Del Mar Race Track, 162
Dentists, 169
Desert Garden, 27
Design Center, 65
D.G. Wills Books, 75–76
Dinosaur Gallery, 77–78
Disabled travelers, 169
Discounts, 30
    arts and entertainment tickets, 127
Diversionary Theatre, 130
Dizzy's, 121
Doctors, 169

E

Eagle and High Peak Mine (Julian), 152
Earp, Wyatt, 35, 46, 49
East Village Tavern & Bowl, 117
Eddie V's, 121
El Campo Santo, 52
Electricity, 169
Ellen Browning Scripps Park, 60
Embarcadero, 18
    neighborhood walk, 55–57
Embassies, 169
Emergencies, 169–170
Emilia Castillo, 79
Encinitas, 147
Estadio Caliente (Tijuana), 155
Europ Assistance, 170

F

Families with children, 29–33
Farmers Insurance Open, 163
Fashion (clothing), 76–77
Fashion Valley Center, 80
Ferry service, 168
Festival of Beer, 162
Festivals and special events, 160–163
Fiesta Cinco de Mayo, 161
Fiesta de Reyes, 51
Fiesta Island, 98
Film, 127
Fishing, Lake Cuyamaca, 153
Fleet Week, 162
Flower Fields (Carlsbad), 149
Flower Fields at Carlsbad Ranch, 161
FLUXX, 119
Folk Arts Rare Records, 79
Football bowl games, 163
Fort Rosecrans National Cemetery, 35
Fossils Exposed, 63

G

Gardens, Balboa Park, 27
Gaslamp Quarter, 5, 10
    neighborhood walk, 45–49
Gay and lesbian bars and clubs, 120–121
Gill, Irving, 64, 67
Girard Gourmet, 61
Glorietta Bay Inn, 68
Golden Poppy Hotel, 46
Golf, 41–42
Go San Diego Card, 30
Grapeline, 148
Green flash, 3
Green Valley campground, 95
Greyhound, 165
G-Star Raw, 77
Guardian of Water (statue), 55
Guild Theater, 65

H

Harbor cruises, 56
Hard Rock Cafe, 49
Haunted San Diego Tours, 38
Health insurance, 170
Hebbard, William, 64, 67
Heritage Park, 35, 53
Hiking, 93–95
Hillcrest, neighborhood walk, 63–65
Hillcrest Sign, 63
Hipódromo Caliente (Tijuana), 155
Historic San Diego, 35–39
History of San Diego, 173–175
Holiday Bowl, 163
Holland America Line, 165
Hope, Bob, 57
Hord, Donal, 55
Hornblower Cruises, 56
Horton Grand Hotel, 49
Horton Plaza, 45, 80
Horton Plaza Park, 45
Hospitality Point, 97
Hospitals, 170
Hotel del Coronado, 18, 67–68
Hotels, 132–144. *See also* Accommodations Index
    best, 132
Hotlines, 170
House of Blues, 122
House of Pacific Relations International Cottages, 24
Humphreys, 122

I

IMAX Dome Theater, 127
Immaculate Conception Catholic Church, 52
Imperial Beach, 84
Inez Grant Parker Memorial Rose Garden, 27
Ingle Building, 49
Insurance, 170–171
Internet and Wi-Fi, 171
I.O.O.F. Building, 47

J

Japanese Friendship Garden, 23–24
Jean Isaacs San Diego Dance Theater, 127
Jewelry, 79
John Wear Memorial, 63–64
Joseph Bellows Gallery, 74–75
Julian, 6, 150–153, 162
Julian Chamber of Commerce, 151
Julian Cider Mill, 152–153
Julian Pioneer Cemetery, 151
Julian Pioneer Museum, 151
June Gloom, 83
Junípero Serra Museum, 36

K

Kayaking, 4
Keating Building, 46
Kendall-Frost Reserve and Northern Wilderness Preserve, 97–98
Kettner Art & Design District, 79
Kids, 29–33
Kita Ceramics & Glassware, 78
Knorr Candle Shop, 78

L

L.A. Cetto Winery (Cava de Vinos; Tijuana), 157
La Casa de Estudillo, 51
La Jolla, 14
    neighborhood walk, 58–61
La Jolla Cove, 60, 84
La Jolla Cove Bridge Club, 60
La Jolla Music Society, 126
La Jolla Playhouse, 130
La Jolla Rough Water Swim, 162
La Jolla Shores, 3, 85
La Jolla SummerFest, 162
La Jolla Village Information Center, 160
Lake Cuyamaca, 153
Lamb's Players Theatre, 67, 130
Landmark Theatres, 127
Lane Field, 57
Large Rock Monument, 51
Laura Gambucci, 77
La Valencia, 61
Leaping Lotus, 78
LEGOLAND California (Carlsbad), 31

Lily Pond, 25
Lips, 122
Liquor laws, 171
Little Italy Festa, 162
Living Coast Discovery Center, 32–33, 94
Livingston House (Baby Del), 67
The Loading Dock, 63
Lodging, 132–144. *See also* Accommodations Index
best, 132
Los Peñasquitos Canyon Preserve, 94
Louis Bank of Commerce, 46
LoungeSix, 118
Lou's Records, 80
Lux Art Institute (North County), 148

M

Mabel's, 76
McCoy House, 50
Mail, 171
Malashock Dance, 127
Mardi Gras, 161
Maritime Museum, 38, 55
Marston Addition Canyon, 64–65
Marston House, 21, 39, 64
Martínez, Alfredo Ramos, 59, 68
Mary, Star of the Sea, 59
MCASD (Museum of Contemporary Art San Diego), 4–5, 56–57, 59
Mead, Frank, 64
Medical insurance, 170
Menghini Winery (Julian), 153
Metropolitan Transit System, 164
Mid-Century, 79
Military Exhibit, Point Loma, 90–91
Mingei International Museum, 22
Miniature Railroad and Carousel, Balboa Park, 27
Miramar Air Show, 162
Mission Basilica San Diego de Alcalá, 37
Mission Bay Park, 85, 96–98
Mission Bay Sportcenter, 96
Mission Beach, 13–14, 85–86
Mission Point, 97
Mission San Luis Rey de Francia, 37
Mission Trails Regional Park, 93
Mission Valley Center, 80
Model Yacht Pond, 98
Moonlight Beach, 87
Museo de Cera (Wax Museum; Tijuana), 155
Museum of Contemporary Art San Diego (MCASD), 4–5, 56–57, 59
Museum of History and Art, 66–67
Museum of Photographic Arts, 25–26
Music
classical, 126
concert and performance venues, 126
Music stores, 79–80
My Own Space, 79

N

Native American reservations, 128
Neighborhood walks
Coronado, 66–68
Embarcadero, 55–57
Gaslamp Quarter, 45–49
Hillcrest, 63–65
La Jolla, 58–61
Old Town, 50–53
The New Children's Museum, 33
Nightlife, 114–122
bars, 117–119
best, 114
dance clubs, 119–120
gay and lesbian bars and clubs, 120–121
live music venues, 121–122
supper clubs, 122
wine bars, 122
North County, 146–149
beaches, 87
Numbers, 120
Nunu's Cocktail Lounge, 118

O

Observatory North Park - North Park Theatre, 126
Ocean Beach, 86
Ocean Beach Antique District, 74
Oceanside, 87, 147
Oceanside Museum of Art, 149
Official Visitors Planning Guide, 160
Old City Hall, 47
Old Globe Theatre, 4, 21, 130
Old Point Loma Lighthouse, 90
Old Town, 35
neighborhood walk, 50–53
Old Town State Historic Park, 9, 35, 50
Old Town Trolley Tours, 48
OMNIA, 119
The Onyx Room/Thin, 119
Opera, 128
Outdoor activities
beaches, 83–87
Cabrillo National Monument, 89–91
hiking, 93–95
Mission Bay Park, 96–98

P

Pacific Beach, 13–14, 86
Pacific Shores, 118
Palacio de la Cultura (Tijuana), 155
Palm Canyon, 23
Panama 66, 23
Park Hyatt Aviara Golf Club, 42
Parq Nightclub, 119
Paso Picacho campground, 95
Passports, 171
PB Shore Club, 118
PETCO Park, 5, 129
PGA Tour, 163
Playas de Tijuana, 158
Plaza Monumental (Tijuana), 158
Poinsettia Bowl, 163
Post offices, 171
Princess Pub & Grille, 118

Q

Qualcomm Stadium, 129
Quiksilver/Roxy, 76
Quint Contemporary Art, 75

R

Requa, Richard, 64
Restaurants, 100–112. *See also* Restaurants Index
best, 100
Restrooms, 172
Reuben H. Fleet Science Center, 26, 31
Richards, Bartlett, 67
Richards-Dupee Mansion, 67
Rich's, 120–121
Riverwalk Golf Club, 42
Robinson-Rose House, 50
Rock 'n' Roll Marathon, 161
RoofTop 600, 120

Rosenthal, Doron, 63
Royal Caribbean, 165

S

Safety, 172
  Tijuana, 158
San Diego Air & Space Museum, 25
San Diego Automotive Museum, 24
San Diego Ballet, 127
San Diego Bay Wine & Food Festival, 162
San Diego Botanic Garden (Encinitas), 149
San Diego Chargers, 129
San Diego Chinese Historical Museum, 49
San Diego City Beat, 163
San Diego-Coronado Bay Bridge, 3–4
San Diego County Fair, 161–162
San Diego Crew Classic, 161
San Diego Cruise Ship Terminal, 56
San Diego Golf Reservations, 41
San Diego Hall of Champions Sports Museum, 25
San Diego Harbor Excursions, 56
San Diego History Center, 39
San Diego International Airport, 164
San Diego-La Jolla Underwater Ecological Reserve, 85
San Diego-La Jolla Underwater Park, 4
San Diego Latino Film Festival, 161
San Diego LGBT Pride Parade, Rally, and Festival, 162
San Diego Magazine, 163
San Diego Maritime Museum, 18
San Diego Model Railroad Museum, 26, 32
San Diego Mormon Battalion Historic Site, 53
San Diego Museum of Art (SDMA), 22–23
San Diego Museum of Man, 21
San Diego Natural History Museum, 26–27
San Diego Opera, 128
San Diego Padres, 5, 129
San Diego Reader, 163
San Diego Repertory Theatre, 130
San Diego Restaurant Week, 163
San Diego Sockers, 129
San Diego Symphony, 126
San Diego Thanksgiving Dixieland Jazz Festival, 162
San Diego Transit Flyer, 164
San Diego Trolley, 167
San Diego Union Building, 51
San Diego Union-Tribune, 163
San Diego Zoo, 17, 29
San Diego Zoo Safari Park, 30
Santa Clara Point, 96
Santa Fe Depot, 56
Santa Fe Station, 165
Santa Maria de los Peñasquitos, 94
Sauvage, 77
The Schoolhouse, 51
SDMA (San Diego Museum of Art), 22–23
SEAL (Sea and Land Adventures) tour, 38
Seaport Village, 57, 80
Seasons, 160
SeaWorld San Diego, 29
Second Hand Prose, 68
Self-Realization Fellowship Hermitage and Meditation Gardens (North County), 147–148
Serra, Junípero, 37
Seventh Avenue, 64
Sevilla, 120
Shakespeare Festival, 4
Sherman-Gilbert House, 53
Shopping, 70–80
  antiques and collectibles, 74
  art galleries, 74–75
  best, 70
  bookstores, 75–76
  children's fashion and toys, 76
  fashion (clothing), 76–77
  gifts, 77–78
  home decor, 78–79
  jewelry, 79
  music stores, 79–80
  shopping centers, 80
Shopping centers, 80
Side Bar, 118
Smoking, 172
Solana Beach, 147
Solana Beach Visitor Center, 160
SoLo, 78
Southern California CityPass, 30
Southern Wildlife Preserve, 97
Spanish Village Art Center, 27, 75
Spectator sports, 129
Spencer-Ogden Building, 46
Spreckels, J. D., 68
Spreckels Organ Pavilion, 24
Spreckels Park, 68
The Sprinter, 167–168
St. Patrick's Day Parade, 161
Starlite, 122
Star of India, 55
Star of India (ship), 18
Stingaree, 48
Stonewall Peak, 95
SummerFest, La Jolla, 162
Sunny Jim Cave, 60
SuperShuttle, 165
Supper clubs, 122
Surprise, HMS, 38, 56
Swami's Beach, 87
Sweetwater Marsh National Wildlife Refuge, 94
Sycuan Resort & Casino (near El Cajon), 128

T

Taboo Studio, 79
Tasende Gallery, 75
Taxes, 172
Taxis, 164–165, 168
Telephones, 172
Temecula, 5, 148
Temecula Valley Convention and Visitors Bureau, 148
Temecula Valley Winegrowers Association, 148
Temperatures, average monthly, 161
Temple Beth Israel, 53
Tepoznieves (Tijuana), 157
Theater, 130
3rd Corner, 122
Tide pools, Cabrillo National Monument, 91
Tijuana, 6, 154–158
Tijuana Convention & Visitors Bureau, 156
Time zone, 172
Timken Museum of Art, 23
Tipping, 172–173
Tipsy Crow, 118
Top of the Hyatt, 57, 118
Torrey Pines Beach, 86–87
Torrey Pines Golf Course, 42, 163
Torrey Pines State Natural Reserve, 4, 93, 147
Tourist offices, 160

Train travel, 165, 167–168
Transit information, 173
Trip cancellation insurance, 171
Trolleys, 167
Tucci, 77
Turista Libre (Tijuana), 156

U

Unconditional Surrender Statue, 57
Urban Mo's, 121
USS Midway Museum, 37–38, 57

V

Viejas Casino (Alpine), 128
The Village, 59
Village Hat Shop, 77
Vin de Syrah Spirits & Wine Parlor, 122
Visitor centers
  Anza-Borrego Desert State Park, 95
  Balboa Park, 23
  Cabrillo National Monument, 89
Visitor Information Center (Tijuana), 156
Vitreum, 78

W

Warwick's, 76
Waterfront, 119
Waterfront Park, 55
Water taxis, 168
Watts-Robinson Building, 46
Wave House, 119
Wax Museum (Museo de Cera; Tijuana), 155
Websites, 163
Wednesday Club, 65
Whale Overlook, 90
Whale-watching, 5, 32, 163
Whaley House, 52
Windansea Beach, 87
Wine bars, 122
Wineries, 5
Wine Steals, 122
Winslow, Carleton, Sr., 59
Witch Creek Winery (Julian), 152
Wizard of Oz House, 67
World Championship Over the Line Tournament, 162
Worldwide Healthcare Plan, 170

Y

Yuma Building, 47

Accommodations

Andaz Hotel, 136
The Beach Cottages, 136
Best Western Bayside Inn, 136
Britt Scripps Inn, 136
Catamaran Resort Hotel, 136
Coronado Inn, 136
Crystal Pier Hotel, 136
The Dana on Mission Bay, 137
Del Mar Motel on the Beach, 137
El Cordova Hotel, 137
Estancia La Jolla Hotel and Spa, 137
Fairmont Grand Del Mar, 137
Gaslamp Plaza Suites, 137
Glorietta Bay Inn, 138
The Grande Colonial, 138
Hard Rock Hotel San Diego, 138
Hilton San Diego Gaslamp Quarter, 138
Holiday Inn Bayside, 138
Horton Grand, 139
Hotel del Coronado, 139
Hotel Indigo, 139
Hotel Palomar, 139
Hotel Solamar, 139–140
Inn at the Park, 140
Inn by the Sea, 140
Keating Hotel, 140
La Jolla Cove Suites, 140
La Jolla Shores Hotel, 140
La Pensione Hotel, 141
L'Auberge Del Mar Resort & Spa, 140
La Valencia Hotel, 15, 61, 141
Les Artistes, 141
The Lodge at Torrey Pines, 141
Loews Coronado Bay Resort, 142
Manchester Grand Hyatt San Diego, 142
Marriott San Diego Gaslamp Quarter, 142
Marriott San Diego Hotel & Marina, 142
Omni La Costa Resort and Spa, 142
Omni San Diego Hotel, 142–143
Pacific Terrace Hotel, 143
Paradise Point Resort & Spa, 143
Park Hyatt Aviara Resort, 143
Porto Vista Hotel & Suites, 143
The Sofia Hotel, 143
Tower 23, 143–144
The US Grant, 144
Wave Crest, 144
The Westgate Hotel, 144

Restaurants

Arterra, 104
Berta's Latin American Restaurant, 104–105
Bertrand at Mister A's, 105
Bino's Bistro & Crêperie, 105
BO-beau, 105
Bracero, 105
Bread & Cie, 105–106
Brian's 24 Restaurant Bar & Grill, 106
Brockton Villa, 106
Bronx Pizza, 106
Burger Lounge, 83
Cafe Chloe, 106
Café La Rue, 15, 61
Café LuLu, 49
Candelas, 106–107
Chez Loma, 107
Clayton's Coffee Shop, 107
Clayton's Mexican Take Out, 68
Coasterra, 107
Corvette Diner, 29
Cosmopolitan Hotel and Restaurant, 52
The Cottage, 107
Cowboy Star, 107
Cucina Urbana, 108
Dobson's Bar & Restaurant, 108
El Agave Tequileria, 108
El Camino, 108
Extraordinary Desserts, 17, 108–109
1500 Ocean, 104
Filippi's Pizza Grotto, 109
The Fishery, 109
The Fish Market/Top of the Market, 109
Georges California Modern, 109
Island Prime/C Level, 109
Jake's Del Mar, 110
Julian Pie Company, 152
Lahaina Beach House, 14
Mamá Testa Taqueria, 64
The Marine Room, 110
Market Restaurant + Bar, 110
The Mission, 97
Mom's Pie House (Julian), 152

New Orleans Creole Café, 36
Nine-Ten, 110
Nobu, 110–111
The Oceanaire Seafood Room, 111
Panama 66, 23
Point Loma Seafoods, 91
The Prado, 10
Puesto, 111
Saffron Noodles and Saté, 111
Sushi Ota, 111
Swami's Cafe (North County), 148
Tepoznieves (Tijuana), 157
Tidal, 112
The Tractor Room, 111–112
Urban Solace, 112
Whisknladle, 112
Wonderland, 112

Photo Credits

p viii: © Dancestrokes; p 3, bottom: © Dancestrokes; p 4, top: © Abdominator; p 4, bottom: © Andre Nantel; p 5, top: © CarlaVanWagoner/Shutterstock.com; p 5, bottom: © meunierd/Shutterstock.com; p 6, top: © Jorg Hackemann/Shutterstock.com; p 7: © Jim Feliciano; p 9, middle: © littleny/Shutterstock.com; p 10, bottom: © f11photo/Shutterstock.com; p 11, top: © Tom Godber; p 13, bottom: © Dancestrokes; p 14, top: © Maybritt Haeling; p 14, bottom: © maratr; p 15, top: © Dancestrokes; p 15, bottom: Courtesy of La Valencia; p 17, bottom: Courtesy of San Diego Zoo/Ken Bohn; p 18, top: © Kimberly Vardeman; p 18, bottom: © Lowe Llaguno; p 19: © Rob Bertholf; p 21, middle: © Mike Liu; p 22, top: © peasap; p 22, bottom: © PJK; p 23, bottom: © Smart Destinations; p 24, top: © Richard; p 24, bottom: © aceshot1; p 25, top: © Joanna Poe; p 25, bottom: © Mike Liu; p 26, top: © Dancestrokes; p 26, bottom: © Mike Liu; p 27, top: © Balboa Park Cultural Partnership; p 27, bottom: © Ming-yen Hsu; p 29, top: Courtesy of San Diego Zoo/Ken Bohn; p 29, bottom: © Roka/Shutterstock.com; p 30, bottom: Courtesy of San Diego Zoo/Ken Bohn; p 31, top: © Shannon Lail; p 31, bottom: © Oleg Shpyrko; p 32, top: © Eileen Maher/Port of San Diego; p 32, bottom: © Dale Frost/Port of San Diego; p 33, top: © Smart Destinations; p 33, bottom: © Mike Liu; p 35, middle: © Ken Lund; p 36, top: © Iriana Shiyan/Shutterstock.com; p 36, bottom: © Gary J. Wood; p 37, top: © littleny/Shutterstock.com; p 37, bottom: © Ray Bouknight; p 39, bottom: © Iriana Shiyan/Shutterstock.com; p 41, bottom: Courtesy of Park Hyatt Aviara Golf Resort; p 42, bottom: Courtesy of The Lodge at Torrey Pines; p 43: © Charles Jellison; p 45, bottom: Courtesy of Indigo Hotel; p 46, top: © f8grapher/Shutterstock.com; p 46, bottom: Courtesy of Balboa Theatre/Nels Akerlund Photography; p 47, top: Courtesy of the Keating ; p 47, bottom: © eileenmak; p 48, middle: © Leonard Zhukovsky/Shutterstock.com; p 51, top: © meunierd/Shutterstock.com; p 51, bottom: © Prayitno/Thank you for (9 millions +) views; p 52, top: © Kimberly Vardeman; p 52, bottom: © Adam Jones; p 53, top: © Bonnie Dean; p 53, bottom: © lowellaguno; p 55, bottom: © Port of San Diego; p 56, top: © lowellaguno; p 57, top: Courtesy of Manchester Grand Hyatt San Diego; p 57, bottom: © lowellaguno/Shutterstock.com; p 59, bottom: © Nancy Rubins/Smart Destinations; p 60, bottom: © jessicakirsh/Shutterstock.com; p 61, top: Courtesy of La Valencia; p 63, bottom: © Aaron Fulkerson; p 64, bottom: © Wendy Cutler; p 67, top: Courtesy of Coronado Museum of History and Art; p 67, bottom: Courtesy of Lamb's Players Theaters/Ken Jacques; p 68, bottom: Courtesy of Hotel Del Coronado; p 69: Courtesy of Sauvage; p 75, top: Courtesy of Africa and Beyond; p 75, bottom: Courtesy of Chuck Jones Gallery/Stephen Russo Media; p 76, top: Courtesy of Joseph Bellows; p 76, bottom: Courtesy of Quint Gallery La Jolla; p 77, top: Courtesy of ROXY; p 77, bottom: © Ming-yen Hsu; p 78, top: Courtesy of Sauvage; p 78, bottom: © Eric Steuer; p 79, top: Courtesy of Kita Ceramics; p 80, bottom: © Prayitno/Thank you for (9 millions +) views; p 81: © Sebastien Burel/Shutterstock.com; p 83, bottom: © Bill Morrow; p 84, top: © Jon Lee Clark; p 84, bottom: © meunierd/Shutterstock.com; p 85, top: © cdrin/Shutterstock.com; p 85, bottom: Courtesy of Catamaran; p 86, bottom: © Maybritt Haeling; p 87, middle: © Abdominator; p 89, middle: © Scott A. Burns; p 89, bottom: © Dancestrokes; p 90, top: © S. Borisov; p 90, bottom: © Maybritt Haeling; p 91, top: © Kara Jade Quan-Montgomery; p 93, bottom: © Chad McDermott; p 94, top: © Patty Mooney; p 94, middle: © Mechanoid Dolly; p 97, bottom: Courtesy of Catamaran; p 98, top: © Dancestrokes; p 98, bottom: © Margaret Hill; p 99: Courtesy of Island Prime; p 105, top: Courtesy of Hotel Del Mar; p 105, bottom: Courtesy of Bertrand at Mister A's; p 106, top: Courtesy of Bo- beau; p 106, bottom: Courtesy of Bracero; p 107, bottom: Courtesy of Brockton Villa; p 108, top: Courtesy of Cowboy Star; p 108, bottom: Courtesy of Cucina Urbana/Singler Photography; p 109, top: Courtesy of Extraordinary Desserts ; p 110, top: Courtesy of Jake's Del Mar; p 110, bottom: Courtesy of Saffron; p 111, top: Courtesy of Nine-Ten; p 111, bottom: Courtesy of Whisknladle; p 112, top:

Courtesy of Wonderland; p 112, bottom: Courtesy of Urban Solace; p 113: Courtesy of Humphreys Concerts By The Bay; p 118, top: Courtesy of San Diego Marriott Gaslamp Quarter; p 119, bottom: Courtesy of Top of The Hyatt; p 120, top: Courtesy of Onyx Room; p 120, bottom: © Photo courtesy of Belly Up Tavern/Daniel Knighton/Pixel Perfect Images; p 121, top: © Laura Luz; p 122, bottom: Courtesy of Starlite; p 123: Courtesy of The San Diego Symphony/David Hartig; p 124, bottom: Courtesy of La Jolla Music Society; p 126, top: Courtesy of Balboa Theater; p 126, bottom: Courtesy of Reuben Fleet Science Center; p 127, bottom: © © Todd Rosenberg Photography 2015; p 128, bottom: © SD Dirk; p 129, top: © Christopher Penler/Shutterstock.com; p 129, bottom: © Danny Baza Blas; p 130, top: Courtesy of La Jolla Playhouse/Kevin Berne; p 130, bottom: © peasap; p 131: Courtesy of Catamaran Resort; p 132, bottom: Courtesy of L'Auberge Del Mar; p 136, bottom: Courtesy of Britt Scrips Inn; p 137, top: Courtesy of Estancia; p 137, top: Courtesy of Fairmont Grand Del Mar; p 137, bottom: Courtesy of Hotel Del Coronado; p 139, top: Courtesy of Hotel Indigo; p 139, bottom: Courtesy of Hotel Solomar; p 140, top: Courtesy of Hotel Keating; p 140, bottom: Courtesy of La Valencia; p 141, top: Courtesy of The Lodge at Torrey Pines; p 141, bottom: Courtesy of Lowes Coronado; p 142, top: Courtesy of Omni la Costa/Don Riddle Images; p 142, bottom: Courtesy of Grand Hyatt; p 143, top: Courtesy of Paradise Point Resort; p 144, top: Courtesy of Tower 23; p 144, bottom: Courtesy of US Grant; p 145: © Adam Cole Barber; p 147, bottom: © Daniel Orth; p 148, top: © Joe Wolf; p 149, middle: © Melinda; p 151, bottom: © Visit Julian; p 152, top: © Visit Julian; p 152, bottom: © Visit Julian; p 155, middle: © f8grapher/Shutterstock.com; p 157, top: © Omar Bárcena; p 159: Courtesy of Catamaran Resort